Facts, Values and Ethics

FACTS, VALUES AND ETHICS

JAMES H. OLTHUIS

a confrontation with
twentieth century
British moral philosophy
in particular G. E. Moore

Second edition

Van Gorcum & Comp. N.V.
Dr. H. J. Prakke & H. M. G. Prakke

Assen, 1969

171
OL8F
114883
July 1980

Printed in the Netherlands by Royal VanGorcum Ltd., Assen

Acknowledgments

On the occasion of the publication of this book, I wish to thank all those who have guided and assisted me during the years of formal academic study. A special word of gratitude is directed to Professor H. E. Runner of Calvin College, Grand Rapids, Michigan who, through his inspired teaching, first awakened and stimulated my interest in philosophy.

To Professors H. van Riessen and J. van der Hoeven of the Free University of Amsterdam, both of whom have read the manuscript in its entirety, I am greatly indebted for their perceptive critique, pertinent questions and helpful suggestions. For the care as well as promptness with which Professor J. P. A. Mekkes of the Hague answered various queries which arose in connection with the last chapter, I cannot but voice appreciation. I also thank Professor R. M. Hare of Corpus Christi College, Oxford for his willingness to discuss matters related to this work.

For the fellowships which it has granted during three consecutive years making possible the writing of this book, I publicly express my gratitude to The Canada Council. At the same time I thank the Netherlands Organization for the Advancement of Pure Research (Z.W.O.) for the subvention which financed a month's study at Oxford University.

Finally, as a token of my thankfulness for her love, encouragement and patience, I dedicate this book to my wife. Moreover, whereas I composed the text, she prepared the manuscript.

To Jean

Table of contents

Abbreviations

Books and articles by G. E. Moore

CPB	*Commonplace Book*
E	*Ethics*
F	"Freedom"
I	"Identity"
LP	*Lectures on Philosophy*
N	"Necessity"
NJ	"The Nature of Judgment"
PE	*Principia Ethica*
PP	*Philosophical Papers*
PS	*Philosophical Studies*
R	"Reply"
RTD	"Russell's 'Theory of Descriptions'"
SMPP	*Some Main Problems of Philosophy*
PGEM	*The Philosophy of G. E. Moore* (ed. P. A. Schilpp)

Further Abbreviations

EL	*Ethics and Language* (Stevenson)
FR	*Freedom and Reason* (Hare)
FV	*Facts and Values* (Stevenson)
LM	*The Language of Morals* (Hare)
LTL	*Language, Truth and Logic* (Ayer)
JP	*Journal of Philosophy*
P	*Philosophy*
PAS	*Proceedings of the Aristotelian Society*
PASS	*Proceedings of the Aristotelian Society Supplementary Volume*
PR	*Philosophical Review*

A setting of the stage

1

The science of ethics, both in its philosophical and theological varieties, is caught up in the throes of transition. Under the impact of irrationalistic underminings, there is a general willingness to break away from the shackling effect of time-less maxims. But the promised deliverance to freedom having boomeranged into a deliverance to fear, uncertainty and anxiety, there is a growing hesitation to accept the appalling consequences of an "every-man-does-what-is-right-in-his-own-eyes-morality." Ethical theories vacillate between casuistry (with its universally valid natural law) and an existentialistic ethics (with its "absolute" freedom).

In contemporary ethical philosophy the main problems involved come to a head in the question of "value."[1] Do "values" exist, or are they figments of the imagination? Do value statements refer to "value realms" (historically, the general trend in Continental Europe), or are they to be interpreted psychologically in the behaviorist pattern (historically, the dominant tendency in the United States and Britain)? Are they objectively real, or are they non-referential in character, perhaps hallucinations or symbols of the conscious mind? Are they like psychosomatic ejaculations, ceremonial utterances, or mathematical formulae? Or are they simply the functions of social, economic and political situations? Such is the sense of bewilderment and frustration which faces a modern ethicist.

It is in this "time of trouble" that a "new" kind of ethics has raised its head and announced itself as the way out of the *impasse* in ethical theory. This novel approach, variously dubbed meta-ethics, critical ethics or analytic ethics, is practiced in a branch of neo-positivism known as Linguistic Analysis.[2] At

---

[1] The same may be said for theological ethics. Joseph Fletcher, a leading proponent of the fashionable contextualist approach to ethics states it plainly: "The basic issue at stake between the situational ethic and natural law theory is the locus of value" (in *Christian Ethics in a Changing World*, ed. J. Bennett, 1966, p. 327).
[2] Not to be confused with the "strong" Logical Positivism of the *Wiener Kreis* or the "weaker" version subsequently advocated by Reichenbach, Carnap *et al.* in the United States. Cf. discussion of Ayer's views Ch. 4, p. 98 ff.

the moment it may be said to be setting the tone in contemporary moral philosophy, at least in the English-speaking world. This being the case, it is necessary that the present developments receive critical attention. The present study is an attempt in this direction. To understand "the revolution in ethical theory,"[3] as it has been recently called, one must become acquainted with its instigators. And thus, we shall give pride of place to the work of George Edward Moore (1873-1958), by all accounts the philosopher with whom this modern interest in and development of ethics first began. Chapters two and three will respectively be expositions of his ethics and general philosophy. Subsequent to the fourth chapter in which attention will be given to the post-Moorean developments, a fifth chapter launches an in-depth critique of Moore's position.

Finally, after catching sight of some inherent problems with which fact-value dualisms must cope in chapter six, this study will conclude by suggesting the outlines of a "new" approach which seeks to do in this dualism. But before we can begin our journey proper, three matters call for attention, albeit in brief. We must sketch the historical context in which Moore moved, as well as characterize the way of philosophizing of which he was a father. Lastly, a quick glance at his person and influence is in order.

THE HISTORICAL SETTING

For the greater part of the history of philosophy the problem of value was, as such, non-existent, or at least incidental. It began to emerge as a full-scale problem when, in reaction to a rationalism which laid all the emphasis on scientific knowledge (Descartes, Leibniz, Spinoza, Hobbes), practical life with its "values" demanded its due in the Aufklärung (Hume, Voltaire, Rousseau). The tension between the two streams was relaxed by the Idealist synthesis: Kant's dichotomic separation of the phenomenal and noumenal worlds.

However, the reconciliation was more fancied than real. Since theoretical reason only wielded sovereign sway in the phenomenal realm, "values," assigned as they were to the noumenal realm, were deprived of logical structure. What heretofore had never been *the* central problem, or the most serious problem — previously there was little doubt that the good could be known, it was even surer than knowledge of the "facts" — became a burning issue: can one really know "values," the good, true and beautiful? See here the value-problem with which modern philosophy is still wrestling.[4]

Then after the brilliant but speculative excesses of the later Idealists (Fichte,

---

[3] G. Kerner, *The Revolution in Ethical Theory* (1966).

[4] It would seem that the concept of "value" first became the center of philosophic interest as a result of the work of R. H. Lotze. The Austrian School of Economics (Menger, Von Wieser) also deserves mention. Cf. also H. O. Eaton, *The Austrian Philosophy of Values* (1930).

Schelling, Hegel), which overextended the noumenal, came the enshrinement of the phenomenal as the *only* real realm and the rejection of any ulterior "metaphysical" explanation. This dramatic shift, from rationalism with its precast moulds set to capture once and for all the "content" of human experience to neo-rationalism which placed its confidence in the methods rather than in the content of reason; from an idealism which did not flinch at remaking the world in the image of the system to a positivism which gave the first and last word to scientifically determined "positive facts," was ushered in by Auguste Comte. Echoing Francis Bacon's cry that knowledge is power, Comte proclaimed *savoir pour prévoir*. By means of a science solely based upon the facts, and the knowledge and foresight such a science affords, mankind can control reality and plan progress.

As it went along, the nineteenth century succumbed in increasing degrees to positivism. The exact sciences were championed as the models of unassailable trustworthiness by which life must be regulated and reformed. Nature can be dominated, the future can be predicted by means of science with its experimental method. The evolutionary hypothesis (Darwin and Spencer) and the genetic method undermined belief in absolute ethical and religious laws. "Natural" and "relative" were the words of the hour.

But positivism as a post-Kantian development could not — intentions to the contrary — make believe that the (positing) subject was irrelevant. (Indeed, the empiricism of John Stuart Mill was through and through psychological.) This became increasingly evident as science was conceived more and more as the means to be employed by human subjects for the subjugation of reality; that is, "prévoir pour gouverner." At the same time, when such supposedly self-evident concepts as "fact" and "law" were found to be replete with problems, "metaphysical" ones at that, science was shaken to its foundations. And as if that were not enough, the gathering cultural crisis abetted by the inattention of science to the fundamental questions of life, as well as the developments in science itself (theory of relativity, quantum-mechanics etc.) helped vitiate the ruling optimistic and utopian belief in progress.

All in all this meant that the attention given to historical relativity and psychology developed (especially in the work of Nietzsche, Dilthey, Troeltsch) into outright relativism and historicism; in short, into irrationalism. Intent on damming the historical stream, neo-Idealism emerged in the form of neo-Kantianism (Cassirer and the "value" philosophies of Richert, Windelband) and especially in England of neo-Hegelianism.

It was in this hyper-idealistic atmosphere of the late 1800's that Moore received his training.[5] He soon saw that the neo-Idealism of Bradley and

[5] At this time curiously enough, traditional roles were reversed. Just when neo-Idealism was exerting its greatest influence in England, there was a renewed German interest in the British empirical tradition.

McTaggart gave short shrift to common sense knowledge and that its victories were at best academic. At the same time he keenly felt the dangers of both psychologism and Naturalism. Moore sought out a new way.

Thus it was that along with the turn of the century came a "turn" in British philosophical thought, hailed by enthusiasts as the harbinger of a second Copernican revolution, derided by dissenters as the prelude to the abandonment of the philosophical task. In any case what Moore initiated — along with Bertrand Russell (b. 1872) and later Ludwig Wittgenstein (1899-1951) — has evolved into a philosophical movement of power and influence.

It is worthy of note that Moore's repulsion of Naturalism finds its counterpart on the Continent in the work of Husserl (and to a lesser extent Brentano). Even as Moore, Husserl and Brentano[6] took up the cudgels against Naturalism at the dawn of this century. And it is a tribute to their greatness that they succeeded in steering philosophy away from Naturalism in their respective areas. Even as Moore stressed the unique character of goodness and the crucial difference between natural and non-natural properties, so Husserl and Brentano rejected the reduction of norms to natural laws as well as the identification of historical facts and norms. And just as in the case of Moore, the work of Husserl and Brentano could be described as an endeavour to maintain values in a strictly scientific philosophy.[7,8]

[6] Whereas Husserl began his attack on Naturalism in the theory of logic, Brentano like Moore took to the battlefield in the area of ethics. For Husserl see especially *Logische Untersuchungen* (1901), "Die Philosophie als strenge Wissenschaft," *Logos* (1910), and *Die Krisis der europäischen Wissenschaften* (1954). For Brentano, see *Vom Ursprung sittlicher Erkenntnis* (1899).

Moore spoke highly of Brentano's book. His opinions resemble mine more "than those of any other ethical writer with whom I am acquainted" (*PE*, xi). Nevertheless, Moore espies a mistaken empiricistic influence in Brentano's contention that psychical impressions can give rise to the concept of *right* loving (Moore's Review in *International Journal of Ethics* XIV, 1903, pp. 115-23).

[7] These parallels — and more of them could be mentioned — are as interesting as they are significant. Nevertheless, they are similarities amid basic differences. Whereas Moore (in *PE*) believed that the world could exist without the consciousness, Husserl (in his last stage) considered the consciousness the source of all being. And although Brentano never took the step to transcendental Idealism, his theory as subject-oriented (psychologism with the intentionality-theme) contrasts with Moore's efforts to develop an object-centered theory.

[8] Ontologically Moore is much closer to the German neo-Idealist Alexius von Meinong, who on account of his position has had little impact on the Continent blanketed as it has been by phenomenology and existentialism. J. N. Findlay has judged that "philosophically, as well as personally, there is no one Meinong so much resembles as G. E. Moore" (*Meinong's Theory of Objects and Values*, 1963, pp. ix-x). It is then no surprise that the American writers of the *New Realism* (1912), among them R. B. Perry, W. P. Montague and E. B. Holt, refer to Russell, Moore and Meinong as their "big brothers overseas." Russell and Moore looked to Meinong for support in their fight to win back a robust sense of reality from the idealistic intoxication with the mind and its

4

Generalizing one could say that whereas in the seventeenth and eighteenth centuries mathematics was the science par excellence (Descartes' *more geometrico*), in the nineteenth the emphasis switched to sciences dealing with the so-called positive facts, physics, biology and psychology. Forced by subsequent crises to an internal critique of science itself, twentieth century philosophy has centered in logic (more and more identified with language). At present, due to the trend away from artificial or ideal languages to ordinary language, neo-positivistic philosophy is acquiring renewed interest in mankind's "practical" problems. As a matter of course this tendency is leading and presumably will continue to lead to a revived, heightened, concern for ethics. In this growing concern for language and ethics Moore has played a powerfully influential role.

Moore, it is becoming clear, was a *transitional* figure. Therein lies a large measure of his philosophic importance. Hopeful of pushing aside the idealistic intrusion into England, he could only fall back upon the British tradition of empiricism (Locke, Hume, Reid). But, enthused as he is by the empiricist emphasis on sense-experience, impressed as he is by the achievements of natural science, he is convinced that there is more to reality than facts. At this point Moore has already begun his attack on the dilemma of that era: Naturalism or Idealism. Naturalism is scientific, but value-less; that is, it is incompetent to answer the important questions of life. Idealism is value-sate, but unscientific; that is, its answers are will-o'-the-wisps which help no one.

The next step is to provide an alternative to a false dilemma. Moore aspires to develop a *scientific* theory doing full justice to the *more-than-factual* character of reality. However, this does not mean that Moore takes flight to a realm of super-sensible existents called values. Such a move would entail going "metaphysical" and that runs counter to the scientific spirit. He determines to walk the tightrope between "the naturalistic philosophers proper — those who are empiricists — and those whom I have called 'metaphysical'" (*PE*, 124). One must, he felt confident, begin with the priority of a mind-independent "objective" world, non-natural as well as natural. This fact; namely, that from out of a mind in many ways congenial to empiricism and positivism Moore struggled to affirm the irreducibility of values (the non-natural) in respect to facts pinpoints his significance for the study of ethics. That he essayed to do this in a new "analytical" way and that present-day conceptions are the continuations and extensions of his work only enhances this significance and witnesses to Moore's far-reaching and profound influence.

fabrications (Cf. Russell's "Meinong's Theory of Complexes and Assumptions," *Mind* XIII, 1904 and Moore's "The Subject Matter of Psychology," *PAS* X, 1909).

It is worthy of note that Max Scheler considered Moore to have in many respects a "similar conception of the problem of value" (*Der Formalismus in der Ethik und die materiale Wertethik*, 1954 Edition, p. 13).

Thus, because Moore not only ended an epoch in philosophy, but initiated a new one, prior to examining his position in detail it is advisable to look ahead and make first acquaintance with the novel way of philosophizing and ethicizing which he adumbrated and, to a degree, practiced. In chapter four this acquaintance will be deepened as we trace in some detail the post-Moorean developments in ethics.

Moore was one of the precursors of linguistic analysis, the name generally applied to the latest phase of neo-positivism. As its name indicates, neo-positivism is a new form of positivism, chastened and shorn of its former rationalistic self-confidence, blind optimism and naïveté. It has not forsworn so much its allegiance to the ideal of science as that instrument by which reality is dominated as it has withdrawn into logico-lingual strongholds in order to consolidate and rebuild its forces for future, hopefully more realistic, conquests.

In its initial stage, the Logical Positivism of the *Wiener Kreis*, neo-positivism sought to do in metaphysics completely by a logical analysis of language. But this flight into logic and artificial languages ended up in the empty tautologies of Wittgenstein's *Tractatus*. In reaction, again under the influence of Wittgenstein, there was a general return to Ordinary Language.

Linguistic analysis itself was born when the later Wittgenstein's language-game approach in which meaning is equivalent with use fertilized Moore's emphasis on the clarification of the dictates of Common Sense. It has since flourished in the so-called Oxford School of Ordinary Language under the leadership of Gilbert Ryle (b. 1900), J. L. Austin (1911-1959) and presently P. F. Strawson (b. 1919), in the more Wittgenstein faithful "therapeutic analysis" of John Wisdom (b. 1904) at Cambridge, and in the philosophizing of many in America, Scandinavia, and the entire English-speaking world. It is not only the dominant philosophical school in the Anglo-American world, it is at present steadily encroaching on the mainland of Europe.

Expressing as it does an irrationalistic distrust as to the possibility of anything fixed and certain, whether it be final truths or ultimate methods, linguistic analysis is known by its style, its type of concern, its way of philosophizing, rather than by a unity of conception and doctrine.

Philosophy means doing, not being. It is an activity as over against a doctrine. It is a game to play rather than a lesson to learn; it is search, never discovery; it is an activity to practice, not a message to preach. Analysis does not affect the world of facts — positively or negatively — "Philosophy ... leaves everything as it is."[9] There is nothing more for philosophy to say: either the

[9] Wittgenstein, *Philosophical Investigations*, par. 124. Cf. also pars. 109, 119, 122, 125 ff. For meaning=use, cf. par. 43.

6

natural sciences will explain it, or common sense already knows it. At least, nothing more *can* be said, the rest is ineffable or hidden. Yet, something must be done — otherwise there will be "nothing" to do and philosophy will (de)cease! There are two possibilities: concentrate on the "saying" or try to *show* what is ineffable. Following the dominant emphasis of the late Wittgenstein, linguistic analysis has followed the first course and ignored the second as an aspect of the to-be-rejected mysticism of the *Tractatus*.[10] Philosophic problems arise from the misuse or abuse of language, from imagining for example, that the logical form of a sentence is the same as the grammatical form. It is not the results which are important — they will come — but the activity, usually taken as technical mastery with language as the instrument. In other words, linguistic analysis thinks of itself as a kind of secretarial-service-for-hire, as a janitor service. It provides a tool-box to be employed as the occasion demands. In disarming fashion, the analyst points out that he has "nothing" to sell, he just offers a new set of tools, or perhaps, just wishes to sharpen old tools. Party banners and school loyalty have no place in philosophy.[11]

Linguistic analysis is thus typified by a "wholesale rejection of programmatic aspirations and zealotry."[12] However, this overly-modest bordering on embarrassed demeanor is only one side of the analytic coin. The analyst on the whole would claim that "this way of approaching philosophical problems was better — more illuminating, more realistic, and more rational — than any other."[13] In effect, this is to say that analysis regards itself as the best, if not the lone, remaining option open to philosophy.[14]

Correspondingly, meta-ethics, the ethical mien of lingusitic analysis, may be described as a linguistic retreat into an enclave purported to be morally antiseptic, an enclave from out of which the ethicists, becoming more and more audacious, launch forays into the arenas of modern life. It claims to (dis)solve the problems under which ethics is staggering by a logical clarification of the

---

[10] Wittgenstein, *Tractatus*, 6.44, 6.45, 6.522, 6.53, 6.54.
[11] Cf. G. Ryle, "On Taking Sides in Philosophy," *P* XII (1937).
[12] In "Introduction" to *British Analytical Philosophy*, eds. Williams and Montefiore (1966), p. 11.
[13] *Ibid.*
[14] The first glimmerings of realization that analysis is not merely a honed tool lacking all metaphysical pretensions is one of the most striking features of the present situation. Strawson, especially, advocates a "descriptive metaphysics" which is "content to describe the actual structure of our thought about the world" rather than a historically popular "revisionary metaphysics" which is "concerned to produce a better structure" (*Individuals*, 1959, p. 9ff.). Strawson's latest book, *The Bounds of Sense, An Essay on Kant's Critique of Pure Reason* (1966), is extremely significant in this respect. The author sets out to separate the cream of descriptive metaphysics from the skim milk of revisionism intermingled in Kant. Kant went awry when he declared the source of the limiting or necessary general features of experience "to lie in our own cognitive constitution" (p. 15ff.).

syntax of descriptive ("formal") and ("material") ethics. It is a second-order (meta-) study of the logic of normative language which prides itself on being "morally neutral,"[15] on seeing issues in a "neutral perspective."[16] Whereas normative ethics is concerned with formulating valid ethical precepts and justifying these principles, whereas descriptive ethics describes the moral views which people in fact have, meta-ethics, its proponents claim, is concerned with the logical, epistemological and semantical questions involved. Meta-ethics deals with the meaning and use of key expressions (e.g. "good," "free," "responsible"), the nature of morality, the distinction moral and non-moral, the nature and possibility of ethical justification, etc.[17] Meta-ethics has approximately the "relation to normative ethics that the *philosophy of science or epistemology or meta-science* has to science."[18]

Meta-ethics does not claim to be the only legitimate ethics, it recognizes its restricted competence. By definition, meta-ethics requires a point from which to move beyond (metá). This means that "ordinary" ethics — as this jumping-off place — fulfills a foundational role for meta-ethics. Neither does meta-ethics claim to solve all the problems, rather it purposively withdraws into a morally antiseptic vacuum and endeavours to absolve itself of responsibility in regard to the "big" questions of life. Thus, having thrown around its shoulders the mantle of neutrality — transforming a lack into a virtue — it reappears as the apostle of peace, volunteering its healing services to all the dissident parties. But, on the other hand, it champions itself as the one and only doctrine-less method which can set free ethics, of whatever stripe, to genuine ethicizing. "Obviously it is necessary to answer the main questions of critical ethics before we have firm grounds for constructing a system of normative ethics."[19]

G. E. MOORE: HIS PERSON AND INFLUENCE

Born of Baptist parents in 1873, educated largely to the exclusion of other subjects in Greek and Latin, having entered Cambridge to read classics, George Edward Moore turned to philosophy in 1894. And for the rest of his rather ordinary uneventful life, philosophy, or more suitably philosophizing,

---

[15] R. M. Hare, *Freedom and Reason* (1963), p. 97. Some ethicists prefer to consider meta-ethics the third level or the third tier. Ethical conduct is on the ground-level, the second level is that of the spectator who with reference to codes, criticizes, evaluates and comments on ethical activity, the third level is reserved for the ethicist who analyzes and systematizes the criteria, the principles and the concepts used by the actors (ground floor) and the critics (second floor). Cf. B. Mayo, *Ethics and the Moral Life*, pp. 9-14.
[16] C. L. Stevenson, *Facts and Values* (1963), p. vii.
[17] W. K. Frankena, *Ethics* (1963), p. 4ff.
[18] R. Brandt, *Ethical Theory* (1959), p. 7.
[19] *Ibid.*, pp. 9-10.

was his main concern. For twenty-six years (1921-1947) he served as editor of *Mind*.

Personally, to take at face value the testimony of his contemporaries, Moore had the touch of greatness, a "combination of clarity, integrity, tenacity" and above all a "passion for truth."[20] And, speaking for a later generation, R. B. Braithwaite testifies that they "would not have written differently."[21] To Leonard Woolf "George Moore was a great man, the only great man whom I have ever met or known in the world of ordinary, real life."[22] To Bertrand Russell Moore fulfilled for some years his ideal of a genius. "He had a kind of exquisite purity."[23]

Although, as Russell himself has described,[24] Moore was the first to descend the Hegelian ladder to firm ground, Moore long stood in the shadow of his friend and colleague — at least outside of philosophical circles. This relative anonymity, in comparison with his influence,[25] may be attributed to two related factors: he published little, and what he did publish was wholly analytical and critical, much too exacting for ordinary consumption. Moore is the philosopher's philosopher. However, since the end of World War II, he has become better known. The influence of Russell and the "early" Wittgenstein of the *Tractatus* (1922) — at a high point in the 1930's — has waned in the proportion that the influence of Moore and the "late" Wittgenstein of the *Philosophical Investigations* (1953) has waxed.

According to Morris Lazerowitz, Moore has done "two most important things" for philosophy. He brought "philosophical talk into connection with ordinary language" and he demonstrated "by the example of his work over the years, how to use the technique of analytical elucidation."[26] Rudolf Metz, the German historian of British philosophy, has called Moore "the greatest,

---

[20] Woolf, *Sowing* (1961), p. 135. Moore's "devotion to truth was indeed palpable. In an argument his whole frame was gripped by a passion to confute error and expose confusion" (in Harrod's *The Life of John Maynard Keynes*, 1951, p. 75). Cf. also Malcolm's essay on Moore in his book *Knowledge and Certainty* (1963).

[21] "G. E. Moore," *Proceedings of the British Academy* XLVII (1958), p. 295. Warnock stresses the influence of "the *character* of G. E. Moore" upon philosophy (*English Philosophy since 1900*, 1958, pp. 11-12).

[22] Woolf, *loc. cit.*

[23] *Portraits From Memory and Other Essays* (1956), p. 68. Also in *The Autobiography of Bertrand Russell 1872-1914* (1967), p. 64, cf. also p. 107.

[24] "With a sense of escaping from prison, we allowed ourselves to think that grass is green, that the sun and stars should exist if no one was aware of them, and also that there is a pluralistic timeless world of Platonic ideas. The world, which had been thin and logical, suddenly became rich and varied and solid" (*The Philosophy of Bertrand Russell*, 1946, p. 12).

[25] Moore's influence came mainly through his teaching. From 1911 to 1939 he lectured at Cambridge at least three times a week and held as many seminars.

[26] "Moore's *Commonplace Book*," P XXXIX (1964), p. 166.

acutest and most skillful questioner of modern philosophy."[27] C. D. Broad, Moore's colleague at Cambridge, has gone even farther: "It is doubtful whether any philosopher known to history has excelled or even equalled Moore in sheer power of analysing problems, detecting and exposing fallacies and ambiguities, and formulating and working out alternative possibilities."[28] Moore has "undoubtedly had a greater influence than any other man on English philosophy in general and Cambridge philosophy in particular during the last fifty years."[29] No further comment is necessary. Moore has played a pivotal role in twentieth century Anglo-Saxon philosophy.

More Moore tributes

[27] *A Hundred Years of British Philosophy*, p. 540. But Metz added that Moore was "an extremely weak and unsatisfying answerer." For Moore's reaction (Metz is right!) cf. R, 677, also *PGEM*, 521.

[28] In his introduction to Moore's *PP*, 12. On Moore's passionate manner of debating, cf. Keynes, *Two Memoirs* (1951), p. 85; Woolf, *op. cit.*, pp. 134-37; Braithwaite, *op. cit.*, p. 305.

[29] Mace, *British Philosophy in Mid-Century* (1957), p. 50. Cf. also *British Analytical Philosophy* (eds. Williams and Montefiore), p. 11. Not that everyone judges that his influence was for the better. Moore — to cite one example — has "messed up philosophy to such an extent that it would require a generation to get it straight again" (Parker, *Philosophy of Values*, 1957, p. 40).

The ethics of G. E. Moore

2

In this chapter on the ethics of G. E. Moore, our orientation point will be his earliest publication in the field — the *Principia Ethica* of 1903.[1] References to other works as well as to his general philosophical position will fulfill an explanatory and explicatory role. In Moore's case this is no "restriction" and, in fact, is to be recommended for a number of reasons. The *Principia* is not only Moore's most important ethical publication, it is one of the most influential ethical works of the twentieth century.[2] More significant for our purposes is the fact that, although Moore later revamped his ethical views, he remained throughout his life "in agreement with its main tendency and conclusions" (Preface to 1922 Reprint). In addition, his later position is only roughly sketched in a few articles, and largely in continuation or rectification of views propounded in *Principia Ethica*. His only other book on the subject, entitled *Ethics*, although it begins the shift on a number of fronts, is a more popular presentation — in reverse order — of the central ideas of the *Principia*.

According to Moore ethics, as well as the other philosophical disciplines, has too often in the past suffered from an embarrassing lack of clarity, and this to such a degree that ethicists, continually wandering about in labyrinths of confusion, have been unable to agree on the most simple matters. Such impasses and conflicts "are mainly due to a very simple cause: namely to the attempt to answer questions, without first discovering precisely *what* question it is which you desire to answer" (*PE*, vii). This, then, is Moore's message to philosophy: purify yourself for your task through pain-staking, resolute, protracted "work of analysis and distinction." And indeed this was Moore's life-witness; "clarification" is the battle-cry, the watchword.

---

[1] References to Moore's writings will be placed in the text accompanied by the appropriate abbreviation. Cf. list of abbreviations.
[2] Although he later changed, in "The Elements of Ethics" Bertrand Russell espoused a Moorean position (*Philosophical Essays*, 1910).

Good-in-Itself and Good-as-Means

Ethics has been unfruitful, ethicists have been perplexed, any kind of consensus has been impossible because the basic questions of ethics have almost always been confused with each other. At all costs and to all ends, Moore argues, the question concerning what is "good in itself" or has "intrinsic value" must be distinguished from the question concerning what one "ought to do" or whether it is a "right action" (*PE*, viii).

This distinction is necessary if one would do justice to the complex state of affairs with which ethics must deal. Mandated to "enumerate all true universal judgments, asserting that such and such a thing was good, whenever it occurred" (*PE*, 21), ethics deals with judgments of the form "X is good." The mistake usually made, argues Moore, is to assume that "good" always means the same thing. But this is not true. In one case the thing in question is said to be *always* good, it is "good in itself," in another case the thing in question is only a *cause or necessary condition* for the existence of some other thing good in itself, it is "good as means." In the former case one has to do with "intrinsic value," "good in itself," in the later case with "value as a means" and "good as means." Failure to distinguish properly at this point is to commit "the fallacy of confusing means and end" (*PE*, 90).[3]

The difference is crucial. If a thing is good in itself in one instance, it is *necessarily* good in all instances regardless of varying circumstances. Its value is constant. But if a thing in a certain instance is merely good as means, there is no guarantee that it will also be good in different situations. What has good effects under some circumstances may well have bad ones under others. In short: Whereas judgments of intrinsic value are, if true, *universally* true, judgments involving causal relations are, if true, at best *generally* true.

If philosopers do not clearly see these matters, regardless of their good intentions and keen argumentation, their conclusions are "totally devoid of weight" and their reasoning "totally irrelevant" (*PE*, ix). They set out to answer the question "what ought we to do" without any awareness that two questions are involved. As a result "two different errors have been rendered almost universal. Either it is assumed that nothing has intrinsic value which is not possible, or else it is assumed that what is necessary must have intrinsic value" (*PE*, 26).[4] But, replies Moore, what once has intrinsic value always has it,

---

[3] The importance of this fallacy is obvious when we hear Moore state that "our ultimate decision with regard to Hedonism will largely turn upon it" (*PE*, 74).

[4] In other words, one assumes that "a thing's reality is a *necessary condition* for its goodness" and further that "the real must be good because it possesses certain characters" (*PE*, 122-23).

the question as to the possibility of its actual existence is irrelevant at this point. On the other hand, what is necessary is often only "good" as *means*.

In general, ethical questions involve a two-fold knowledge. "We must know *both* what degree of intrinsic value different things have, *and* how these different things may be obtained" (*PE*, 26). When one knows what is good in itself, he can by means of "causal generalisation" (*PE*, 146) calculate his duty. An action is right, it ought to be done, if it in all likelihood will result in the existence of an intrinsic good. Separating the good-in-itself and good-as-means questions (or, the questions concerning "what is good"[5] and "what is right"), Moore is able to defend the "objectivity" of moral judgments even as he declares that right and wrong depend upon "consequences." He is able to do justice to the contingencies of life without abandoning his belief in constancy (intrinsic value).

In light of the foregoing, it is no surprise that Moore concludes that the "primary and peculiar business of Ethics [is] the determination [of] what things have intrinsic value and in what degrees" (*PE*, 26). The "fundamental question of Ethics" is the question: "'What things are goods or ends in themselves?'" (*PE*, 184; cf. 8-9, 77, 138-39, 223). A "judgment that certain effects are better, in themselves, than others" is "an ethical judgment proper." The secondary ethical question — the question of practical Ethics — is "what things are related as *causes* to that which is good in itself." To inquire "what kind of actions we ought to perform, or what kind of conduct is right, is to ask what kind of effects such action and conduct will produce" (*PE*, 146; cf. 27). Ethical philosophy must "classify all the different sorts of things which *would* be good or bad, right or wrong" (*SMPP*, 26; cf. *E*, 153).

All this leads one to expect Moore's work to be a full-fledged attempt to discover answers to these two questions. But this is not so! In spite of his numerous and lucid declarations as to the proper task of ethics, he spends relatively little time in such proper pursuits. The only comparatively extended treatment in his writings of what things are good in themselves (*PE*, ch. VI)[6] ends with the caution that the results are not, in the first place, valuable in themselves, but only as illustrations of the method. In his *Ethics* of 1912 Moore highlights the importance of classifying, only to continue that he has no "space to attempt it here" (*E*, 153). After 1912 he never explicitly returns

---

[5] When "good" is employed without further specification, it should always be read as "good in itself."
[6] This chapter has been of negligible importance in the field of philosophy proper. But, ironically, it alone of Moore's work has had significant influence outside the circles of philosophy. To the distinguished economist John Maynard Keynes and the Bloomsbury Group of which he was a member, Moore's *Principia* (especially ch. VI) was the model of a way of life. Cf. p. 51 for further discussion, and a listing of relevant bibliographic material.

to this question again. He does devote relatively more space to the question as to what is right (especially chapter V of *Principia* and large sections of *Ethics*), but it never becomes his main preoccupation.

Moore's Innovation

Since these were the two main questions in the field of ethics, this creates — certainly at first glance — a passing strange situation. It is well at the outset to face this discrepancy or seeming discrepancy in Moore's ethics. Noticing it, and discussing it will enable us to receive a valuable insight into why his work has been of such importance and influence in modern times. How did Moore reconcile these matters? How could he emphasize that *the* primary task of ethics is the discovery of what kinds of things are good (and bad) and, at the same time, for the most part, systematically avoid addressing himself to this self-assigned task? To what did he untiredly bend his energies? Does he contradict himself as to the main task of ethics? Or is he guilty of careless, ambiguous writing? Is there, perhaps, a third possibility?

The answers to these questions are, formally at least, surprisingly simple. Moore is neither guilty of confusion, contradiction or sleight of the hand. His writing is generally a model of clarity, and when it is not, it is more from over-attention than inattention. Moreover, Moore can be characterized as a philosopher with one passion: honesty. He sought the truth and to find the truth he pleaded for clarity of expression. Although the answer we are about to present is simple, it must not — as subsequent history has amply evidenced — be underestimated either in its depth or importance. To clear up the seeming confusion in Moore's thought, it is advisable to sketch-in the main lines of the situation which led him to choose the road he did, the road which made him famous.

Moore began by disentangling the two basic questions of ethics proper. However, having effected this initial clarification, he discovered almost immediately that he was still unable to answer these key questions. Prior to determining what (kinds of) things are good, one must first learn the *meaning* or *analysis* of the adjective "good." Moore then drew his revolutionary conclusion: "how 'good' is to be defined, is the most fundamental question in all Ethics." Unless this question is "fully understood" and its answer "clearly recognised" the rest of ethics (that is, consideration of the two basic questions) is "as good as useless from the point of view of systematic knowledge" (*PE*, 5; cf. 143).

And here we stand at the cradle from which arose modern meta-ethics. Neutral, logical analysis of the term involved (i.e., the adjective "good") is explicitly separated from and considered prior to treatment of the normative questions of ethics (what kinds of things are good in themselves?, what ought

14

we to do?). Thus, whereas Moore announces *two* main questions in the Preface to *Ethica*, his investigations led him promptly to a *third*. And from that moment on he speaks of *three* questions. As the "new" question is a question which must be answered at the outset, it is henceforth termed the first question. His subsequent absorption in matters surrounding the first question stems partly from the simple but stubborn fact that he was never satisfied with his answers to this first and preliminary query, and partly because he was concerned to write, taking a cue from Kant, the "'Prolegomena to any future Ethics that can possibly pretend to be scientific.'" His main objective was the discovery of the "fundamental principles of ethical reasoning; and the establishment of these principles, rather than of any conclusions which may be attained by their use" (*PE*, ix).

In *Principia Ethica* this state of affairs is crystal clear. Moore is overwhelmed by the realization that much trail-blazing awaits doing *before* ethics will be able to find its way out of the dark forests of confusion and suspicion, before ethics can constructively begin her proper task. His hope and his trust is that future generations will begin where he left off and tread the cleared-path to proper ethicizing. In summary: without an answer to the preliminary question of analysis, ethics would always be barking up the wrong tree. Without answering the two normative questions, ethics will always have failed in its purpose. Analysis is indispensable, but it is only a means to a greater end.

All this implies that the work of Moore, certainly in ethics, can only be understood when one sees the old and the new. Moore is a *transitional* figure and it is unfair to pass him off as out-of-date, or as the first full-fledged analyst. He is often reverenced as a patron-saint of analysis, as the philosopher's philosopher who practiced what he preached, who taught what needed teaching: philosophy is analysis, period. "For the metaphysical and Copernican discovery of how nearly philosophy is really logic," intones the leading Cambridge philosopher John Wisdom, "Moore did as much as, and perhaps more, than any other man."[7] It is true that the all-important, but nevertheless preparatory search to discover the meaning of the adjective "good" occupied Moore — in ethics — for the remainder of his life. And as he was never satisfied with the analyses, he felt incapable of full-scale investigations of the basic questions of ethics. It is likewise indisputable that in his general philosophizing Moore "restricted" himself more and more to matters of analysis. Nevertheless, it must be emphasized that Moore did not at any time in his life restrict ethics, or for that matter, philosophy, to analysis. Thus he reminds Wisdom that it is evidence of careless thinking to move from the fact that most of his philosophical work was analysis to the conclusion that he equated

---

[7] "Moore's Technique," in *PGEM*, 450. (Reprinted in Wisdom's *Philosophy and Psycho-Analysis*, 1953.) Wisdom has since admitted his error. Cf. *Paradox and Discovery* (1965), p. 83.

analysis and philosophy (R, 675-76). As it is a sub-division of philosophy, the same reasoning holds true in respect to ethics. As we shall see, it holds in particular for ethics. Of direct relevance, albeit an argument from silence, is his treatment of the task of ethics in *Some Main Problems of Philosophy*. Although these fascinating lectures were delivered in the winter of 1910-11, they were only published in 1953. To bring the lectures in line with his position of 1953, Moore now and then changed words, added footnotes as well as a short appendix. However, in total there are amazingly few corrections and there is not the slightest indication that his conception of the task of ethics ("to classify all the different sorts of things which would be good or bad, right or wrong") has undergone metamorphosis.[8]

The Three Basic Questions

Now that the stage has been set, it is time to examine Moore's ethical philosophy in detail, set by set and prop by prop. As we have hinted, the three previously mentioned questions are the blueprint as well as the sub-structure of his ethics. They give order to the ethical structure as a whole. Considering their importance it is well to examine the questions more closely. An insight into what Moore envisions is obtained by a study of the various ways in which he formulates the three questions.

Question I (QI)   What is *meant* by good (*PE*, 37, 77)?

Variations: How is good to be defined (*PE*, 5, 6)?
      What is the nature of the predicate peculiar to ethics (*PE*, 37, 180)?
      What "good" — the adjective "good" — means (*PE*, 142)?

Question II (QII)   What kinds of things are good in themselves (*PE*, 27, 118, 184)?

Variations: What is good (or best) in itself (*PE*, viii, 26, 118)?
      To what kinds of things (and in what degree) does the predicate "good" attach directly (*PE*, 37, 180)?

---

[8] Thus, although contemporary meta-ethics has largely followed Moore's lead in its preoccupation with analyzing ethical concepts and judgments in lieu of a treatment of more concrete problems, Moore would no doubt have raised a sympathetic ear to the growing chorus of voices clamoring for a return to the "content" of moral life. For Moore, in distinction from many of his epigoni, did not in principle confine ethics to analysis. Analysis was the unavoidable "door" through which one must pass if he would properly engage in "normative" ethics.

16

What has intrinsic value (*PE*, viii, 26, 187, 224)?
What kinds of things ought to exist for their own sakes (*PE*, viii, 188)?
What ought to be (*PE*, 115, 118)?
What ought to be real (whether it exists or not) (*PE*, 118, 119)?

Question III (QIII)   What ought we to do (*PE*, viii, 26, 115, 146, 180, 223)?

Variations: What is right (or wrong)? What is my duty (*PE*, viii, 146, 180)?
What is good as means (*PE*, 18, 21, 24, 27, 180)?
What will bring about the best possible (*PE*, 26, 224)?
By what *means* shall we be able to make what exists in the world as good as possible? What causal relations hold between what is best in itself and other things (*PE*, 27, 37, 146, 180)?

For the sake of convenience, the three divisions of ethics will henceforth be referred to as QI, QII, and QIII. Each of these questions forms a complex in its own right, and the ethical edifice as a whole has three complexes. To facilitate understanding of inter-mural as well as intra-mural relations, we shall go ahead of ourselves and sketch the basic patterns in the three complexes.

Moore is convinced that the separation of QII and QIII is of supreme importance because it becomes plain that, for answers to the second question (QII), "no relevant evidence whatever can be adduced: from no other truth, except themselves alone, can it be inferred that they are either true or false." As for question three (QIII), "it becomes equally plain, that any answer to it *is* capable of proof or disproof." Complex QII is the "self-evident class," the class of "first principles" which must simply be "accepted or rejected." One can only present "indirect proof." Although QIII is capable of proof, there are so many relevant considerations that the "attainment of probability" is extremely difficult and of certainty "impossible" (*PE*, viii). However, whereas QII is only open to *indirect* proof and depends in the last analysis on intuition, and whereas QIII is open to *direct* proof although certainty is never attained, QI is open both to direct proof and is "capable of strict proof" (*PE*, 77). In more technical language: QI deals with the meaning of "simple" notions in reference to which ethical propositions become by definition synthetic, QII involves universally true judgments (synthetic *apriori*) and QIII involves causal judgments which may be true (synthetic *aposteriori*) (*PE*, 7, 16, 21-24, 58, 144).

17

What is Ethics?

Having in hand the ground-plan of the ethical edifice, we can begin to examine the furnishings. Ethics, defines Moore, is "the whole truth about that which is at the same time common to all such judgments [ones employing terms such as virtue, vice, duty, right, ought, good, bad] and peculiar to them" (*PE*, 1). Assuming that "good" is the most often utilized word to refer to this common element, Moore defines ethics as "the general enquiry into what is good" (*PE*, 2). "The peculiarity of Ethics is . . . that it investigates assertions about that property of things which is denoted by the term 'good,' and the converse property denoted by the term 'bad'" (*PE*, 36).

But this will not do as a mandate for a scientific ethics; certainly for the clear-thinking Moore further specification is necessary. As it stands, the definition is open to sundry interpretations. Since ethics, in distinction from history and geography, does not deal with the "unique, individual and absolutely particular," the question cannot be read as "what *particular* things are good?" Such a question is simply outside the domain of ethics as a science.[9] The question can be read as asking "what sorts of things are good" (QII)? However, although this is certainly the ultimate goal of ethical investigation for Moore, this "cannot be safely attempted at the beginning of our studies but only at the end" (*PE*, 5). Thus, as we have already noticed, he prefers another interpretation: "how good is to be defined." To this question (QI) and its answer must be granted logical as well as chronological priority.

"Goodness"

In what may be called an initial aside, Moore assures his readers that he is not the least interested in discovering a dictionary definition. Such "verbal" definitions are of little or no philosophic interest, and their existence or non-existence is irrelevant to the question at hand. Lexicography is concerned with "usage," it does not concern itself with presenting an "analysis" of the objects for which certain words are employed. "My business," he exclaims, "is solely with that object or idea, which I hold, rightly or wrongly, that the word is generally used to stand for" (*PE*, 6). He is searching for *the* notion of goodness — although it would be amiss not to note the caution expressed in the words "generally used to stand for." In 1912 Moore begins to emphasize the ambi-

---

[9] Moore proceeds and draws from this argument what has turned out to be a far-reaching and extremely influential conclusion; namely, "it is not the business of the ethical philosopher to give personal advice or exhortation (*PE*, 3). See, for example, Bernard Mayo, *Ethics and The Moral Life* (1958), ch. 1.

guity of good, and in 1932 as well as in 1942 he explicitly recognizes diverse senses of goodness (*PP*, 89-90; R, 582).

It is, however, not permissable to envision this as a basic change in Moore's thought. His search for the meaning of "goodness" was always in fact a search for the meaning of a sense of good ordinarily used in common speech, a sense he called "intrinsically good" (R, 554). The point is that Moore, to the end of his life, considered "intrinsically good" to be in a class by itself. All of the other senses of good (some of which he already recognized in *Principia*) are simply ways of expressing rightness (good as means, good as part). That is, only "intrinsically good" belongs to complexes QI and QII, the other senses of good belong in complex QIII. Something has intrinsic value, it is good in itself if it would have value "even if it existed *quite alone*, without any further accompaniments or effects whatever" (*E*, 42).

What is the meaning or analysis of good? "Good is good," replies Moore, "and that is the end of the matter." Good "cannot be defined and that is all I have to say about it" (*PE*, 6). A definition for Moore is by definition only possible of a "complex" object. To define is to break down into simplest parts. Since "goodness" is a "simple notion" lacking "parts," it is not susceptible to definition. Rather as a simple notion, it is uni-cellular and serves only with other such "units" as that "out of which definitions are composed and with which the power of further defining ceases" (*PE*, 8). "Good" and "bad" are the only simple notions peculiar to ethics in *Principia* (*PE*, 5).[10,11] Moore means by indefinable: not capable of further decomposition or division. This is worthy of special emphasis as he does believe that good can be "distinguished" — and in this way "defined" — from other notions. "We can ... describe its relations to other things, but define it we can *not*" (*PE*, 13). In fact, he urges us to "become aware ... that it [good] is different from other notions" (*PE*, 17).

The quality of goodness which is present in everything that is good intrinsically is simple, unanalysable, indefinable, and non-natural. Goodness, Moore explains later, is a quality in the sense that the "character of being worth having for its own sake *was* a character and was *not* a relational property: that and

[10] Later Moore is moved to add "ought" to the list of indefinables. Cf. p. 53.
[11] As the pendant of intrinsic goodness, "intrinsic badness" appears in *Principia* to be more than a deficit or lack of intrinsic goodness. Moore terms badness an "evil quality" (219). He talks of "intrinsic evil" (213, 218), "intrinsic odiousness" (210), "intrinsically evil" (214, 218), evil and bad in itself (158, 160, 178, 181). However, in *Ethics* badness seems to be conceived of as a lack: "While if B be intrinsically *bad*, that is to say, if its intrinsic value is less than O" (150). He further mentions that B could be "intrinsically *indifferent*, that is to say, if its intrinsic value = O." But can Moore talk of a deficit in degrees of intrinsic goodness? A thing either has it or it does not have it. If the latter is the case, the thing is not indifferent, it must be intrinsically bad. The difficult problem of "negativity" which we only announce here also confronts Moore in relation to his views of truth and falsehood. See pp. 86-90.

19

nothing more" (*PP*, 97).[12] From the belief that goodness is a "quality" or that it is "simple," it follows that "x is intrinsically good" does not include nor is identical with "I ought to do x" (R, 577).[13]

Goodness is a "simple" notion because it cannot be broken down into parts. In 1942 he admits that "I used 'simple' . . . to mean the same as indefinable" (R, 594). Since yellow, a natural property, is also a simple notion, Moore stresses that goodness is a non-natural property. In the universe there are natural objects ("something of which the existence is admittedly an object of experience" *PE*, 38) as well as natural properties ("their existence does seem to me to be independent of the existence of those objects").[14] Goodness is a non-natural property because it is unable to exist "by *itself* in time," it must always appear as a "property of some natural object." Being a "mere" predicate (*PE*, 41), one can take goodness away without confiscating the object itself. Goodness is non-natural, non-existent and non-temporal. "It is immediately obvious that when we see a thing to be good, its goodness is not a property which we can take up in our hands, or separate from it even by the most delicate instruments, and transfer to someting else. It is not, in fact, like most of the predicates which we ascribe to things, a *part* of the thing to which we ascribe it" (*PE*, 124), Goodness is a member of a class of objects or properties of objects (along with numbers and universal truths) which are "not therefore parts of Nature, and which, in fact, do not *exist* at all." It is not the "adjective 'good,'" or as Moore interchangeably says "*goodness*, but only the things or qualities which are good, which can exist in time — can have duration, and begin and cease to exist — can be objects of *perception*" (*PE*, 110). Nevertheless, although it does not *exist* (in time as part of Nature), goodness *is*; it has *being*. See here the ontological framework on which Moore strings his ethics. Moore carries over these basic distinctions in the natural/non-natural polarity.

But there are grave difficulties involved, some of which did not escape Moore's perceptive glance. In 1942 he admitted that *Principia* failed to present a "tenable explanation" of the natural/non-natural distinction. He is now "perfectly sure" that Broad is right in questioning whether any property, natural or non-natural, can exist in time by *itself* (R, 581-82). He even calls his

[12] Here the post-Kantian as well as anti-Kantian strain in Moore's ethicizing comes to the fore. He is particularly concerned to demonstrate the impossibility of conceiving goodness as a relation between an object and a state of Mind.

[13] But, from the belief that goodness is "intrinsic" (as distinct from goodness as a "quality" or even an "intrinsic quality"), it does follow that it *would* be the duty of a *possible* agent to produce it, though not of *actual* agents. That is, an "ought-implying" property is inherent in Moore's use of the term "intrinsic value." Cf. p. 22. For a discussion of the good-ought relation, cf. p. 53.

[14] Nature includes "all that has existed, does exist, or will exist in time." Only objects which "may be said to exist now, to have existed, or to be about to exist" are *natural* (*PE*, 40).

earlier view "utterly silly and preposterous." Lewy has pointed out that Moore had recognized certain mistakes already before 1922 (thus anticipating, on points, Broad's critique by some twenty years). However, Moore's new formulations as given by Lewy cannot be said to shed much light on the matter at hand.[15] But even this was not his earliest attempt to develop an alternative view. During the time-span 1914-1917 he concentrated on regarding goodness as intrinsic value. *"To say that a kind of value is "intrinsic" means merely that the question whether a thing possesses it, and in what degree it possesses it, depends solely on the intrinsic nature of the thing in question"* (*PS*, 260). And this implies, concludes Moore, that "A kind of value is intrinsic if and only if, it is *impossible* that x and y should have different values of the kind, unless they differ in intrinsic nature," or again, "A kind of value is intrinsic if and only if, when anything possesses it, that same thing or anything exactly like it would *necessarily* or *must* always, under all circumstances, possess it in exactly the same degree" (*PS*, 265).

This necessary "dependence"[16] of intrinsic value on natural intrinsic properties marks a shift in emphasis for Moore. In *Principia* he had stressed the "independence" of goodness in respect to natural properties: goodness could be plucked from an object without the object losing its identity. Now, although he still holds to the "independence" of good, in order to avoid any appearance of arbitrariness, he stresses the "necessary dependence" of goodness on natural properties. If X is good, it is bearer of A, B, and C. The connection is "necessary." If X is good, it is "impossible" that Y (only numerically different from X) is not good. But in what way "impossible," in what way "necessarily" or "must always": here Moore confesses to be at a loss. He is certain that it is neither "factual necessity" (the necessity sought involves not only what is or will be, but also what *could* be or could have been the case), nor "causal necessity" (the necessity sought must hold even if entirely different causal laws ruled our universe). Even "logical necessity" is ruled out (the necessity sought cannot, it seems, be deduced from any logical law). From the fact that X has

[15] "A 'natural' property is a property with which it is the business of the natural sciences or of psychology to deal, or which can be completely defined in terms of such." Casimir Lewy, "G. E. Moore on the Naturalistic Fallacy," *Proceedings of the British Academy* L (1964), p. 254.

[16] In 1942 Moore reaffirms his views on dependence. "It is true, indeed, that I should never have thought of suggesting that goodness was 'non-natural,' unless I had supposed that it was 'derivative' in the sense that, whenever a thing is good (in the sense in question) its goodness (in Mr. Broad's words) 'depends on the presence of certain non-ethical characteristics' possessed by the thing in question: I have always supposed that it did so 'depend,' in the sense that, if a thing is good (in my sense), then that it is so *follows* from the fact that it possesses certain natural intrinsic properties, which are such that from the fact that it is good it does *not* follow conversely that it has those properties" (R, 588).

21

A, B, and C, it cannot be logically deduced that X is good — even though if X is good, it is necessarily because it has A, B, and C.[17]

Approaching the matter from another tack, Moore points to the difference between "intrinsic properties" (such as 'yellow' and 'being a state of pleasure') and "not intrinsic properties," those of intrinsic value. But, admitted Moore in 1942, this only added to the confusion. The natural/non-natural distinction ought to be described rather as that between "natural intrinsic properties" and "non-natural intrinsic properties" (R, 585). In 1942 he further exemplifies his earlier stand.

The account is that an intrinsic property is "natural" if and only if, in ascribing it to a natural object, you are *to some extent* "describing" that object ... [and] not "natural" if, in ascribing it to a natural object you are not describing that object *to any extent at all*. (R, 591)

However, he admonishes, "I am no more able to specify the sense of describe in question" now than I was in 1914-17.[18]

Later in the same "Reply" (603-06) he again attempts to explain the natural/non-natural distinction. Intrinsic value possesses a peculiar "ought-implying property" which places one under obligation to produce intrinsic value. Is this perhaps the unique characteristic of non-natural intrinsic properties? Closer examination forces Moore to admit that natural intrinsic properties, for example, pleasantness, are also "ought-implying" (the only requirement to be ought-implying is intrinsicness). What now: is there any reason to distinguish the natural from the non-natural? Yes, affirms Moore, for *intrinsic value*, though it cannot be identical with each of a number of different intrinsic properties, or with the disjunction of them all, is entailed by *each* of them. This is not true of any other intrinsic property (no other property which is also ought-implying is at the same time entailed by all the others). Thus, intrinsic value is a unique kind of intrinsic property, a uniqueness which he prefers to designate with the term "non-natural." But, since Moore is at a loss as how to explain the type of "necessity" and "entailment" involved in the relation of natural and non-natural intrinsic properties (as we have just noted), the explanation grinds to an abrupt halt.

The Naturalistic Fallacy

Nevertheless, in spite of difficulties of explanation, Moore held throughout his life to the natural/non-natural distinction. He has observed only too often

[17] For an expanded treatment of necessity, see pp. 62-70.
[18] Cf. also *PS*, 272ff. In this situation it is understandable that Moore in 1942 was "partly inclined" to accept Stevenson's position that in saying "X is good," a person is not making an assertion at all which could be true or false. Good in this case would be non-descriptive and would have only emotive meaning (R, 540ff.).

the consequences of a failure to abide by the distinction. To confuse a natural with a non-natural property is to commit the naturalistic fallacy (in one of its forms). The fallacy is committed when one denies that "good is indefinable," i.e. when one tries to define the non-natural notion good in terms of some natural notion.

Positively, the naturalistic fallacy "consists in identifying the simple notion which we mean by 'good' with some other notion" (*PE*, 58; cf. 10, 73, 124). Negatively, it is the "failure to distinguish clearly that unique and indefinable quality which we mean by good" (*PE*, 59). In more general terms, those who commit the naturalistic fallacy "confuse the first and second of the three possible questions which Ethics can ask" (*PE*, 38). They "hold that from any proposition asserting 'Reality is of this nature' we can infer, or obtain confirmation for, any proposition asserting 'This is good in itself'" (*PE*, 114).

The danger, Moore never tires of warning, is confusing goodness as a *unique* quality with the other qualities in virtue of which something is called good.[19] It is fallacious to identify the value of any object with some "ordinary" property of it. In essence the naturalistic fallacy is perpetrated by anyone who attempts to define ethical concepts in non-ethical terms. This fallacy is inevitable unless one holds to the "unique nature of ethical truths" (*PE*, 114). Anyone who begins from a definition of "good" automatically, as it were, disqualifies himself as an ethicist. He has reduced ethics to physics, biology, psychology, metaphysics etc. depending on the area from out of which he extracts the "definition" (*PE*, 40; *LP*, 196). In accepting a definition one ties himself to a certain position and is thus unable to engage in the "open" logical reasoning which characterizes scientific activity. He no longer has an open mind. On the one hand, any definition logically pre-determines what ethical principles one can accept, on the other hand, all other definitions and principles are wrong *before-hand* (*PE*, 11, 20-21). In effect, logical reasoning is reduced in such instances to the status of a "handmaid" carrying out previously issued instructions. Moore's conclusion: When one begins with a definition of good "no reason at all, far less any valid reason" (*PE*, 20) can be offered in support of an ethical principle; at the same time, "it is then impossible either to prove that any other definition is wrong or even to deny such definition" (*PE*, 11). Not only is the naturalist (or any "definist") unable to offer any *valid* reasons in support of his ethical principles (the reasons given are merely deductions *from* the definition which itself requires proof), but the definition itself is non-

---

[19] As Broad formulates it: When one defines good he makes himself guilty of confusing his own *criteria* for what is good (good-making characteristics) with the essence of good itself. Cf. *PGEM*, 64. That this is an accurate portrayal of Moore's intentions becomes evident in *Principia* when he accuses modern Epistemology à la Kant of holding the "self-contradictory assumption that 'truth' and the criterion of truth are one and the same thing" (*PE*, 133).

ethical and thus self-contradictory (*PE*, 11, 19, 20, 38, 139). Any attempt to define "good" involves one in logical contradictions. That is, one is guilty of what Moore labelled — and the label has "stuck" — the naturalistic fallacy. The only way of escape is to declare good indefinable. Moore's proof of indefinability is essentially negative; if good is not indefinable, it can only be a) "a complex, a given whole" or b) "it means nothing at all." But both possibilities "may be dismissed by a simple appeal to facts" (*PE*, 15). In his refutation of the first possibility Moore developed what has become known as *the* refutation of Naturalism, the *famous open-question argument*.

Take any suggested definition of good. Then consider if it is not possible "with significance" to question the goodness of the object offered as the definition of the good. If it is possible to ask this question meaningfully, if it makes sense to ask if the object in question is good, the definition is proved without a shadow of doubt to be wrong. For if the "property" or "object" is indeed the definition, it is sense-less to raise the query, it would be pointless. One would be asking "is goodness good," and this, as Edwards has aptly called it,[20] is a self-answering question. For example, if good *means* pleasure, there is no need to inquire if pleasure is good. That's like asking if "pleasure is pleasure," or "good, good." However, the query, "is pleasure good," is constantly being raised and this fact itself suffices to refute the definition. The conclusion of the matter: "The point that 'good is indefinable,' and that to deny this involves a fallacy, is a point capable of strict proof: for to deny it involves contradictions" (*PE*, 77).

The only remaining alternative is that good "means nothing at all." In such cases differences in regard to "good" are merely verbal. The word "good" is merely a synonym for some other concept and we have to do with tautologies (*PE*, 11-12, 19, 38, 73, 139). Since in all such instances no ethical propositions (by definition synthetic for Moore) are involved, Moore feels justified in disposing of this possibility even as he announces it. At the same time he realizes that no one would be willing to allow that his ethical teachings lacked (ethical) meaning. Naturalists too are anxious to persuade us that "what they call the good is what we really ought to do" (*PE*, 12). But neither information about how words are employed, or a listing of synonyms, etc. is capable of providing the slightest substantiation for such views. What such intentions do demonstrate is that everyone — naturalists included — are "constantly aware" of the unique property of things called good (*PE*, 17). This awareness is in itself sufficient refutation of the position that good has no meaning of its own.

The crucial importance of indefinability for Moore is further illustrated at every turn in *Principia*. At the key points in his argument he refers back to the discussion in chapter one (the naturalistic fallacy and open-question). Chapter

---

[20] Edwards, *The Logic of Moral Discourse* (1955), p. 209.

II is mainly directed at illustrating further "the positive result, *already established* in Chapter I" (*PE*, 58). The central idea of chapter IV that metaphysics "can have no logical bearing whatever upon the answer to the fundamental ethical question... *follows at once* from the conclusion of Chapter I, that 'good' denotes an ultimate, unanalysable predicate" (*PE*, 139-40; cf. 118, 129). In chapter V, prior to considering the answer to QIII, Moore summarizes the argument thus far: "So much, then, for the first step in our ethical method, the step which *established* that good is good and nothing else whatever, and that Naturalism was a fallacy" (*PE*, 144, my italics in all cases).

It all sounds very simple and most convincing! Indeed, Moore won the day with his open-question argument. But it is a deceptive simplicity in more ways than one. Despite the central place which the refutation of the naturalistic fallacy has enjoyed since Moore first introduced it in 1903, the exact nature of the fallacy has been and is subject to acute and continual controversy. Is Moore's fallacy a re-working of Hume's is-ought distinction? Or is it unrelated? Is the open-question argument logically anterior or posterior to intuitionism?

The naturalistic fallacy has enjoyed a rather unusual history of interpretation.[21] Immediately after its birth it was hailed by the philosophical avant garde as the unsurmountable obstacle to Naturalism. Naturalism, Moore had proven, is not the alternative to Idealism. Mankind must return to the realities of the Universe, but he must not reduce everything in reality to that which is "natural." In face of Moore's argument it was generally agreed that the philosophical traffic no longer dared to enter the dead-end streets of Naturalism. One glance at Moore's "Danger Ahead" sign was enough to cause the traffic to seek new routes. Perhaps the most remarkable aspect of this whole affair is the almost naive, unquestioning manner in which his argument was received, acclaimed and heeded. It was not until 1939 that the fallacy was subjected to a comparatively detailed investigation. In his now famous article Frankena claims that the fallacy argument is only valid *after* one has first proven the intuitionist position. He argued that since the fallacy involves "confusion or identifying two properties," it can more fittingly be termed the "definist fallacy." However, as such it has no "essential connexion with the bifurcation of the ethical and non-ethical." Rather than functioning as the *apriori* instrument certain to insure victory in any skirmish, it is *logically posterior* to intuitionism and "can enter only at the end of the controversy."[22] The real dispute between intuition-

---

[21] In his *Logic and the Basis of Ethics* (1949) A. N. Prior has called attention to precursors of Moore's naturalistic fallacy argument, in particular, eighteenth-century intuitionists (most strikingly, Richard Price), Bishop Whately and Henry Sidgwick.

Consult W. Hudson, *Ethical Intuitionism* (1967) for a concise introduction to eighteenth-century intuitionism and for bibliographic references to relevant literature.

[22] Frankena, "The Naturalistic Fallacy," *Mind* XLVIII (1939), pp. 464-77 (reprinted

ism and definism, centering around the existence or non-existence of certain ethical qualities, does not involve a *logical fallacy*. What is involved is moral color blindness (on the part of definists, if they are wrong) or moral hallucinations (on the part of intuitionists, if they are wrong). Despite the weight of Frankena's critique it was still regarded as disastrous to commit the naturalistic fallacy. One avoided perpetrating it as he avoided the plague; the more amazing since intuitionism had soon passed its zenith. So complete was the annihilation of Naturalism as a respectable ethical position that its defenders to this day are few and far between. Contemporary philosophers brave enough to break a lance for Naturalism (and their number is multiplying in recent years) do so without the stridency and bravour reminiscent of the pre-Moorean era. And either they advocate a chastened version which (they believe) avoids the naturalistic fallacy or they initiate action to render the Moorean argument ineffective.[23] However, the majority of philosophers, still viewing the fallacy as a yawning chasm, have occupied themselves with sprucing up the logic and streamlining the technique involved. Paul Taylor has recently noted at least four versions in circulation.[24]

This development forces one question to the fore: if Frankena is right and the naturalistic fallacy is only *valid* after one has first adopted intuitionism, why the continued (un)popularity of the fallacy in a time when intuitionism is out of grace? This is not a simple question to answer. One is confronted with a paradoxical situation: although many are under the influence of Frankena's conclusions, they cannot rid themselves of the feeling that the fallacy is not as innocent as it is made out to be. There are contemporary scholars who, sharing Frankena's idea that the naturalistic fallacy is in essence the definist fallacy, challenge his conclusion that the fallacy is logically posterior to intuitionism. A. White, for example, in spite of his disagreement with intuitionism, considers Moore's arguments to be still valid "because these refutations rest on the use of the naturalistic fallacy argument and not, even if he often thought so, on his own particular view of the meaning of 'good'."[25] But does this prove that Frankena is wrong and White right? It would seem not. What it does do is question whether one must consider the fallacy to be so intimately related to intuitionism as Frankena suggests. Is it not more reasonable to assume that a

in Sellars and Hospers, *Readings in Ethical Theory*, 1952). As late as 1958 Frankena saw need to challenge those who consider the argument a potent weapon. Cf. *P* XXXIII (1958), pp. 158-62 where Frankena questions the effectiveness of Alasdair MacIntyre's use of the argument.

[23] See the concluding section of chapter four for a brief discussion of the "New Naturalism."

[24] Taylor, *Normative Discourse* (1961), p. 242ff.

[25] White, *G. E. Moore* (1958), pp. 126-27. Thus, he is able to accuse the pragmatistic and coherence theories of truth of committing the naturalistic fallacy ("Truth as Appraisal," *Mind* LXVI, 1957, p. 323).

naturalistic fallacy type argument is logically posterior to *any* position one might care to hold?

The Naturalistic Fallacy: Its General Sense

In an effort to advance the discussion, let us go back to Moore and examine the place and meaning of the naturalistic fallacy in his work. To begin with it must be allowed that Moore's descriptions of the fallacy elicit two rather diverse types of interpretations. Many are inclined to view it as the intractable result of efforts to reduce one simple notion to another. As we have seen, William Frankena aptly dubbed this the "definist fallacy." With characteristic pith and whimsicalness, John Wisdom has termed it the "Idiosyncracy Platitude"; to wit, "every sort of statement has its own meaning."[26] E. F. Carritt in a similar vein suggests "heterogenous" as an appropriate substitute for "naturalistic."[27] The Moorean scholar A. White also interprets the naturalistic fallacy in this "definist" way.[28]

Although Moore invoked a special name (naturalistic fallacy) for the confusion of two notions in ethics, the detection of this fallacy was one of his major philosophical preoccupations. Thus, he accused Idealism of continually acting as if one can treat blue and a sensation of blue, existence and a thought of existence as single notions. To make such confusions is to stand condemned. In our discussion, we shall refer to this interpretation as the naturalistic fallacy *in its general sense.*[29]

The Specific Sense of the Fallacy

There is another sense; to which we shall affix the name, the naturalistic fallacy *in its specific sense.* Under the impact of Moore's stress on the autonomy, uniqueness and independence of ethical notions (such as goodness) over against natural science and metaphysics, one is led to consider any attempt to define

---

[26] Wisdom, *Philosophy and Psycho-Analysis* (1953), p. 51. Compare with J. O. Urmson's epigram, "every statement has its own logic" (*Philosophical Analysis*, 1952, p. 79).
[27] Carritt, *Ethical and Political Thinking* (1947), p. 17.
[28] White, *op. cit.*, pp. 122-27. Most recently, Fogelin, *Evidence and Meaning* (1967) p. 127 ff.
    A. N. Prior in *Logic and the Basis of Ethics* also considers Moore's set-up the argument from trivialization. However, later he insists that the argument can be broadened to include the more basic fallacy of deducing an ethical conclusion from non-ethical premises.
[29] More technically Moore castigates in the general sense of the fallacy-argument any inference from *extensional* equivalence to *intensional* equivalence. The fact that two propositions are constantly cojoin does not empower one to infer that they are identical.

ethical concepts in non-ethical terms illicit. In this view one begins from the supposition that ethical propositions are logically independent of any other kind of truth. The fallacy is perpetrated if one denies this autonomy and interprets ethical propostions in terms of "reality" (as naturalists are inclined to do) or in terms of a "higher reality" (as metaphysicians tend to do). Thus, H. Osborne has objected that the naturalistic fallacy is not simply confusing an adjective with a noun, rather the defining of "value" in terms of psychological or empirical fact.[30] More recently, R. M. Hare felt compelled to point out that there is more at issue than the "definist" fallacy. There is the basic mistake of moving from purely factual or descriptive premises to moral or evaluative judgments.[31] According to Nowell-Smith the fallacy involves identifying ethical properties with natural properties.[32]

However, in spite of the obvious difference between these two interpretations, this difference has to my knowledge never received the stress that it deserves.[33] As a result, the discussion of the naturalistic fallacy is still shrouded in fog. As we have already intimated, and as could be gleaned from the various quotations that we have cited from *Principia*, Moore himself often confused the two senses of the fallacy. It is noteworthy in this connection that Moore, although basically concerned with the specific sense, graces the title page of *Principia* with an epigram borrowed from Bishop Butler, "Everything is what it is, and not another thing," that can only bear the general interpretation.

Nevertheless, Moore's intentions are clear. "If indeed good were a feeling, as some would have us believe, then it would exist in time. But that is why to call it so is to commit the naturalistic fallacy" (*PE*, 41). The fallacy to which he is pointing in this case involves more than a mistaken identification of two notions. The fallacy is committed by anyone who treats a non-natural notion which "is" as a natural notion which "exists in time." The fallacy "consists in

[30] Osborne, *Foundations of the Philosophy of Value* (1933), p. 67.
[31] Hare, *The Language of Morals* (1952), p. 83ff. Hare asserts that the logical rule, "No 'ought' from an 'is'," (*Freedom and Reason*, 1963, p. 108), which he names Hume's Law in reference to *Treatise on Human Nature* iii, I, i, "was the point behind Professor G. E. Moore's celebrated 'refutation of naturalism'" (*LM*, 30).
[32] Nowell-Smith, *Ethics* (1954), p. 33; cf. also p. 36.
[33] This is perhaps best reflected in the general failure to distinguish the naturalistic fallacy and the open-question argument. Cf. discussion below. Frankena called attention to the possibility of various interpretations. But it appears that he, wrongly in my view, considered the special sense of the fallacy the doctrine of intuitionism itself. There is indeed an intimate connection in Moore's work. However, there are at present many ethicists who share Moore's basic critique of Naturalism without sharing his intuitionism.
It may be objected that it is out of place to term the naturalistic fallacy in its special sense a "fallacy." I have continued to employ the term because Moore used it in both senses. Lewy informs us that Moore realized that he was using the term "fallacy" in an "extended, and perhaps improper, sense." Lewy, *op. cit.*, p. 256.

the contention that good *means* nothing but some simple or complex notion, that can be defined in terms of natural qualities" (*PE*, 73). Mill's basic mistake was not merely that he defined good, but rather that he defined good in *natural* (rather than non-natural) terms. Naturalists have failed to detect a most important characteristic of the Universe — the non-natural. The metaphysicians have, to their credit, seen the more-than-natural character of the Universe, but they have wrongly assumed that the non-natural must "exist" as a "super-sensible Reality" (*PE*, 125). "The naturalistic fallacy ... rests upon the failure to perceive that any truth which asserts 'This is good in itself' is quite unique in kind — that it cannot be reduced to any assertion about reality" (*PE*, 114). Here in a nutshell we have Moore's basic critique: the naturalists and the metaphysicians define good in terms of "existence" and "reality" — natural or supersensible — and thus commit the naturalistic fallacy (in the specific sense).

At this point it is imperative to recognize that Moore's fundamental objection to Naturalism and Metaphysics (ultimately based, as we shall see, on inspection) must be distinguished from the technical argument (the open-question approach) by which he sought to give his views scientific standing. One sees the difference and the relation in the opening sections of chapter II (*PE*, 37-38). Moore begins by stating his major objection to Naturalism. For Naturalism "there is only *one* kind of fact, of which the existence has any value at all." But, he does not set out to prove that there is another kind of fact, or even to challenge the view that this single kind of fact is "held to define the sole good." His concern is rather with "another characteristic"; namely, that this single kind of fact is "held to define what is meant by 'good' itself." With this subtle, but very real shift from "the sole good" (complex QII) to the meaning of "good itself" (complex QI), he begins his descent to the logical level. He proposes to prove that any definition of the adjective "good" (QI) is logically self-contradictory.

Similarly in relation to metaphysical ethics, Moore is not concerned to deny that "something which is real possesses all the characteristics necessary for perfect goodness" (*PE*, 113) — this may well be true. The fallacy is that the metaphysician implies that the "realness" involved has *logical bearing* upon the "goodness" (*PE*, 114, 118, 125, 126). His strictures against Naturalism and *mutatis mutandis* against Metaphysics clearly fall into two categories. A) On the logical plane, Naturalism is *fallacious* because it confuses goodness with some other concept; consequently it does not allow the "openness" necessary for scientific ethicizing. As it closes the mind to any but a naturalistic solution, the arguments it employs both to defend its own position and refute that of others are invalid. Here we have to do with the naturalistic fallacy in its general sense. B) On a deeper level, Naturalism is guilty of *overlooking* the fact that "goodness" is a unique non-natural quality which cannot be reduced to, or identified with, or exhausted in "natural" properties. See here the fallacy in its specific sense.

After the analysis given above was completed, Casimir Lewy's Dawes Hicks Lecture on Philosophy for the British Academy (1964) came to my attention. In this lecture Lewy gives a synopsis of an unpublished draft originally intended as the Preface to the second edition of *Principia Ethica* of 1922. It appears that Moore's unpublished Preface provides strong substantiation for my analysis of the naturalistic fallacy.[34] Butler's dictum, Moore declares, may be interpreted in three diverse ways, all of which, since he had not distinguished them as such, had been used interchangeably in *Principia*. It may mean "*either* 'Good is different from everything other than Good' *or* 'Good is different from everything which we express by any word or phrase other than the word 'good'" or finally, that "Good was not identical with any natural or metaphysical property." The first alternative is now dismissed by Moore as trivial (it holds true for any concept, definable or indefinable), the second is judged to be obviously false (in fact we do employ synonyms for 'good'); only the third is tenable and justifiable (and it is what Moore desired to assert all along). As Lewy tells it, Moore also confessed that he had made an analogous mistake in respect to the naturalistic fallacy. He had "confused the three entirely different propositions (1) 'So-and-so is identifying Good with some property other than Good'; (2) 'So-and-so is identifying Good with some *analysable* property'; and (3) 'So-and-so is identifying Good with some *natural or metaphysical* property'." As a result he had accused others of committing the naturalistic fallacy and not only when they held (3), in which case the charge is justified, but also when they — innocently it turns out now — held (1) and (2). Moore is anxious to explain that Good retains its uniqueness (it is not identical with any natural or metaphysical property) regardless of whether it is analysable or unanalysable. But, adds Moore, if Good "is analysable at all, it involves in its analysis *some* unanalysable notion which is not natural or metaphysical."[35]

From a reading of Lewy's lecture it becomes clear that Moore understood that affirmative answers to the question of *analysability* do not necessarily entail negative answers to the question of *uniqueness* (the reverse also holds true) and further that the latter question is the all-important one. In the Preface Moore was concerned to separate his concern with indefinability in senses (1) and (2) (comparable with what we have termed the naturalistic fallacy in its general sense) from his major thesis asserting the uniqueness of Good (3) (comparable with the fallacy in its specific sense). In one sentence: Moore no

---

[34] It remains a puzzle that Moore did not publish the "Preface" — be it in some other form. That he did not publish it as the preface to a second edition is perfectly understandable. With his clarified insights into the matters at hand he either had to rewrite the book or keep silent. In the Preface to the second edition which was published Moore thus says: "it is reprinted without alteration, because I found that, if I were to begin correcting what in it seemed to me to need correction, I could not stop short of rewriting the whole book" (*PE*, xii). Cf. p. 36.

[35] All the quotations are from Lewy, *op. cit.*, pp. 251-55.

longer supposes that "Good is not identical with any such property [as pleasure] *rests* on the contention that Good is unanalysable."

The Open-Question Argument

Having determined that it is necessary to distinguish between the naturalistic fallacy in its general and specific senses, the critical question surfaces. Does Moore's refutation of the fallacy hold in respect to both senses? To discover the answer one must first take a closer look at the technical make-up of the argument itself.

There is more to the open-question than first meets the eye. Moore was well aware of what was involved. To explain to readers "familiar with philosophical terminology" that good is indefinable, he states "That propositions about the good are all of them synthetic and never analytic; and that is plainly no trivial matter" (*PE*, 6-7). In concluding chapter II he adds that he has previously established that the "fundamental principles of Ethics must be *synthetic* propositions" (*PE*, 58). In a later key passage, to which we will return again, he declares:

In fact, it follows from the meaning of good and bad, that such propositions are all of them, in Kant's phrase, "synthetic": they all must rest in the end upon some proposition which must be simply accepted or rejected, which cannot be logically deduced from any other proposition. ... the fundamental principles of Ethics must be self-evident. (*PE*, 143)

Careful scrutiny reveals that these (and other references) are not the literary touches applied to give the ethical edifice its "finished-off" look, but the few remaining evidences of the "girders" which support and buttress the entire structure. We have hit upon the (logical) substructure of Moore's "house": the Kantian analytic-synthetic distinction (*PE*, 18, 33 ff., 38, 58, 143 ff., 220-21). The open-question argument (as well as his refutation of Idealism, and his treatment of the problems of perception etc.) is a worked-out version of the analytical-synthetic distinction. Or in his own words those who commit the naturalistic fallacy fail

to perceive that their conclusion 'what possesses this property is good' is a significant [synthetic] proposition: that it does not mean either 'what possesses this property, possesses this property' [= analytic] or 'the word "good" denotes that a thing possesses this property' [= analytic]. And yet, if it does *not* mean one or other of these two things, the inference contradicts its own premise. (*PE*, 38)

Stripped to its steel (technical and logical) skeleton, the lines in Moore's argument run as follows. One can begin with any proposed definition of good. Let us take one that was also in the center of Moore's attention: "good is pleasure."

31

In order for this to be meaningful, good and pleasure must be distinct terms. Otherwise the phrase is a tautology, one is asking if pleasure is pleasure, or if good is good. If they are distinct terms, then pleasure, being distinct, is not identifiable with the *whole* of good and must *only* be one of the terms that can be attributed to good. That is to say, "good is pleasure" asserts a connection between *two* different notions and is therefore "significant." It is a synthetic proposition in that it "adds" information and not an analytic proposition, an *identical* proposition with only *one* notion, one whose contradictory is self-contradictory (*PE*, 16). This implies that one can as meaningfully say "good is *not* pleasure" as that "good is pleasure" (which is precluded if an analytic proposition is involved). Thus to assert that "good is pleasure" means that to say "good is *identical* with pleasure" is self-contradictory. At one and the same time one is asserting distinctness (implying synthetic) and identity (implying analytic) of the two notions. Since good cannot be logically defined without self-contradiction his logical apparatus allows him but one alternative: good is (logically) indefinable. That is the negative side of the coin, the positive side reads: "Good is good and that is the end of the matter" (*PE*, 6).

The key to the open-question argument as employed by Moore lies in the word "meaningful." If it is found meaningful or significant to question a definition of good, it is by that very fact, and that fact alone, declared fallacious (*PE*, 14, 15, 38). He declares good to be "indefinable" because the question of meaning is always raised about any suggested definition of a simple concept. By *whom*? Everyman? The man of Common Sense? Moore? Even if everyone questioned the assertion that "good is pleasure," this only proves that *no one* defined good as being pleasure. In which case the proof is expendable and superfluous, or if one wishes, the proof can be considered valid in that it "proves" what was already believed, that good is not pleasure. However, does everyone question whether good is pleasure? It would seem not. Is it *meaningful* for one who defines good as pleasure (or considers the terms synonymous) to question the definition? Certainly, that would be a sense-less question. (If such a naturalist — one who defines good as pleasure — accepts the question whether good is pleasure as being significant, he is inconsistent. And then, but only then, does the open-question technique "work." Even here, however, it does not prove anything about the definitions concerned; only that there is inconsistency in the vicinity.)

The problem or "crux" for Moore is the criterion by which one is to judge significance. If there was one universally accepted criterion for meaningfulness, his open-question argument could be redeemed. But that is just the problem: there are as many criteria of meaning as there are recognizable positions. Moore assumes that *his* criterion is *the* criterion; that is, he operates as if the criterion is the same for everyone. This is his mistake. For one who believes that "good = sex" it has no *meaning* in the sense required by Moore to question whether sex is good. "Good=sex" is the very criterion by which he judges whether anything else has meaning. It is excluded *before-hand* that such a person will question his definition. If he does, he is abandoning his starting-point. But even then, he is not able to judge impartially, for he has already adopted another position which has now become his criterion of significance. All this means that the open-question argument only succeeds in convincing one of the validity of his own beliefs and of the untenableness of everyone else's. If he already stands with Moore and believes that "good is indefinable, and thus simple," the open-question confirms his "faith." Any definition of good is found wanting — but only because of the previously-accepted (before-the-argument) position that good is indefinable (simple). That is to say: if one considers "good" to be "pleasure," from his *point of view* he is not guilty of the naturalistic fallacy in any sense; because — for him — good is what it is (pleasure) and not another thing. He would only be guilty of the fallacy if he inconsistently defined good as desire (granting for the moment that desire is a separate notion, and not a synonym for pleasure). Then he is confusing two irreducible notions: pleasure and desire. The whole affair is a vicious circle. The logical open-question technique (no matter how sharply honed) is impotent to prove any definition wrong or right. Depending on the starting point, the operator sets the bite of his (logical) "saw." In each case the conclusion is foregone. In every instance, one's own stand is affirmed and the opponent's is found wanting.

Assumptions and Confusion

To answer the query with which we began this discussion, the open-question argument is only able (at best) to refute the naturalistic fallacy in its *general* sense. Although Moore's basic attack on Naturalism is expressed in what I termed the *specific* sense of the fallacy, his refutation is directed at the *general sense.* And whereas the former is not basically *logical* in nature, the latter is taken to be purely logical. Or in other words: Moore's open-question argument does not take to the field against the fallacy in its specific sense. And even in regard to the general sense, as we have seen, the open-question argument is power-less since it begs the question at issue. Only when good is "simple" and not a complex or part of a complex whole[36] is it self-contradictory to define good — but the simplicity of good is just what is being challenged by a definition of good. However, even granting the assumption of simplicity, the argument proves nothing about the ethical nature of goodness. That is to say, Moore

[36] It is also a possibility that a person wishes to put forth a *synonymous* definition. Moore seems to have forgotten that goodness can be expressed by other words, by synonyms. Once again he seems to have realized his mistake later, cf. Lewy, *op. cit.*, 253.

assumes not only that good is *simple* (and in this *general* sense indefinable) but also that it is a *unique* simple; that is, a non-natural simple (and in this specific sense indefinable).[37]

The difficulty is, and it has bred confusion, that in *Principia* Moore did not admit that the open-question argument is at best only capable of refuting the fallacy in its *general and not in its specific sense*. In *Principia* he did not distinguish the two senses of the fallacy nor did he sense the concomitant ambiguity surrounding his use of indefinability. However, there is implicit recognition. If the open-question argument is to confute the special sense of the fallacy, it must invalidate any movement from the natural ("is") to the non-natural ("ought"). It does not do this, it cannot do this, as it is *in*different to the argument whether "good" is ethical (non-natural) or non-ethical (natural). As Moore himself confessed at one point: "Even if it [good] were a natural object, that would not alter the nature of the fallacy nor diminish its importance one whit" (*PE*, 14). In other words the logical open-question stands in the way of a reduction of an ethical object to a non-ethical object in the *same degree* that it frowns on the confusion of two natural notions or even two non-natural notions. Moore provides countless examples of the former (pleasure and red, self and pleasure, yellow and orange) as well as of the latter (metaphysical ethics in its various forms). The fallacy is the same in all cases. "If anybody were to say, for instance, that pleasure *means* the sensation of red . . . . Well, that would be the same fallacy which I have called the naturalistic fallacy" (*PE*, 13).[38] By wielding the logical sword, Moore not only did in the naturalist who claimed that "pleasure is good" but also the idealist who confessed "*esse*

[37] But what feature grants goodness its unique non-natural (ethical) character in relation to other concepts? This is not a simple question to answer. On the one hand, good = good, *period*. On the other hand, "good ought to be." Thus, as we have seen, the question QII, "What things are good in themselves?" can also take the form "What ought to be?" (to be sharply distinguished from QIII, "What ought we to *do*?"). Indeed, in his refutation Moore continually trades on the fact that defining good amounts to defrocking it of its normative, ought character (for example, *PE*, 73). But in such cases Moore himself appears guilty of confusing two notions — goodness and oughtness — and thus of committing the fallacy in its general sense. Ought X to *be* simply because it possesses the quality of goodness? Moore can only avoid violating the is-ought distinction (the heart of the fallacy argument) by identifying goodness and oughtness. Then X ought to be merely because it is good. But this does away with the simplicity of goodness! Cf. the discussion of this problem in chapter three, p. 64ff.

For arguments of a similar nature addressed to intuitionists, cf. Nowell-Smith, *Ethics*, pp. 36-43 and Ayer, "On the Analysis of Moral Judgments," *Philosopical Essays* (1954). Cf. also, R. M. Hare, *The Language of Morals*, p. 30.

[38] Thus, the name of the fallacy is most inappropriate. Even within Moore's ethics this is abundantly clear. Not only the naturalists, but also the metaphysicians are guilty of the fallacy. But the name is not the important consideration and Moore was untouched by critique at this point. "I do not care about the name, what I do care about is the fallacy" (*PE*, 14).

is percipi."[39] In line with his refutation of the subjectivist conclusion that "being true is identical with being cognised," he challenged the concomitant conclusion in ethics that "being good is identical with being willed" (*PE*, 133). According to the open-question argument, a reduction of a non-natural to a natural notion is proscribed because the two objects are not identical; it has nothing to do with the supposed invalidity of moving from an "is" to an "ought." It only proves that X cannot be reduced to A, if it is X, without self-contradiction. As far as the argument is concerned, it is wholly accidental that sometimes one of the diverse objects is ethical and the other non-ethical. Even when one infringes on the is-ought, natural/non-natural demarcation, the *mistake* is not the infringement as such, but merely that *two* different objects are treated as being identical.

In conclusion, the open-question argument is only apropos to the naturalistic fallacy and definability in the general sense. Concretely: whereas it claims to prove that "good is indefinable," in actuality it only shows that "good" is as indefinable as *any other simple notion*. Thus considered, it becomes embarrassingly clear how little is gained. The open-question argument is simply the logical form of Butler's dictum, and as such, it defends with all the power of logic the sacredness of individual identity. It does not in the least tend to prove that "good" is unique, primus inter pares, among the class of indefinables. Yet, this is what Moore desires to prove and intends to prove and even, at least in *Principia*, considers proven. He not only declares an attempt to define one simple notion in terms of the other an instance of the naturalistic fallacy, he also, and with stress, links up the fallacy with a neglect to acknowledge the *unique* nature of good as a non-natural ethical object.

Thus, Moore relates that his purpose in chapter II is to "illustrate the fact that the naturalistic fallacy is a fallacy, or, in other words, that we are all aware of a certain simple quality, which (and not anything else) is what we mainly mean by the term 'good'" (*PE*, 38).[40] The explanatory phrase "in other words" is bound to confuse. One receives the misleading impression that the logical proof (referred to in the first clause) is on the same level as the "awareness" of good (referred to in the second clause); as if one is saying the same thing. This is not at all the case, Moore has confusedly telescoped two matters into one.

Indefinability of Good: Later Views

Thus far we have limited ourselves largely to Moore's explanation of the indefinability of "good" as expressed in *Principia*. This is not accidental. For although Moore has become (in)famous for his views of indefinability, he never

[39] See, for example, Moore's famous "The Refutation of Idealism" (*PS*, 1-31).
[40] Again; "It is, indeed, only when we have detected this fallacy, when we have become clearly aware of the unique object which is meant by 'good'" (*PE*, 61).

again subjects the whole matter to a full-scale investigation. This is the more strange since he had difficulties with his explanation in *Principia* immediately after it was published in 1903.

> In *Principia* I asserted and proposed to prove that 'good' . . . was indefinable. But all the supposed proofs were certainly fallacious; they entirely failed to prove that 'worth having for its own sake' is indefinable. And I think that perhaps it is definable; I do not know. But I also still think that very likely it *is* indefinable. (*PP*, 98)

Moore nowhere explained why he regarded the previously air-tight arguments as fallacious. And prior to 1964 one could only guess. In that year, as we have previously noted, Lewy published the contents of a draft written by Moore sometime prior to 1922. In this document Moore discredits any talk of the naturalistic fallacy in other than what we termed the *specific sense*. In view of this, and recalling our previous conclusion that Moore's open-question argument was only apropos to the fallacy in its general sense, is it too much to surmise that he considered the arguments irrelevant to the point at issue? The arguments of *Principia* are fallacious because they either proved something trivial (indefinability in a general sense, the definist fallacy) or something wrong, but in any case not what required proof: "indefinability" in the specific sense.

A following question is whether Moore realized that no valid proof could ever be constructed which convicted anyone of the trespassing of the fallacy in its specific sense; or positively, did he still dream that one could prove that "goodness" was indefinable, that is non-natural and also non-metaphysical? These are moot questions. No answers can be given with any confidence. There are indications however which lead one to suppose that he believed a new and valid proof to be a real possibility. It would appear that his chief problem was his inability to fabricate a new proof, not the possibility of such a proof.[41]

In any case a remarkable state of affairs has announced itself. Despite this hesitancy and even confession of error, Moore's argumentation continues — without offering new proofs — to presuppose the indefinability of good in the specific sense. It is, thus, ill-advised to move from Moore's infrequent treatment of indefinability in his post-1920 period to the conclusion that the whole matter has lost its importance. In his post-*Principia* period, as we noticed, he had begun to sense that he had formerly employed indefinability in at least two totally different senses. Although the matter of decomposition is not without interest,[42] indefinability in the specific sense or the non-natural nature of goodness is his real concern. In this connection, perhaps to avoid confusion,

---

[41] It is remarkable that Lewy presents a reformulation of Moore's open-question argument which he believes validly refutes the fallacy in its specific sense (his number 3) in the same paper as he reveals Moore's second thoughts on the matter. Cf. his British Academy Lecture, section II.
[42] Lewy, *op. cit.* p. 254.

he talks of "intrinsic value." The notion involved, Moore assures us, is "simple enough; and everybody will recognize it at once, as a notion which is constantly in people's heads" (*PS*, 259). But, when it comes to "defining it precisely," he runs into difficulties which he confesses appear to him insolvable (*PS*, 260-75).[43] Again Moore attempts and again he admits his failure to furnish a logical (read: scientific) explanation of the uniqueness of goodness. He is unable to explain the *distinction* between non-natural intrinsic properties and natural intrinsic properties. Nevertheless, he knows, everyone knows, that there is a tremendous difference — but to prove it, that's a different and difficult matter. One thing is certain: there is a difference.

Inspection

Our discussion has indicated that, even though in *Principia* Moore claims more, the open-question argument is only structurally able to relate itself to the naturalistic fallacy in its *general* sense. The weight of our results would, so to speak, double if we could discover that Moore himself was unable to proceed *as if* the open-question argument was sufficient to prove the indefinability of good. If our argument was valid, it would appear that he could not remain on the strictly logical level in complex QI. And this, indeed, turns out to be the case. No sooner has he launched the open-question argument than he appends by means of a "moreover" another argument of a different type. "Moreover any one can easily convince himself by inspection that the predicate of this proposition — 'good' — is positively different from the notion of 'desiring to desire'" (*PE*, 16). There would be no strangeness or difficulty with this "moreover"-argument if it were another logical consideration brought in to strengthen the case. The newness and strangeness, and thus importance, of this argument lies in the fact that it is not an appeal to "logic" (even though Moore is in the midst of logical complex QI and is assembling a logical argument). It is an appeal to *inspection* — and inspection belongs to complex QII.

It is possible that one could argue that this is simply a misplaced or, lacking that, a mis-phrased argument. Recalling the painstaking thoroughness of

---

[43] In an apparent attempt to alleviate difficulties surrounding the notion of intrinsic value; in other words, to make it easier to see what notion Moore is pointing at, Moore in 1912 announced that "no state of things can be intrinsically good unless it *contains* some feeling towards *something*" (*E*, 104). In 1921 he introduced the further restriction that intrinsic value is limited to "actual occurrences, actual states of things over a certain period of time — not such things as men, or characters, or material things" (*PS*, 327). In 1932 Moore redefined "intrinsically good" as "worth having for its own sake" (*PP*, 93-96). As Moore employed "having" in a sense which nothing "but an experience can be 'had'," only "experiences" could be intrinsically good. However, in 1942 he withdrew this latter restriction and, so it seems, abandoned this line of approach altogether (*R*, 555).

Moore, neither alternative is very likely. Moreover, and this is conclusive evidence it would appear, in order to refute the second alternative to the indefinability of the good ("that it might mean nothing at all"), Moore appeals to this "same consideration"; that is, to inspection.

But whoever will attentively consider with himself what is actually before his mind when he asks the question 'Is pleasure (or whatever it may be) after all good?' can easily satisfy himself that he is not merely wondering whether pleasure is pleasant. ... Everybody is constantly aware of this notion ["the unique property of things — which I mean by 'good'"], although he may never become aware at all that it is different from other notions of which he is also aware. But, for correct ethical reasoning, it is extremely important that he should become aware of this fact; and, as soon as the nature of the problem is clearly understood, there should be little difficulty in advancing so far in analysis. (*PE*, 16-17)

And neither of these instances is Moore's first appeal to inspection. He had no sooner introduced his division-method of analysis and the indefinability of "simple" notions when he exclaims:

But when you have enumerated them all, when you have reduced a horse to his simplest terms, then you can no longer define those terms. They are simply something which you *think of* or *perceive*, and to any one who cannot think of or perceive them, you can never, by any definition, make their nature known. (*PE*, 7, italics added)

Although, as these quotations evidence, Moore does not hide his appeal to inspection, the complicating factor is that inspection according to his set-up plays its decisive role in complex QII and not QI (the area of logic). That Moore regardless of his own system appeals to inspection in matters of complex QI leads to a confused situation. A striking example of this ambiguity is given in his treatment of metaphysical ethics.

In face of this direct perception that the two questions are distinct, no proof that they *must* be identical can have the slightest value. That the proposition 'This is good' is thus distinct from every other proposition was proved in chapter I. (*PE*, 126)

In one sentence he invokes inspection to disallow any possible logical proof that the propositions are identical; in the next he appeals to the logical proof (given in chapter I) that the propositions are distinct. If inspection can annul any logical proof, how can he proceed as if his own logical proof is safe from possible annulment. One can answer that he appeals to his logical proof because it was certified by inspection. This may indeed be the case. But, according to his own use, he is not permitted to speak of proven in such cases. Inspection for Moore never offers proof, it is simply the last court of appeal (which may still be right or wrong). But when something is proven, it is universally valid.

It is well to withhold judgment on this matter until more materials are gathered. One thing is certain, we have come across another key concept in Moore's ethics, a concept which asserts itself as the corollary of logical argumentation. In itself this complementary character is not surprising: Moore had explained that whereas complex QI was accessible to logical proof, complex QII was only open (in the final analysis) to inspection. What is surprising is that he should appeal to inspection in answering the question concerning "good" (which belongs to complex QI). In other words, even as he argues as if QI is "capable of strict proof" (*PE*, 77), he appeals to extra-logical inspection.

This discovery sheds at once more light on the whole matter. What Moore is really saying and doing — without stating it, and even perhaps without always being conscious of it — is this: Good is *logically* indefinable in that it cannot be confused with other simple notions without contradiction, and good is *intuitively* (by inspection) recognized as a "unique," "simple," and in that sense, indefinable object. The former stands over against the naturalistic fallacy in its general sense; the latter stands over against the fallacy in its specific sense. And whereas the former is insufficient by itself (good is no different from other simple notions) and requires the look of inspection (good is unique); the latter needs the former to give it the show of science (which is after all a logical activity).

COMPLEX QII: INTUITIONS, INTUITION AND THE METHOD OF ISOLATION

Once having ascertained the meaning of the adjective "good" (QI), one can proceed and ask what kinds of things are intrinsically "good" (QII). Having previously demonstrated that good (and bad) are simple and indefinable notions (QI), it is obvious that all propositions describing something as "good" are synthetic in character. Further that all such propositions "must in the end rest upon some proposition, which must be simply accepted or rejected . . . the fundamental propositions of Ethics must be self-evident" (*PE*, 143). These self-evident truths or "intuitions" (synthetic a priori) are beyond the reach of logical proof: they cannot be proven true or false, they are self-evident. That is to say: in crossing over the threshold from complex QI to complex QII, one moves from an area where final logical proof is possible to an arena where it is impossible in principle; from a region where direct proof is the order of the day, to a region where indirect proof is all one can hope for and expect. QII is the domain of self-evident intuitions.

From the vantage point of the inquiring subject, the migration from one area to another means that the answer to what kinds of things are good depends in the last analysis on *intuited* judgments (not as in QI, on logical reasonings). Ultimate truths are self-evident. They are intuitively recognized as such, they are immediately seen to be self-sufficient, they are believed without question, they are themselves their only and best certification. There is nothing more to be said. To ask for justification, validation or authorization is to demand the impossible. At best one can have his own reasons for *holding* such propositions to be self-evident, but he must never imagine that these subjective reasons are applicable to the propositions themselves. In themselves they are inaccessible to logical probing.

Intuitions

Thus a bird's-eye view of the terrain of QII. Now to retrace our flight, this time on foot. "Intuitions" are self-evident (ethical) truths to which "no relevant evidence whatever can be adduced: from no other truth, except themselves alone can it be inferred that they are true or false" (*PE*, viii). Later, Moore stresses the "objective" character of intuitions in even stronger words:

The expression 'self-evident' means properly that the proposition so called is evident or true, *by itself* alone .... The expression does *not* mean that the proposition is true, because it is evident to you or me or all mankind, because in other words it appears to us to be true. ... we mean emphatically that its appearing so to us, is *not* the reason why it is true: for we mean that it has absolutely no reason. (*PE* 143)

The self-evident character of certain propositions is beyond dispute. But, and this is a major difficulty for Moore, he is forced to introduce another "way of knowing." Moore is very cautious at this point and does not go into details. He is content to assert that "intuitions" are known. One perceives — no more need, nor can be said. Nevertheless, he cannot evade giving this organ of reception some more precise designation. It is intuition. The (subjective) intuition intuits (objective) Intuitions.[44] Answers to the question "What kinds of things are intrinsically good?" are self-evident. At a certain point no evidence can be brought forward, no logical proof is possible; the question must be answered *intuitively*. Questions in complex QII "must be settled by intuition alone — by the properly guarded method which was explained in discussing Hedonism" (*PE*, 173). Again, he terms a judgment of self-evidence a "judgment of that intuitional kind ... a direct judgment" (*PE*, 79,; cf. 92, 149).

In spite of this clear-cut appeal to intuition as the ultimate tribunal, Moore tries to minimize its importance. He continually stresses that it is intuitions (what is intuited) that are important and not their receptor. In the Preface of *Principia* (x) he assures us that he "*merely*" means by "Intuitions" to assert that certain propositions are incapable of proof, "I imply nothing whatever as to the manner or origin of our cognition of them." But, as if Moore sensed that the psychological intuition would still try to steal the show, he proceeds to deny that a proposition is true "*because* we cognise it in a particular way ... in

---

[44] Moore makes a habit of "objectivizing" subjective terms. It is not only intuitions which are considered to be mind-independent entities, but also propositions, ideas, judgments, and concepts.

every way in which it is possible to cognise a true proposition it is also possible to cognise a false one."

In other words, the subjective intuition can fail. Intuiting is no guarantee that what we intuit is true, it may be false. The intuitions are true in themselves, they are self-evident; that we recognize them as true is only a reason *for us* to hold them as true, they may still be true or false in themselves (*PE*, x, 75, 143-44). The best that can be had are persuasive reasons for believing certain propositions to be true.

As is apparent, Moore has worked himself into a strange, not to say, paradoxical position. Intuitions are true (self-evident), but we cannot be sure of intuiting truly. On the other hand, logical reasoning, if valid, can be known as being true, but such reasonings depend, in the last analysis, on intuitions. Later we shall discover what led Moore to assume this precarious stance.

One facet of Moore's intuition demands more attention: Moore has no desire to introduce an esoteric faculty.[45] He distinguishes between intuition and reason because of the different natures of the *knowable*,[46] it is only because self-evident truths are in a class by themselves that he sees no recourse but to introduce a special organ, namely intuition. (As to the difference, if there is such a difference, between intuition and reason, Moore refuses to say.) The appeal to intuition is much rather the result of logical impotence, it is no alternative to logical reasoning in the sense that intuition questions the competence of, or encroaches on the domain of logic. Moore rejects even the shadow of a hint that he would give the psychological intuition an exalted place. But this is not to affirm that he succeeds in his efforts, for as a matter of fact, by pointing to the necessity of turning to intuition for the last answers, he does give the intuition an exceptional, all-important place. Granted that Moore denies infallibility to the organ of intuiting, it remains incontested that the intuition is the last court of appeal. It alone has the capabilities of "seeing" truths. It is the indispensable "camera" which views the "objective" scene. The camera may be out of focus, nevertheless we depend upon the pictures which it takes.

The intuition does not provide reasons for the truth of any proposition; it only furnishes reasons for *subjectively holding* a certain proposition to be true, which reasons may indeed be the cause of our asserting it to be true. This, however, it must do "when any proposition is self-evident, when in fact, there are no reasons which prove its truth" (*PE*, 144). Both reason and intuition provide "reasons," but they are of different, non-competing types. A logical

---

[45] In fact Moore avoids referring to the subjective intuition as much as possible. Cf. fn. 47.

[46] Volition and feeling differ from cognition "only in respect of the kind of object of which they take cognisance, and in respect of the other mental accompaniments of such cognitions" (*PE*, 141).

reason is the "reason why something is true ... why *the proposition itself* must be true."

This almost grudging admittance of the uniqueness of intuition is altogether understandable within Moore's perspective. His stress cannot be on the subjective intuition, it must be on the objective intuitions. When he places the spotlight on the subject — and he must at some point, despite his qualms — he prefers to do it when the subjective operator has on his logical "garb." Then at least one moves within the confines of the reasonable (read: predictable and universally valid). However, logical reasoning is not self-sufficient, it must end by appealing to something, something which it cannot prove, and this something is a self-evident proposition. Thus, precisely because Moore restricts the power of the reasoning subject in order to rehabilitate propositions as objectively independent, he is forced (these objective propositions must be known in some way!) to allow subjective intuition to play a substantial role. This is so, as we shall see, not only in complex QII or in ethics as a whole, but in every part of Moore's philosophy — but then usually under another name, inspection.[47] Intuition or inspection refers to the ability of the knowing subject to have immediate knowledge or insight into a state of affairs when recourse to logical proof is no longer possible. In all situations Moore's procedure is the same: distinguish clearly, isolate the thing in question, bring it before the mind; and then the rest is up to inspection. "If the question is reduced to these ultimate terms, it must, I think, simply be left to the reader's inspection. Like all ultimate questions, it is incapable of strict proof either way" (*E*, 54; cf. 104, 112, 145, 147).

The Method of Isolation

Although intuition is the last word in complex QII, this does not exclude all reasoning. Even though it is a fact that one cannot *prove* a certain answer right or wrong (it must be seen), it is possible to *prepare* the intellect in a way analogous to leading a horse to water. Reason may not be the last word, it can speak the word-before-the-last. The significance of this reprieve for reason in

---

[47] Whether intuition and inspection are identical is not clear in Moore's writings. It is certain that inspection and intuition are both called in when logical reasoning can go no farther. Moreover he does employ the terms interchangeably. "Intuition" is the last resort in complex QII (*PE*, 173). In another place he relates that in regard to the "method of isolation ... the sole decision must rest with our reflective judgment" (*PE*, 197). Later in summarizing the argument, he substitutes inspection-terminology in place of intuition-language: "our only means of deciding upon their intrinsic value and its degree, is by carefully distinguishing exactly what the thing is, about which we ask the question, and then *looking to see* whether it has or has not the unique predicate 'good' (*PE*, 223, italics added). Cf. pp. 73-74, 76-79.

QII only dawns on one when he examines the method which Moore developed to "prepare the way."

This technique, which he dubbed the "method of isolation," grew naturally out of Moore's views of goodness as "intrinsic value." The notion or idea which we have generally termed "goodness" or "good" is often, and more precisely, referred to by Moore as "intrinsic good," or "intrinsic value" in order to distinguish it from other senses of the word good, "good as means," "good as a part," etc. (all of which are assigned to complex QIII). "Intrinsic" generally means in Moore's writings "in itself," "for its own sake," "if quite alone" (e.g. *PE*, 188; *E*, 37, 42ff.; *PS*, 326; *PP*, 93ff.). Whereas all other senses of good derive their goodness, at least in part, from their relation to something else, "intrinsic goodness" is a quality whose goodness does not depend on its relations with anything else. It is self-sufficiently, autonomously good. In order to discover what things have this quality, one must employ the "method of isolation." "This is, in fact, the only method that can be safely used, when we wish to discover what degree of value a thing has in itself." It consists in considering if the item in question would be intrinsically good, "if it existed in absolute isolation, stripped of all its usual accompaniments" (*PE*, 91; cf. 93-95, 187, 197; *E*, 37ff.; *PS*, 328; R, 557). The question is "whether it would be worth while that it should exist, even if there were absolutely nothing else in the Universe besides" (*E*, 101).[48]

Moore, quoting Mill with agreement, considers it to be the task of the method to marshall "'considerations . . . capable of determining the intellect either to give or withhold its assent to the doctrine'" (*PE*, 74-75). These considerations serve as "indirect proof." Thus, Moore cautions:

I could do nothing to *prove* that it was untrue; I could only point out as clearly as possible what it means, and how it contradicts other propositions which appear to be equally true. My only object in all this was, necessarily, to convince. But even if I did convince, that does not prove that we are right. It justifies us in *holding* that we are so; but nevertheless we may be wrong. (*PE*, 144-45)

In the same context Moore avers that he may justly pride himself in believing that he has answered the questions better "than Bentham or Mill or Sidgwick or others who have contradicted us. For we have *proved* that these have never even asked themselves the question which they professed to answer. . . . For all we know, the whole world would agree with us, if they could once clearly understand the question upon which we want their votes."

One begins to feel the atmosphere. We cannot prove that we are right, but meanwhile . . . we can do as well, no better, than anyone else. Notice the

---

[48] Moore cites Socrates as an important figure who also practised this method. He points to Plato's *Philebus*, 21A (*PE*, 88).

analogous situation in relation to self-evident propositions: there too we cannot be certain that the propositions we intuit as self-evidently true are really true, but we ought to be sure that our reasons for *holding* them to be true are valid. Actually it is wrong to talk of an analogous situation, the method of isolation is the device, the technique to make sure that we have the proper reasons, and what is more, it is the contrivance for clearing the brush and undergrowth away in order that one can be as sure as possible that he intuits propositions true in themselves.

This method of isolation, Moore is certain, will guard against the all too common errors which have plagued philosophers. No one will henceforth confuse what is only good as a means with what is good in itself. The "intrinsic worthlessness" of the former will become apparent as soon as we isolate it by itself (*PE*, 187, 93). Further, we shall evade the more subtle error of assuming that the value of a whole is the same as the sum of the values of its parts.[49]

In short, the method involves "carefully distinguishing exactly what the thing is . . . and then looking to see whether it has or has not the unique predicate 'good'" (*PE*, 223). With this last quotation we have placed the method in its proper niche in the complex QII. The method helps unravel the network of problems in which we are enmeshed. The result is *clarity*, the perspicuity mandatory if one would see correctly. Once having applied the method, one need only "look." He is guaranteed, in as far as possible, clear vision. Logical reasoning cleared the way, intuition provides the answers. Moore's answer:

By far the most valuable things, which we know or can imagine, are certain states of consciousness, which may be roughly described as the pleasures of human intercourse and the enjoyment of beautiful objects. (*PE*, 188)

It is only for the sake of these things

that any one can be justified in performing any public or private duty; . . . they are the *raison d'être* of virtue; . . . it is they — these complex wholes *themselves*, and not any constituent or characteristic of them — that form the rational ultimate end of human action and the sole criterion of social progress. (*PE*, 189)

In *Ethics*, in lieu of a compilation, he is content to announce that "there are an *immense variety* of different things, *all* of which are intrinsically good" (153).

The Relation of Intuition and Isolation: A Quandary

A striking as well as tell-tale feature of this section is Moore's treatment of the role of intuition. Prior to divulging the answers of intuition, he intones: "Indeed, once the meaning of the question is clearly understood, the answer to it, in its main outlines, appears to be so obvious, that it runs the risk of seeming

---

[49] Cf. p. 47ff.

to be a platitude" (*PE*, 188). He has no sooner recorded the "results" than he plays down the significance of the receiving organ. "No one, probably, who has asked himself the question, has ever doubted that personal affection and the appreciation of what is beautiful in Art or Nature, are good in themselves." It is not that he wishes to minimize or detract from the significance of the intuitions as such. Rather it would seem that the contrary is true; Moore is out to demonstrate that it makes little difference that the intuitive answers cannot claim the certainty of a valid logical proof. But as scientifically-concerned ethicists begin to mill around in panic at the thought of something so arbitrary as intuition, Moore assures them by referring to the fact that the answers correspond to what everyman believes and experiences. No right-minded, clear-thinking person will even think of questioning the intuitions, not because they are *intuited*, but because we simply cannot help holding them — they are common sense. In this way, the appeal to intuition is de-mythologized of any possible mystical, arbitrary character. The results of intuition are self-evident, obvious; it is almost a platitude to recount them. Moore applies the isolation test and then appeals "with confidence to 'the sober judgment of reflective persons'" (*PE*, 94). In the Index of *Principia* (xvii) Moore summarizes his view with characteristic pithiness. "I conclude, then, that a reflective intuition, if proper precautions are taken, will agree with Common Sense that it is absurd to . . . ."

The ultimate tribunal is without a doubt intuition. But it is the intuitions that count. And what intuitions are "received" by the intuition depends, to say it mildly, for a large measure on the preparatory method of isolation.

We must be quite sure that the same question has been put, before we trouble ourselves at the different answers that are given to it. . . . Certain it is, that in all those cases where we found a difference of opinion, we found also that the question had *not* been clearly understood. Though, therefore, we cannot prove that we are right, yet we have reason to believe that everybody, unless he is mistaken as to what he thinks, will think the same as we. It is as with a sum in mathematics. If we find a gross and palpable error in the calculations, we are not surprised or troubled that the person who made this mistake has reached a different result from ours. We think he will admit that his result is wrong, if his mistake is pointed out to him. . . . And so in Ethics. . . . The only difference is that in Ethics, owing to the intricacy of its subject-matter it is far more difficult to persuade anyone either that he has made a mistake or that that mistake affects his result. (*PE*, 145)

Thus, although he is adamant in his belief that logical argumentation does not have the last word, he takes away much of the impact of this stance by granting a logical method (of isolation) free play. In this spirit Moore confesses at one point that "the considerations which I am about to present appear to me to be absolutely convincing" (*PE*, 76).

All this confirms our earlier observation that Moore wishes to reduce his reliance on subjective intuition to a bare minimum. This is wholly in line with his wish to anchor his certainty in mind-independent intrinsic value. His problem, as we have seen it develop, is that one can only gain access to this objective "realm" by means of intuition. Moore accepts this fact, how bitter it is for him — but never misses the opportunity to portray the psychological organ of intuition as a kind of rubber stamp (providing official certification of a foregone conclusion). Intuition is enthroned as the last court of appeal more out of necessity than out of conviction. Recalling, on the other hand, Moore's undisguised confidence in the validity of logic and logical reasoning (albeit within certain limits), it becomes all the more credible that he would usher in and accentuate the logical method of isolation.

It is worthy of notice that we have an analogous situation in complex QII to that of complex QI in respect to the relation of intuition and logical reasoning — except that the roles are reversed. Whereas in QI logic has in principle the last word, we discovered that Moore cannot avoid a final appeal to intuition; in QII as we have just discovered, although intuition has in principle the last word, Moore in practice depends on the "method of isolation." Intuition enjoys veto power, but it wields this power in respect to candidates singled out by the logical method. All that Moore or any ethicist can do is to marshall evidence, seeking to persuade others to "see" things his way — but that "all" threatens to become just that, everything. Our claim that the method of isolation is more than a subordinate help for intuition, and in fact is guilty of insubordination in practice, is clearly reflected in his practical ethicizing. Thus, for example, in combating the hedonistic principle accepted by Sidgwick that "Pleasure alone is good as an end," Moore employs the method of isolation. "Pleasure" is completely isolated and *then* Moore asks for the judgment of intuition. Obviously pleasure is not the sole good because without the *consciousness* of pleasure, pleasure is comparatively valueless (*PE*, 89). He then isolates "consciousness of pleasure" (even from one's consciousness of being conscious of pleasure) and repeats the question. Moore has no doubt that everyone will reject "consciousness of pleasure" as the sole good (*PE*, 91-95).

The moral is clear. One can only reasonably disagree with Moore in regard to the results of intuition if he has already challenged Moore's method of isolation. And as the method is beyond disrepute for Moore, the fact that final proof is not possible is almost inconsequential. No wonder that the major share of his energy, and thus of his writings, is devoted to persuasion aimed at enticing others to accept his beliefs as worthy of adoption. All this makes it apparent that the dual-appeal to intuition and reason and the relation involved must be discussed in our critique.

46

All of the intrinsic goods are what Moore terms "highly complex *organic unities*" (*PE*, 189). The great evils are also such organic unities and have the same make-up. This holds for two such evils at least (love of ugly or evil, and hatred of good or beautiful). A third great evil, consciousness of pain, appears to be something of an exception; cognition of pain by itself, without the accompanying emotion, is evil in itself (*PE*, 208-14). A random-selection of some other results: belief, if true, adds to the value of the total state and takes away if false; knowledge does contribute towards intrinsic value; material objects, though possessing little or no intrinsic value in themselves, are "essential constituents" in the largest group of wholes having such value on the whole; if the evil element in a "mixed good" actually exists, the total sum of value is always negative; essential to the Ideal is some cognition of evil things. The details are not important, Moore informs us, they are only illustrative of "the method which must be pursued in answering the fundamental question of Ethics" (*PE*, 223).

It remains to explain Moore's doctrine of organic unities. This doctrine plays a crucial, largely preventive role for Moore in guarding against what may otherwise turn out to be costly errors. His main evidence for the principle is contained in the example of "aesthetic enjoyments" (*PE*, 28, 189 ff.). Appreciation of a beautiful object is composed of three elements: the cognition or consciousness of the beautiful qualities possessed by that object, the appropriate emotion and true belief. By themselves, the elements have little value; a beautiful object of which no one is conscious has little value, neither does mere consciousness always confer great value upon the whole of which it forms a part. And if one adds up the value of the parts, the resultant is comparatively meagre. Nevertheless, together these elements constitute a whole which is good in itself, in fact, one of the two most valuable things we can "know or imagine." This paradox (Moore himself considers it such) takes on general form in the principle of organic unities: "*The value of a whole must not be assumed to be the same as the sum of the values of its parts*" (*PE*, 28).

This principle has an intimate relation with Moore's total position. He must guard against the for him relativistic-subjectistic position that one and the same thing under the same circumstances is in one instance intrinsically good and in another instance not.[50] This seems indeed to be often the case. But, argues Moore, it is only appearance. If something has no intrinsic value in isolation, it has no intrinsic value when part of a more valuable whole. It is a

---

[50] "Judgments of intrinsic value have this superiority over judgments of means that, if once true, they are always true" (*PE*, 166). Moore's fundamental objection to any "subjective" interpretation and to any "objective evolutionary interpretation" is that "the very same kind of thing which, under some circumstances, is better than another, would, under others, be worse" (*PS*, 256-57).

"self-contradictory belief that one and the same thing may be two different things" (*PE*, 35) which it would be, says Moore, if it can have two different values. It is illegitimate to infer that a "part" has intrinsic value just because the whole it belongs to is intrinsically valuable. Of course, as a *part* of the whole, it is a necessary condition for the existence of the whole; but in such a case, its value is strictly *instrumental* in character.

As a transition to complex QIII, a number of observations are in order. Once again as in complex QI, Moore has fabricated a logical expedient to serve his ends. In both instances he has started with the assumption of the autonomy and independence of "goodness." In complex QI the indefinability-face was exposed, in complex QII it is the constancy-face of the goodness-coin. Moore begins from the assumption that intrinsic value is constant and stedfast. Indeed this fixity, to-be-counted-on character is inherent to intrinsic value. The principle of organic unities enables him to maintain this view of constancy in every situation. The "method of isolation" was set up, not as a test for intrinsic value, that it presumes but to separate intrinsic and instrumental value and thus avoid the common fallacy of confusing means and end. At the same time, it enables one to avoid violating the principle of organic unity (cf. *PE*, 93, 187). As in the case of its twin-sister in QI (the open-question), the argument is in essence the working out of a previously accepted stance (the constancy of value). However, what if one does not believe in the autonomy or constancy of goodness or of the sharp division between end and means? Then the method is of questionable value. Such a person might easily argue that absolute isolation robs value of its very value-character (constituent to its value-character is its *relation* to other factors).[51] Abstraction from the concreteness and wholeness of life no doubt characterizes scientific activity. But abstraction is certainly not "absolute isolation."[52] Nothing exists in itself and nothing has value in itself.[53]

COMPLEX QIII: RIGHTNESS

What is Right?

It remains to make a reconnaissance of the third and last complex to be found in Moore's ethical edifice. In philosophic circles this complex has received little attention in comparison to I and II. However, in many ways it functions

[51] As Bosanquet already did in his review of *Principia Ethica* (*Mind* XII, 1904, p. 255).
[52] Edel is certainly correct when he judges that the method could only be significant as a method of variation (isolating one factor in a situation to check the value of what it is, in itself, contributing to the situation) and not as "absolute isolation." Cf. "The Logical Structure of G. E. Moore's Ethics" in *PGEM*.
[53] Moore himself is unable to escape this fact. His intrinsic goods are all, as we have seen, "highly complex *organic unities*" (*PE*, 189).

48

as the proof of the pudding. Here we face the questions of the "third great division of ethical enquiry," practical ethics: "What ought I to do? What is right? What is my duty?" And here too, as in the previous complexes, there is a special technique, the "method of empirical investigation." "To ask what kind of actions we ought to perform, or what kind of conduct is right, is to ask what kind of effects such action and conduct will produce" (*PE*, 146).

For this reason no "single question in practical Ethics can be answered except by a causal generalization." Judgments of intrinsic value (intuited synthetic a prioris of QII) are also involved, but they are "causually connected with the actions in question." Thus, to answer the practical query, a double know-ledge is involved; "we must know *both* what degree of intrinsic value different things have, *and* how these different things may be obtained" (*PE*, 26; cf. ix). Judgments of practical ethics always take the form; "This is a cause of that good thing." All moral laws are "merely statements that certain kinds of actions will have good effects." "Right" can mean nothing but "'cause of a good result,' and is thus identical with 'useful'" (*PE*, 146-47).[54]

Rightness is definable in terms of goodness. "That the assertion 'I am morally bound to perform this action' is identical with the assertion 'This action will produce the greatest possible amount of good in the Universe' . . . is demon-strably certain" (*PE*, 147). And it is the latter statement which defines the former. One's moral duty is "that action, which will cause more good to exist in the Universe than any possible alternative." The requirements for what is "right" are slightly less rigorous: "what will *not* cause *less* good than any possible alternative" (*PE*, 148). Often Moore groups these notions under the um-brella of "good as means" (e.g. *PE*, 21, 22, 24, 159, 180; *E*, 154-55). An action is right, it is a duty, it ought to be done when it will have good effects, when it will be a means to good and thus "good as means."

A duty differs only from an "expedient" action, and a virtue differs only from other favorable dispositions, in that whereas we are often tempted to avoid duties and to forget virtue, we have a natural inclination to do the expedient and to be favorably disposed. This difference is in both cases non-ethical in character and does not affect the question whether X ought to be done (*PE*, 169). Generally, virtues as "habitual dispositions to perform actions which are duties" are not good in themselves.

The End Results

As we have noted, answers to the third question (what ought I to do?) are

---

[54] Moore is obviously not to be classed with those intuitionists who claim that duty is self-evident. He takes great pains to distantiate himself from the "Intuitional school of moralists" (*PE*, 148; x). Sir David Ross has called Moore's amalgam of intuitionism and utilitarianism, "Ideal Utilitarianism." Cf. *The Right and the Good* (1930), p. 9.

"capable of being confirmed or refuted by an investigation of causes and effects" (*PE*, 149). Nevertheless, Moore is immediately thwarted in his intention to designate duties. And for a simple reason; his "definition" of duty makes it impossible that such investigations can ever arrive at *conclusive* results. To know what action will cause more good, or at least as much good as any other in the Universe, demands knowledge, not only of present conditions, but of how our actions will affect events "throughout an infinite future." This is of course impossible; "no sufficient reason has ever yet been found for considering one action more right or more wrong than another" (*PE*, 152). The most that can be done is *generalization*: not a listing of fixed duties or best possible actions, but a determining of "which, among a few alternatives possible under certain circumstances, will, on the whole, produce the best result" (*PE*, 151). This implies that what is good as means in one instance need not be so in another situation (*PE*, 22-23). The end result is a "defence of most of the rules most universally recognised by Common Sense. . . . it seems possible to prove a definite utility in most of those [rules] which are in general both recognised and practised" (*PE*, 156, 160).

Almost as if he sensed the disillusionment and anticipated the critique which his acceptance of the status quo caused, Moore attempts to assuage by pointing out that even if *new rules* had been advisable it is 1) doubtful if one person could bring about general observance and 2) there is no reason why a person would have to observe such a law in absence of general observance (*PE*, 161). It is doubtful if this explanation really helps. Even more discordant is Moore's conclusion that, although we know that the violation of an existing rule is sometimes the best course of action, "we can never know which those cases are, and ought, therefore, never to break it." It is preferable "*always* to conform to rules which are both generally useful and generally practised."[55] By such reasoning Moore is forced, for example, to decree that "it is undoubtedly well to punish a man, who has done an action, right in his case but generally wrong, even if his example would not be likely to have a dangerous effect" (*PE*, 162-64). Further, he accepts the fantastic conclusion that "there is, therefore, a strong probability in favour of adherence to an existing custom, even if it be a bad one." In *Ethics* he admits being "committed to the paradox that a man may really deserve the strongest moral condemnation for choosing an action, which *actually* is right" (121).

Moore's ethical philosophizing has come to a rather surprising conclusion. Whereas in complex QII questions about intrinsic value are declared in the final instance to be a matter of personal "intuition," in complex QIII mankind is admonished to adhere to the rules commonly recognized and practised. On

---

[55] Ewing in *Second Thoughts in Moral Philosophy* (1959, p. 146) informs us that Moore "has not retained the view that it ought to be done *always*."

the one hand, man is thrown back on his own intuition, on the other, he is faced with the duty to obey the conventions of society.

In our critique we must return to this, at first sight at least, puzzling situation. Here it only remains to append the interesting note that this contrast was keenly felt in the Bloomsbury Group, the social and literary avant garde of the early 1900's.[56] Moore's *Principia* was to this circle the philosophic Bible. A member of Bloomsbury, the renowned economist J. M. Keynes, hailed *Principia* as a "stupendous and entrancing work, the greatest on the subject."[57] He praised Moore's chapter on "The Ideal" as the best since Plato, "and it is better than Plato because it is quite free from fancy."[58] As Keynes reminisces in his *Two Memoirs*:

The influence [of Moore] was not only overwhelming; but it was the extreme opposite of what Strachey used to call *funeste*; it was exciting, exhilarating, the beginning of a renaissance, the opening of a new heaven on earth, we were the forerunners of a new dispensation, we were not afraid of anything.[59]

But, continues Keynes:

There was one chapter in the *Principia* of which we took not the slightest notice. We accepted Moore's religion, so to speak, and discarded his morals. Indeed, in our opinion, one of the greatest advantages of his religion, was that it made morals unnecessary — meaning by 'religion' one's attitude towards oneself and the ultimate and by 'morals' one's attitude towards the outside world and the intermediate.[60]

This disregard for chapter five of the *Principia* (in which Moore defends the status quo) is altogether understandable. Bloomsbury saw in the "clarity,

---

[56] For information on the remarkable Bloomsbury Circle and Moore's influence on its members, consult J. K. Johnstone, *The Bloomsbury Group* (1954); J. M. Keynes, *Two Memoirs* (1951); R. F. Harrod, *The Life of John Maynard Keynes* (1951); Leonard Woolf, *Sowing* (1961).

[57] In a letter to B. Swithinbank, 7th October, 1903 (quoted in Harrod, *op. cit.*, p. 75).

[58] John Maynard Keynes, *Two Memoirs*, p. 94.

The measure of Moore's influence can be the better estimated when we realize that Keynes considered the notion of "probability" unique and indefinable. "Moreover, the failure to explain or define 'probability' in terms of other logical notions, creates a presumption that particular relations of probability must be, in the first instance, directly recognized as such, and cannot be evolved by rule out of *data* which themselves contain no statements of probability." Cf. *A Treatise on Probability* (1921), pp. 52-53, also p. 8.

[59] Keynes, *op. cit.*, p. 82.

[60] Keynes, *loc. cit.*

Woolf has stated that Keynes is guilty of distorting the true state of affairs at this point. "It is not true . . . that we neglected all that Moore said about 'morals' and rules of conduct." Indeed, "Moore himself was continually exercised" by "questions of what was right and wrong, what one *ought* to do." And "we followed him closely in this as in other parts of his doctrine." Cf. *Sowing*, pp. 148-49. Cf. also Russell, *Autobiography*, p. 71.

freshness and common-sense"[61] of *Principia* a revolt against the code of conduct and morality of bourgeois Victorianism. No longer must rules of society be obeyed just because they happen to be the rules; every moral law, every duty and even every virtue must prove its worth. And then Moore's plea for adherence to the status quo!

Objectivity

It is not unimportant in this connection to note that lack of conclusive certainty as to what is right does not in the least jeopardize the "objectivity of moral judgments" (*E*, chs. III & IV). This objectivity, or, as Moore prefers, intrinsicness,[62] is non-negotiable. If ethical judgments are subjective in the sense of being simply statements about a speaker's feelings, "then there is absolutely no such thing as a difference of opinion upon moral questions" (*PS*, 333). But there are such moral disagreements and therefore there must be a property (e.g. goodness or rightness) about which interested parties can contradict one another.[63] Only then can moral judgments be true and false (*PS*, 330ff.). Right and wrong are not in themselves intrinsic, but "they have a fixed relation to a kind of value which *is* 'intrinsic.' It is this fixed relation to an intrinsic kind of value ... which gives to right and wrong that kind and degree of fixity and impartiality which they actually are felt to possess, and which is what people are thinking of when they talk of their objectivity" (*PS*, 257). It is not that a certain act is right or wrong, good or bad because someone, perhaps God, has so ordained or commanded. Much rather an act is recommended or

[61] Woolf, *Ibid.*, p. 147. Woolf becomes ecstatic when he records Moore's influence. "The tremendous influence of Moore and his book upon us came from the fact that they suddenly removed from our eyes an obscuring accumulation of scales, cobwebs, and curtains, revealing for the first time to us, so it seemed, the nature of truth and reality, of good and evil and character and conduct, substituting for the religious and philosophical nightmares, delusions, hallucinations, in which Jehovah, Christ, and St. Paul, Plato, Kant and Hegel had entangled us, the fresh air and pure light of plain common-sense."
[62] It is not that Moore doubts the "objectivity" (or as he could better have said, the "universal validity") of moral judgments. On occasion he does talk of the "objective predicates of value" (*PE*, 201) even though reference to objectivity is inherent in the usual terminological designations; namely, "quality" and "predicate." He usually avoids use of the term "objective" because naturalists also make much of objectivity. "Intrinsicness" is for Moore a more suitable word. It is the intrinsic character of predicates of value which is "the strongest ... objection to any subjective view." Indeed, "from the proposition that a particular kind of value is 'intrinsic' it does follow that it must be 'objective', the converse implication by no means holds" (*PS*, 255).
[63] X is good" and "X is not good" are logically contradictory according to Moore. A subjective analysis of good (good = approval) is impossible because "*A approves* of X" is compatible with "B does not approve of X."

52

forbidden by God, or the Pure Will, *because* it is right or *because* it is wrong (*E*, 93-96).[64]

Revisions

In *Principia*, Moore was not prepared to identify goodness and rightness. He stressed that duty and obligation are logically subordinate to goodness and excellence. But the nature of this subordination, and the nature of the logical relationship in general, remained obscure. Moore appeared to have doubts at this point. In *Principia* duty was defined without any remainder in terms of expediency (productiveness of best possible consequences), later he wishes to speak of equivalence rather than identity between that which is a duty and that which is expedient (*E*, 38-39; cf. *PE*, 147; R, 558). The two characters are no longer identical, nor does the one contain the other in the sense in which a bicycle is two wheels in tandem. Related as being colored is to being extended (color is impossible without extension of some sort), so being a duty is impossible without having a tendency to promoting good.

Ethics also contains, as Ross discovered,[65] the first hint of a shift in Moore's views on the good-right relation. Productiveness of good is treated not so much as the definition of rightness as a criteria for rightness (*E*, 8). Lewy has further informed us that Moore had begun serious reconsideration of the relationship as early as 1921.[66] But it was not until 1942 that Moore explicitly rejected the idea that "right" or "ought" can be defined in terms of "intrinsically good."

So far as I can see, there is just as much reason for supposing 'ought' to be definable in terms of 'intrinsically good' as the other way about; and the reason for rejecting the view that 'intrinsically good' or 'intrinsically better' are definable in terms of 'ought' is of precisely the same kind and just as strong as the reason for rejecting the view that 'ought' is definable in terms of 'intrinsically good.'

My present view is that both views should be rejected, and that, in the case of *all* the functions, which I have stated to be equivalent, the functions in question, though equivalent, are *not* identical. (R, 610-11)

"Ought" too, it appears, is a simple, indefinable notion. There is no longer identity, but only logical equivalence between certain ought-statements and certain statements of intrinsic value. Certain ought judgments follow from, or may be inferred from, certain judgments of intrinsic value and vice versa.

[64] Since rules or laws are willed by "subjects," they are relative for Moore and must, finally be determined by objective intrinsic values.
[65] *The Right and the Good*, pp. 8-11.
[66] Lewy, *op. cit.*, p. 252. Moore considered the possibility that "right is unanalysable and Good is to be analysed partly in terms of right." Actually, even though Moore declares in *Principia* that right and ought must be defined in terms of good, he does at times give the impression that intrinsic goodness can be at least partly defined in terms of "ought." Thus, his practise of employing "what *ought to be*?" as an alternative formulation for the question "what things are good in themselves?" Cf. p. 17 and fn. 37, p. 34.

The philosophic substructure 3

On repeated occasions during the previous chapter we have curbed our desire to wander farther afield — even when the argument led in that direction. Throughout the discussion it became obvious that a knowledge of Moore's general philosophic position is a prerequisite for a proper understanding of his ethics. In this chapter our aim will be to gain such knowledge. Various facets of Moore's philosophy will be discussed. The scope and depth of the exposition will vary as the philosophic repercussions for his theory of ethics are more or less decisive.

Moore's philosophizing, with the exception of his early years, always bore the neo-positivistic signature. After having written two articles clearly neo-Idealistic in tone, in 1899 with "The Nature of Judgment" Moore launched his attack on neo-Idealism. From that date until his death in 1958, thus for nearly sixty years, he gave his energies to the defence of Mind-independent entities and endeavoured to establish what could be termed a post-Kantian "objectivism," or a neo-Realism.[1]

During the first decade, roughly from 1899 to 1911, in which Moore did not hesitate to set forth his positive views, he developed an ontological position which we shall describe, employing Vollenhoven's terminology, as a Platonizing Subsistence theory.[2] Although, due to the scarcity of material it is difficult

[1] Moore in effect strove towards a Kantianism-in-reverse (cf. *PE*, 133). Objects ought not to conform to knowledge in the post-Kantian manner, but knowledge ought to conform to objects (cf. Kant's Preface to *Kritik der reinen Vernunft*). Moore is an "objectivist" in his concern to maintain the independence of the world in respect to the mind.

In that Moore in contrast to many a neo-positivist also had an eye for the non-natural, and in order to call attention to the similarity with as well as difference from Plato's Realism, one can also aptly speak of "neo-Realism."

[2] Cf. fn. 47 and Vollenhoven's *Kort Overzicht van de Geschiedenis der Wijsbegeerte* (1956), p. 27f. Unfortunately comparatively little of Vollenhoven's work has been officially published and almost none in English. He has developed the "Problem-Historical" method of philosophic historiography which centers attention on the

to be certain, there is strong evidence that prior to 1899 he worked with the same ontological pattern, but then neo-idealistically. And though, subsequent to 1911 — thus for the greater part of his life — he became reluctant to issue declarations too general and too firm, and though it would appear that only a skeleton of his earlier position remains, there is no compelling evidence which leads one to conclude that he adopted another position.

Before beginning our exposition of Moore's neo-positivistic views, it is well to preface a succinct note on his neo-Idealism. Not only does it provide a good idea of the kind of position he later so passionately rejected, but, as we shall see, it furnishes evidence that in his later thought the same basic onto-logical schema is maintained — but then, rethought, refurbished in the neo-positivistic spirit. For the early Moore the fundamental contrast is that "in which the world as it really is stands to events as we know them. It is the relation of Reality to Appearance" (F, 183). This relation Moore conceives of as something special, it is neither the "notion of causal dependence between empirical things in time" or that of "logical dependence . . . between concepts" (F, 202). It is both at the same time, *existent* AND *logical*: it is *synthetic a priori*.[3]

To mention one other matter: as Moore considers Bradley's arguments establishing "the unreality of Time . . . perfectly conclusive" (F, 202), he ac-knowledges that this amounts to a "thorough-going rejection of almost all the content with which our world is filled up." Reality remains "little more than a Ding an Sich."[4] Moore, nevertheless, opting for a unique form of perception insists that reality does remain *knowable*.[5]

---

regular recurrence of certain systematic problem-patterns, be they in conjunction with new personalities and different historical currents. For studies in English employing this method, cf. H. E. Runner, *The Development of Aristotle Illustrated From the Earliest Books of the Physics* (1951) and H. Hart, *Communal Certainty and Authorized Truth* (1966).

[3] Cf. also F, 203. According to Moore Kant's Transcendental Freedom is the same type of special connective concept in that it belongs to both phenomenal and noumenal realms. Moore's article entitled "Freedom" deals specifically with Kant's views.

[4] Cf. "In what sense, if any, do Past and Future Time Exist," *Mind* VI (1897), pp. 235-40. "Time must be rejected wholly, its continuity, as well as its discreteness if we are going to form an adequate notion of reality" (p. 240).

[5] Moore's neo-Idealism schematically represented:

Reality	Concepts	Abstract (Time-less Changeless)	Logical Necessity (Analytic)
			Synthetic A priori
Appearance	Things (Objects) Events	Existence Time	Causal Necessity

Compare with schema of later period, fn. 47, p. 83.

Although Moore was not given to long discourses on the nature of philosophy or philosophizing, he realized that it was impossible to avoid such basic questions altogether. In 1910 he declared that the "first and most interesting problem of philosophy" (*SMPP*, 23) is to furnish a "general description of the *whole* of the Universe, mentioning all the most important kinds of things which we *know* to be in it, considering how far it is likely that there are in it important kinds of things which we do not absolutely *know* to be in it, and also considering the most important ways in which these various kinds of things are related to one another" (*SMPP*, 1). In the wake of answers to the first question, a host of subordinate questions have risen: the questions of Metaphysics (what kind of things exist in the universe, how does one more clearly define the differences between the kinds); the questions of Logic (classifying ways of knowing, examining the event of knowing, analyzing the nature of truth, investigating the ways a proposition can be proved true); and the questions of Ethics (classifying sorts of things according to their goodness and badness, rightness and wrongness).

In his *Lectures on Philosophy*, edited by Casimir Lewy, there is a selection from a course of lectures given in the years 1933-34 which offers us Moore's *later* views on the nature and purpose of philosophy. Philosophy, summarizes Moore, considers:

(1) Questions about the meaning of words, phrases & forms of expression: Analysis,

(2) Questions about Reality as a whole,

(3) A number of questions about human knowledge,

(4) Still more questions about what it's *reasonable for us to believe & in what degree.* (*LP*, 190)

Centering his discussion around Broad's distinction between critical and speculative philosophy, Moore equates critical philosophy with Analysis (1) and speculative philosophy with questions concerning reality as a whole (2). Only towards the end of his discussion does he allow that "he ought perhaps to have mentioned" (*LP*, 196) ethics as another sub-division of philosophy.

Philosophy as Analysis

The first question which requires discussion is the place and function of analysis in Moore's philosophizing. The immediacy of this question arises from a comparison of the above-mentioned quotations which report Moore's earlier and later views as to the task of philosophy. First he talks of "description," later the emphasis is on "analysis." There is no denying that he increasingly throughout his life restricted himself to analysis. Thus, although he labels only one of the four categories of philosophic questions "Analysis," analysis seems to have the built-in necessity to usurp and appropriate (recall the designs of ethical complex QI). For when Moore expands on the matter, analysis begins to play an important, if not all-dominating role. Insofar as logic is philosophy (and not the working out of a formal system), it deals with analysis. Even a general question of inductive logic such as: "*What is a good reason for believing what? . . . may* be a question of analysis." The same holds true for psychology: insofar as psychology is philosophy (and not the discovery by observation and experiment of laws with regard to mental facts), it is "simply a department of philos.: the analytic part." Only when it comes to ethics does Moore draw a line — and only then, if his own ethical views are correct. Ethics is indeed "partly analysis of what's meant by 'good,' 'ought,' 'right,' 'wrong,' 'valuable,' etc." It is *more* only if certain "naturalistic analyses are wrong." Otherwise ethics is exhausted in analysis and the "more" is usurped by "Psych., Sociology, or the theory of Evolution" (*LP*, 195-96).

Further, Moore registers his agreement with Broad's definition of analysis as the defining or analyzing of "very *general* concepts which are constantly used both in ordinary life & in the special sciences" (*LP*, 155). Later he adds to the definition: and "the analysis of concepts *only* occurring in special sciences" (*LP*, 195). Through such analysis, argues Moore, arguments and reasonings in ordinary life and science become less confused. But this undoubted virtue is not to be regarded as the *raison d'être* of analysis, much rather, the very fact that analysis effectuates clearness in philosophizing as such is its justification.

Nevertheless in 1942 Moore insisted (R, 676) that he not only "had no preference for any one method" of philosophizing[6] but also that he had never regarded analysis as the only proper business of philosophy. But then why this restriction, certainly in practice, to matters of analysis? It is not coincidental that we faced the same question at the beginning of the previous chapter, albeit in an ethical context. And the answer is the same. "Logically" the question of meaning (= analysis) is "presupposed" in all the other questions of philosophy (cf. N, 290). Thus, regardless of the importance of the other questions, one must first search out meaning and that is to analyze. Only then is one able to furnish a general "description" of the Universe. And as the discovery of meaning penetrates, as we shall see, to what stands behind the words and expressions, to analyze or at least to relate the results of analysis is itself to engage in description of the kinds of things populating the Universe. Taking all these matters into consideration one need not ascertain a basic change in his view as to the task of philosophy, but only an increased awareness of and incessant preoccupation with the initial, that is analytic, concerns. A misleading feature

[6] Cf. also *LP*, 171.

in this situation is Moore's increased tendency to discuss matters of ontology in the idiom of logic and linguistics.

Turning now to analysis: Analysis is in the strict sense for Moore "definition," or "decomposition." This is clearest in his earliest writings. "A thing becomes intelligible first when it is analysed into its constituent concepts" (NJ, 182). As we have already seen "goodness" cannot be analyzed or defined because it is indivisible and simple. His "Refutation of Idealism" demonstrates that "things" taken to be one and the same are actually composed of various *elements*, e.g. a sensation is dissected into the object of the sensation, the awareness of it, and a relation of the two elements. Although he always retained this division-view of analysis, in practice he often analyzed by "distinguishing" and "differentiating" how one notion differed from the other.[7] This was the only remaining possibility when the notion to be examined was "simple" rather than "complex." But, due to his theory of meaning which we shall later discuss, the "division" view maintained the primacy.

Analysis is the search for *meaning*. And this pursuit of meaning, Moore exclaimed already in 1900, is of "fundamental importance for philosophy" (N, 289). Not, it is necessary to stress, everyday meaning, or dictionary meaning, or even the meanings with which the natural sciences are occupied; but philosophic meaning.[8] He is confident that propositions (such as "This is an ink-stand") are most often true, and what is more, that they are *known* to be true. In this sense he is not concerned with truth, knowledge or meaning — they are already known. But to say that we understand the everyday meaning of a certain proposition or that we know it to be true, is *not* to say that "we *know what it means*, in the sense that we are able to *give a correct analysis* of its meaning." Such questions are profoundly difficult, and "no one knows the answer" (*PP*, 37; cf. 53). Or again, Moore is convinced that a philosopher need not inquire "whether this is a finger or whether I know that it is," rather the philosophically interesting question is "*what*, in certain respects, I am knowing, when I know that it is" (*PS*, 228). Philosophic definitions as analyses differ from dictionary definitions

---

[7] "For no discussion about the meaning of a word is *merely* about the meaning of a word, it always involves some discussion as to the way in which the things or notions, for which the word may stand, are distinguished from or related to one another" (*SMPP*, 206).

Moore's theory of meaning did not enable this emphasis on distinguishing to develop into the late Wittgenstein's concern for meaning as use. Thus, it is gratuitous to appeal to Moore as the adumbration of this typical late Wittgensteinian view. Wittgenstein himself only developed his view after rejecting a theory of meaning very similar to Moore's, cf. *Philosophical Investigations*, Pars. 1-120.

[8] In 1942 Moore cautioned that he had often inadvertently confused every-day meaning with philosophic meaning in earlier writings (R, 664).

because they're all of them definitions of words or forms of expressions *you already understand* — you already *know* their meaning, in the sense that you *attach the common meanings* to them when you use them or hear or read them, though you mayn't *know their meanings* in the sense of being able to make true props. of the form "this *means* so-&-so." (*LP*, 166)

Finally, one must distinguish philosophic concerns from natural scientific ones. Questions such as the age of the earth; whether Darwin's theory of the Origin of the Species is correct; whether millions of stars existed a million years ago; whether Newton's Law of Gravitation or Einstein's is more accurate; etc. are typical non-philosophical questions, questions of which it is "not the business of philosophy to discuss whether it's true or not." What questions are philosophical? Moore replies:

It's quite clear that the question I've discussed about whether the word "Nature" has a connotation, & if so what it is, *is* a philosophical question: nobody but a philosopher would discuss it: but it isn't about *Nature*, but about the word Nature, or about a certain concept.

To illustrate his point, Moore then formulates five philosophical questions about Nature as a "certain property."

(1) Is Nature Real? Or is it an appearance, an illusion?
(2) Do we *know* that Nature is real?
(3) If we do, *how* do we know that Nature is real?
(4) What is the analysis of the concepts that occur in the connotation of "Nature"?
(5) Is Nature, in any sense, dependent on "mind"? (*LP*, 11)[9]

For Moore it is a concept or proposition which is the analysandum (that which is to be analyzed). (By accident he sometimes speaks as if a *verbal expression* can serve as analysandum, but that is contrary to his theory and general practice.) Concretely this means that he avoids examining things or words as such. He concerns himself with *predicates* (which make up or attach to things and which are expressed in words). In ethics, for example, to ask "what is *meant* by good?" is to raise "the question What is the nature of that peculiar predicate, the relation of which to other things constitutes the object of all other ethical investigations?" (*PE*, 37). In such analysis he attempts to manipulate or analyze until the left-hand expression (the analysandum) and the right-hand expression (the analysans) have the same meaning. But how does one judge such an identity? Moore was most reticent when it came to explaining, he preferred simply to go about his analytic labors. However, under the urging of critics, he laid down various criteria for correct analysis in his 1942 "Reply."

(a) both *analysandum* and *analysans* must be *concepts*, and . . . in some sense the *same concept*, and
(b) that the *expression* used for the *analysandum* must be a different *expression* from that used for the *analysans*. . . .

⁹ Cf. also *LP*, 3-11, 184-85, 190, 194.

(c) that the expression used for the . . . *analysans* . . . must differ in this way, namely, that [it] . . . must *explicitly mention* concepts which are not explicitly mentioned by the expressions used for the *analysandum* . . .

(d) *the method of combination* should be explicitly mentioned. (R, 666)[10]

Analysis clarifies concepts, dissolves philosophical puzzles, and shows up contradictions. As the search for meaning, it does not affect the real world of facts (the world is there already and continues undisturbed),[11] but concentrates on analyzing, describing and investigating the components of our beliefs and knowledge of the world. Although it is satisfied that the beliefs of common sense are on the whole trustworthy and true, it is far from satisfied that we know the ins-and-outs of what we believe. Our knowledge must be clarified and, in the process, deepened.[12]

A good definition of the sorts of things you hold to be in the Universe, obviously adds to the clearness of your view. And it is not only a question of clearness either. When, for instance, you try to define what you mean by a material object, you find that there are several different properties which a material object might have, of which you had never thought before; and . . . of which you would never have thought, if you had merely contented yourself with asserting that there are material objects in the Universe, without enquiring what you meant by this assertion. (*SMPP*, 24)

In the process of analysis, Moore discovered that grammatical similarities have often mistakenly been read as implying logical similarity. Insistence on clearly distinguishing at this point has since become a hallmark of Linguistic Analysis. Due to the commonness of subject-predicate propositions asserting "a relation between two existing things" (e.g. 'somebody is in the room'), efforts are made to force "This is Good" into this pattern, and one illegitimately

[10] Previously Moore had also legislated that "(a) nobody can know that the *analysandum* applies to an object without knowing that the *analysans* applies to it (b) nobody can verify that the *analysandum* applies without verifying that the *analysans* applies, (c) any expression which expresses the *analysandum* must be synonymous with any expression which expresses the *analysans*" (R, 663). Cf. White, *op. cit.*, pp. 88-98 and *CPB*, 255-57.

[11] It is significant to notice that, just as in ethics the analysis of QI did not predetermine *what* things were good? in QII, knowledge of the (technical) *meaning* of words does not predetermine the answers to the far more important, but subsequent questions, as to *what things* have these properties. Although it may influence answers to the latter questions (*what things* are real, do exist, have being, are facts and are true), the meaning of the idea is not "logically relevant" (*SMPP*, 206).

[12] Philosophic problems "as to the meaning of words" are "worth discussing for their own sakes" because every discovery about the notion conveyed by a certain word (eg. 'real' or 'true') is "a new discovery which applies to the whole range of things which *are* real or true: it is, in that sense, a new discovery about properties which would belong to the Universe, even if there were no such things as words at all, and properties which are exceedingly general — which belong to an enormous number, if not to the whole, of the most important constituents of the Universe" (*SMPP*, 206-07).

concludes that good "exists" (*PE*, 124). Idealists have been fooled by the grammatical *identity* of words such as "blue," "green," and "sweet" which refer both to the subjective sensation and the object causing the sensation (PS, 19).

And Moore, in a well-known essay, has shown the logical difference which holds between "Tame tigers exist" and "Tame tigers growl" despite their grammatical similarity. "Existence" is not an ordinary property, if a property at all; "growling" is (*PP*, 113-26; cf. *PS*, 216-19 for other examples).

In summary as an illustration of Moore's method, a glance at his discussion of necessity in the century's first analytic paper will serve well:

My primary object in this paper is to determine the *meaning* of necessity. I do not wish to discover what things are necessary; but what that predicate is which attaches to them when they are so. Nor, on the other hand, do I wish to arrive at a correct verbal definition of necessity. . . . My main object is not to discover whether any or all propositions of the form "A is necessary" are true or false, nor yet whether they are correctly expressed; but what their *meaning* is. (N, 289, 290)

The Paradox of Analysis

"To be a brother is to be a male sibling" may be regarded as Moore's paradigm of analysis. The analysans is to make explicit what is implicit in the analysandum, and that is what it does. The knotty point or Gordian knot is to find two expressions which are different from each other (in more than a verbal way) and which yet have the same meaning. C. H. Langford has aptly dubbed the predicament the Paradox of Analysis.

And the paradox of analysis is to the effect that, if the verbal expressions representing the analysandum has the same meaning as the verbal expression representing the analysans, the analysis states a bare identity and is trivial; but if the two verbal expressions do not have the same meaning, the analysis is incorrect.[13]

If the left-hand expression has the same meaning as the right-hand expression, the analysis threatens to be trite. But if they do not have the same meaning, the analysis is incorrect. Moore's answer: "Now I own I am not at all clear as to what the solution of the puzzle is." If, continues Moore, in his exemplary fashion, one asks why the concept "X is a male sibling" is *identical* with the concept "X is a brother," while "X is a cube with 12 edges" is only logically *equivalent* and not identical with the concept "X is a cube," I cannot answer. "To raise this question would be to raise the question how an 'analytic' necessary connection is to be distinguished from a 'synthetic' one" (R, 665-67).

When we recall that Moore had earlier compared the relation "X is good"

[13] "Moore's Paradox," *PGEM*, 327. See R. Carnap's "Solution," in *Meaning and Necessity* (1947), pp. 63-64; N. Goodman's "On Likeness of Meaning," *Analysis* X (1949) and White's comments, *op. cit.*, p. 109.

and "I ought to do X" with the relation "X is a cube" and "X has 12 edges" (R, 575 ff.), one's ethical ears prick up. When we further recollect that the open-question argument depended on and was built around the analytic-synthetic distinction, we begin to sense the scope of the issues involved.

It is perhaps well to notice at once that A is A is not an analysis for Moore. Simple, indivisible concepts such as good cannot be defined, neither can they be analyzed. Analysis and analyticity have to do with the whole-part relation (in complex concepts). The whole analytically contains its parts. The problem in analysis hinges on this containment relation: does the whole contain — analytically necessary — the part or not? If not, the "part" is an independent concept and the relation, if necessary, is synthetic. Thus, for example, in the first entry of Notebook VI (*CPB*, 256-57) Moore faces the difficulty that in some instances in which the apodosis follows logically from the protasis he is unable to consider that the apodosis is "contained in" or "part of," or "included in" the protasis. And it is just this "containment" which he requires in order for an analysis to be correct, only then do the analysandum (protasis) and analysans (apodosis) have the *same* meaning. The important point is that whereas as a rule logical entailment and analyticity are considered mutually inclusive, this is not the case with Moore. Moore-analyticity is so narrow that logical entailment is at times broader.

Although Moore agrees that if X has an intrinsic property, say yellow or beauty, which Y also has, one can calculate *a priori* that X and Y are insofar exactly alike, he is prohibited by his view of analyticity from considering the necessity logical in character. Only when there is evidence of "containment" can one speak of analytic necessity. For him logical necessity is *only* "the kind of necessity, which we assert to hold, for instance, when we say that whatever is a right-angled triangle *must* be a triangle, or that whatever is yellow *must* be either yellow or blue" (*PS*, 271). Whereas a right-angled triangle "contains" the triangle-concept, one yellow or beautiful patch X does not "contain" another yellow or beautiful patch Y.

In view of the fact that uncovering the "parts" of a whole need not devolve into a fatuous exercise, it is by no means immediately obvious why Moore felt compelled to accept the dilemma. Light is shed on the matter when we realize that this matter of "containment" is a sensitive point with Moore. Although he grants that "parts" are *analytically necessary* to a whole (the whole-part relation), he is at the same time concerned to maintain that the concepts (which are on the one hand "parts") have an *independent* existence in regard to the whole. Thus he refuses to term the non-causal type of necessity at work in the part-whole relation analytic (*PE*, 29, 30, 206; cf. *PS*, 288-89).

In such a situation it is indeed problematic if one is dealing with parts of *one* concept, or if he must speak of as *many* concepts as there are "parts." And now the paradox of Analysis takes on its clearest form. If A and B are synonymous, they have the same meaning. But by mentioning A as well as B, are we not implying that the meanings of A and B are different? (RTD, 205-12). However, if A and B are not identical, the analysis is incorrect. A correct analysis states that A and B are identical, or that their expressions are synonymous, or that the statement "A is B" is analytic. But can such an analysis avoid being trite and tautological? In his earlier years Moore even doubted whether one could speak of such *analytic a priori* statements as being true; after all they are only tautologies, they say nothing (N, 294-96; *PS*, 11-12).

Moore's 1942 confession of puzzlement in regard to the paradox becomes even more significant when we learn that he was already consciously struggling with the problem in 1901.[14] The problem concerned the concept of "identity." He was convinced that to say "this is identical with that" differs from saying "this is identical with itself." Whereas the former states that A is B, the latter represents the Law of Identity, A is A. But there is an enigma involved: $A = B$ must differ from $A = A$, otherwise the Law of Identity implies its contradiction. On the other hand, $A = A$ must signify a relation between two things if it is not pure nonsense and if it can have a contradictorry (I, 119).

Moore approaches the problem from two sides. A is A, everything is self-identical, does not imply difference. Yet it is meaningful. For only in respect to its subject can a proposition differ from all others. Any predicate assignable to a subject could also belong to other things. Thus when one wishes to highlight the absolute uniqueness of a subject, one can only state that the subject is what it is; e.g. A is A, good is good, mind is mind.[15] At the same time, when two things have common predicates, there is identity of content which is not affected by the fact that there is numerical difference. Or, more generally, two notions can be *conceptually one* (same predicate) and yet *numerically different* (there are two).[16] Here identity does imply difference.

Later, as we have seen, Moore discussed the problem in more linguo-logical terminology. Instead if asking whether a predicate remains the "same" when borne by different things, he puzzles as to whether it is a "part" of the whole. And in his 1942 and 1944 papers he considers whether two synonymous expressions express the one and same concept (or proposition) or if one must conceive of two identical concepts. Or is there no difference here?

[14] "Identity," *PAS* 1 (1901), pp. 103-27. This similarity in problematics is one indication that Moore's ontological position remained basically the same from 1899 onward.
[15] Here we receive an additional insight into Moore's intentions when he says that "good is good."
[16] Moore also contends that universals differ *numerically* but not conceptually from their particulars (I, 114).

Moore employs his narrow view of analyticity as a logical weapon safeguarding the integrity and individual identity of the myriad "concepts" and objects populating the Universe against the idealistic emphasis on interdependence and Absolute Unity. Thus, he fabricates a logical argument "proving" the uniqueness of good. He demonstrates the idealistic confusions of thinking and what is thought of, of the sensation of blue and the color blue. Further, he is enabled to defend his thesis that *only* necessary relations need be internal (*PS*, 276-310). This is all well and good, but Moore is faced with the illusion-breaking fact that he desired to maintain the existence of a non-causal, non-factual "logical" necessity outside of the logical necessity inherent in analyticity. As we already noted, this is true in certain cases of logical entailment between two, at least numerically, different objects. There are also other, and for our purposes more important, situations which caused Moore concern.

One we have already met in the previous chapter: the natural/non-natural or fact-value relation. Whereas Moore treats natural properties as parts analytically necessary to the whole, he denies this status to non-natural properties, i.e. goodness and beauty. In that it cannot exist "*by itself* in time" and thus cannot as natural properties be "parts of which the object is made up" (*PE*, 41), goodness is an adherent, supervenient factor enjoying a special relation to the object. But what relation?

In *Principia* the nature of the relation is vague. Moore only allows that material (natural) qualities are "essential constituents" of valuable wholes (*PE*, 206). Later, concerned to avoid appearances of arbitrariness, he posits the *necessary* dependence of goodness on natural intrinsic properties. Intrinsic value itself depends "*only* on the intrinsic nature of what possesses it "(*PS*, 273). *Nevertheless*, goodness is not itself a natural property. This is the Paradox of Goodness.[17] Moore can only conceive of goodness as an analytically necessary part at the cost of a fall into Naturalism. Goodness must, thus, be supervenient. At the same time, goodness depends *only* and *necessarily* on these other analytically contained natural properties. But when it comes to explaining the nature of the relation and the kind of necessity involved, he confesses that he is at a loss.

"Good Ought To Be"

What is all involved — in particular for his theory of ethics — in the postulation

---

[17] Robert S. Hartman claims that Moore, especially in his Paradox of Goodness, was a pioneer in scientific axiology. See Robert S. Hartman, "Definition of Good: Moore's Axiomatic of the Science of Ethics," *PAS* LXV (1964-65). Cf. also *Kant—Studien* XLV, pp. 67-82 and XLVI, pp. 3-18; and his recent book, *The Structure of Value: Foundations of a Scientific Axiology* (1967).

of another type of logical necessity besides that of analyticity becomes clearer when Frankena's essay in *The Philosophy of G. E. Moore* and Moore's "Reply" are taken into consideration.[18] Frankena zeroes in on Moore's contention that good "ought to exist" (*PE*, 17) or "ought to be" (*PE*, 115, 118) or "is worth having for its own sake" (cf. *PE*, 188).[19] The argument is roughly as follows: If good is simple and thus indefinable, it cannot be claimed that "good ought to exist." The latter is a complex involving two notions, goodness is only one. The conclusion is obvious: Moore contradicts himself.

In more detail: since good is "simple," argued Frankena, any notion of "normativity" or "oughtness" is missing in "X is good." If Moore conceives of "X is good" as including such a concept of normativity, "good" may retain its nature of being analytic a priori, but certainly "good" is no longer simple. (In other words, by identifying goodness and oughtness, Moore would himself be committing the naturalistic fallacy.) If he retains the simplicity of good, "X is good" can only attain normative status in a synthetic, *contingent* way. And this is contrary to the weight of evidence that goodness brings with itself the concept of "oughtness" (which Moore himself recognizes by stating that "good ought to exist"). Thus, Frankena is convinced that Moore can only maintain the built-in or inherent normativity of intrinsic value at the cost of self-contradiction. The dilemma with which Frankena confronts Moore is clear: either goodness includes oughtness (involving analytic a priori, but with a loss of simplicity) or goodness does not include oughtness (in which case the connection becomes contingent, and goodness is non-normative or natural).

Frankena's clearly formulated critique depends, it is clear, on the assumption that logical necessity is exclusively analytic; in other words, synthetic a priori propositions are self-contradictory. His case receives strong support from the fact that it is easy to read Moore's own open-question argument as a refutation of synthetic a priori. Although Moore himself never drew this conclusion, he certainly gave occasion for it by not drawing a clear distinction between "identity" and "necessity." Often, as for example in his discussion of the relation between "X is good" and "X is thought" (*PE*, 129, 137) and "X is true" and "X is thought" (*PE*, 133), logical necessity appears synonymous with logical identity.

Moore argued, we recall, that a definition of good is self-contradictory because at one and the same time one is asserting distinctiveness (implying synthetic) and identity (implying analytic) of two notions. If one substitutes

---

[18] W. K. Frankena, "Obligation and Value," *PGEM*, 91-111. See also H. J. Paton, "The Alleged Independence of Goodness," *PGEM*, 111-35.
[19] In 1932 Moore explained that he had used the word good "Sometimes, though perhaps, not always . . . to mean the same as 'worth having for its own sake'" (*PP*, 98). In *Principia* (17) Moore inconsistently asserted "good ought to exist" instead of "good ought to be."

"necessity" for "identity," the argument turns out to presume (or prove) the self-contradictory character of synthetic a priori. When two notions (synthetic) are involved, there can never be talk of necessity.

Moore, however, wastes no time in answering Frankena's critique. On the one hand, he affirms, he has not contradicted himself (leaving aside certain inadequate phrasings and "slips"); on the other hand, he is unable in any sense to recognize the dilemma which Frankena has erected. Frankena's problem, relates Moore, is that he mistakenly assumes that "statements about obligation can only *follow from the very nature*' of statements about intrinsic value, if the statements of the latter sort *include or are identical with* statements of the former sort" (R, 575). On the contrary, although a connection between value and obligation is certainly synthetic in nature and not analytic, "a statement about obligation *follows from the very nature* of a statement about intrinsic value." Thus Moore considers it perfectly consistent to maintain on the one hand that good is "indefinable" and "simple" and on the other that "good ought to exist." The necessary connection between intrinsic value and obligation is synthetic and not analytic. "X is good" does not include "I ought to do X" just as "X is a cube" does not include "X is a cube *and* has 12 edges." This is true, but nevertheless there is in both instances a necessary and reciprocal connection between the propositions.

Moore terms the peculiar relationship of necessity or entailment which holds between such statements *logical equivalence* (in contrast to the logical identity characteristic of analyticity). This "new" relation is introduced when neither identity (analytic) nor contingency (synthetic a posteriori) is involved.

Logical Equivalence

In effect Moore's appeal to logical equivalence is a defense of synthetic a priori. And such a defense is completely in line with his earlier work. Ethics, as we have seen, is mandated to "enumerate all true universal judgments" (*PE*, 21, 4, 143) of which there are two species. One species (of Q II) asserts that "this unique property does always attach to the thing in question." In 1910, over against Hume, Moore chooses for Kant and the importance of synthetic a priori (*SMPP*, 152-53).[20]

The concept of logical equivalence itself is first introduced by Moore in his *Ethics* of 1912 (38-9). This in itself is revealing. It quickly comes to mind that Moore employed the concept in order to avoid some of the difficulties of *Principia*. And the supposition is valid: witness Moore's own testimony that

---

[20] Already in 1903 Moore praised Kant's "great discovery" that "all mathematical propositions are ... synthetic" ("Kant's Idealism," *PAS* IV, pp. 129, 130). Cf. also F., 203; NJ, 188; N, 294-96; *PS*, 11, 12; *PP*, 237; *CPB*, 266.

he introduced it under the influence of Bertrand Russell's critique.[21] In the "Reply" of 1942 he defends and further explains his utilization of logical equivalence. He transfers his accent from identity to equivalence because "it certainly seems as if this proposition were not a mere tautology" (*E*, 40) and yet it expresses a necessary relation. As this concept allows Moore the freedom of maintaining a necessary reciprocal connection — without falling backward into the tautologies of analyticity or forward into the contingencies of causal reality — he appeals to it increasingly after 1912 (his "Reply" is largely an appeal to logical equivalence).

Moore describes "equivalence" as "'logically' follows" (R, 606), but then 'logically' in the widest sense, synthetically as well as analytically. One proposition follows from another when it is true that to deny the first and affirm the second is contradictory. "X is a cube with 12 edges" follows from "X is a cube," but the two propositions are not identical. In the same way, "I ought to do X" follows from "X is good." In both cases there is logical equivalence and not logical identity, yet it is self-contradictory to deny the first and affirm the second. There is mutual entailment without identity. Thus, Moore is able to say that although intrinsic value has an "ought-implying property" which places one under obligation, there can be no justification for defining good in terms of ought (R, 604ff.). In a refinement of his position in the *Principia*, he further recognizes a logical equivalence of propositions re the "will" (which are identical with ought-propositions) and those re intrinsic value (R, 615ff.). Logical equivalence is the necessary but not the sufficient condition for identity (R, 601); which is to say that logical equivalence is the *necessary* but not *sufficient* criterion for a correct analysis (cf. *SMPP*, 275-76; *PP*, 81-83; R, 667; RTD, 196-97).

Another telling example of the reprieve which logical equivalence affords is the famous "two-worlds argument." In *Principia* Moore had defended the view that it was not irrational to maintain that beauty and ugliness would still exist without the presence of consciousness. The world would still be beautiful, even if no one saw it, and it would be far better that the beautiful world should exist rather than the ugly world, even if no one lived in either world (*PE*, 83-84). By asserting that there is no ground for choosing either world, as colors unseen, sounds unheard, are valueless without consciousness, Moore in 1942 modified his extreme view. And thanks to the concept of logical equivalence, he is able to write:

I agree . . . as I did not when I wrote *Principia*, that the existence of some *experience* is a proposition which does follow from the hypothesis that there exists a state of affairs which is good. (R, 618)

---

[21] *Independent Review* II, March 1904, pp. 382-83; cf. R, p. 558.

There is a necessary connection between "experience" and "goodness." But, since it is synthetic, good retains its "simplicity" and independence.[22]

Finally, it is important to point out that Moore could have employed logical equivalence as the solution to his "necessity" problem in relation to the natural/ non-natural distinction. Implicitly he did make this appeal, but never, at least to my knowledge, explicitly. The necessity involved in the relation of value (goodness) to certain facts (intrinsic natural properties) is not analytic in character, but neither is it factual or causal. Since there is no other choice, it must be the necessity of logical equivalence, the necessity holding between two concepts. Thus, we have to do with synthetic a priori. However, the presence of synthetic a priori could not serve as *the* mark or as the logical proof of the natural/non-natural relation for which Moore searched. For he discovered other properties *besides* goodness, natural properties that is, which also enjoy this supervenient, consequential relation to objects. "Pleasantness," for example, is a natural property which cannot be considered a constitutive part of an object; it too is supervenient (R, 587).

Logic and Inspection

It is time to take inventory. We have discovered that Moore avoided the antinomy of both maintaining synthetic a priori (QII) and of refuting it (QI). "Good ought to be" is not self-contradictory. There is necessity and universal validity outside of analytic concepts. In this way (through logical equivalence) he seeks to safeguard the "distinctness" (of goodness and in general of the material, external world) essential to the maintenance of "objectivism" without being thrown in naturalistic, but also in historicistic or relativistic fashion, into the maelstrom of contingency. "X is good" does not include any other notion than good and yet it follows by logical entailment that "what has intrinsic value ought to be promoted."

At the same time he must maintain his narrow concept of analyticity. Any expansion would not only torpedo the proofs for indefinability, but Moore's stance would resemble (at least some forms of) Naturalism in that the unbridgeable chasm between facts and values — and this is what Moore's ethics

---

[22] However, Moore adds that although one can deduce the existence of "experience" from the proposition "X is intrinsically good," it does not entail the *existence* of a "rational will." Neither does it imply that a good state of affairs "*depends* on the *existence* of a rational will." There is no dependence on the existence of a rational will because a proposition to the effect that a certain state of affairs would be good, if it existed, is a "statement which, if true, would have been true, even if *nothing at all* had existed." What the implication does mean is that a good state of affairs "*depends* on the fact that a rational will, if any had existed in certain circumstances, would have made a certain choice" (R, 617).

is all about — would have been bridged (the "necessity" involved would become "logical" in the narrow analytic sense).

By distinguishing logical identity and logical equivalence Moore can avoid scuttling his own position even as he lays low the opponent — at least, so he intends. Although his sustained appeal to logical equivalence does not torpedo the open-question argument as such, it does generate clouds of confusion. The clouds move in on the clear logical lines of the argument when it becomes mandatory to distinguish two kinds of necessity, apparently only differing in that one (logical identity) is an intra-mural affair (within the confines of one concept) and the other (logical equivalence) is an inter-mural affair (between two concepts). But how does one determine whether he has to do with one notion (analytic) or with two notions (synthetic)? And suddenly we are back at the open-question argument, be it in other terms. The ethical question would be something like this: how do we know that goodness is a different concept from the qualities in virtue of which an X is called good? Here we have the Paradox of Goodness. Why is goodness not a "part," seeing that it necessarily depends on these other "properties"?

Moore at this point jumps down from (or climbs above, if you prefer) the logical level. For him "inspection" answers the question. One *sees* whether one or two concepts are involved. He admits as much in forthright fashion in many instances. In answer to Frankena he insists that mutual entailment between *definiendum* and *definiens* can exist without analyticity. The test whether this is indeed the case is to ask the question: "Can I think of the one without *ipso facto* thinking of the other?" (R, 598) If this is possible, two notions are involved and logical equivalence is the pertinent relation. In other words, the final word belongs to *inspection* and not to logic.

In an article setting forth Moore's latest ethical views C. A. Broad comes to the same conclusion:

The final objection [which Moore could offer] would have to be that one can think of intrinsic goodness without *ipso facto* thinking of even so indeterminate a notion as that expressed by the phrase 'some intrinsic natural ought-inclining characteristic or other'. But is that really at all certain.[23]

But — and this is a telling confession — Moore later concedes that he is no longer sure of what he "sees."

To raise this question would be to raise the question how an "analytic" necessary connection is to be distinguished from a "synthetic" one — a subject about which I

[23] "G. E. Moore's Latest Published Views on Ethics," *Mind* LXX (1961), p. 453. In his article Broad also provides an interesting side-light on the fluidity of the analytic-synthetic distinction. Whereas Moore refused to believe that the proposition "X has 12 edges" is included (analytically) in the proposition "X is a cube," Broad cannot think otherwise (p. 445).

am far from clear. It seems to me that there are ever so many different cases of necessary connection, and that the line between "analytic" and "synthetic" might be drawn in many different ways. As it is, I do not think that the two terms have any clear meaning. (R, 667)

And this is not the first or the last time that with admirable integrity he admitted his inability to determine whether identity or equivalence is involved.[24]

If it depends in the last analysis on sight, or insight, whether one or two notions are involved, Frankena was no doubt right when he concluded: "It is a *petitio* for the intuitionists to say that what the definist is taking for a definition is really a universal synthetic proposition."[25] It is a begging of the question because that is just the matter at hand; whereas the definist sees but one notion (thus considering it analytic), the intuitionist sees two notions (and takes it to be synthetic). But neither disputant has the right to consider his position (what he "sees") as established. This must first be demonstrated, it is the very issue at stake. In the final analysis it resolves into a conflict between those who "see" and those who "do-not-see"; with all parties concerned confidently assigning their opponents to the latter camp. This entire state of affairs points to the fact that the issues at stake are more-than-logical. Even in matters of logic it has become clear that this "more" is articulated.[26]

COMMON SENSE BELIEFS AND INSPECTION

The Common Sense View

In order the better to understand the place of inspection or intuition in Moore's philosophy, and at the same time to obtain a clearer idea of the role of supralogical motives, it is well to emphasize that Moore restricts himself in his analytic endeavours to the statements of common sense as they come to expression in ordinary language.[27] The common sense view "which seems ob-

---

[24] Cf. also for example, *SMPP*, 279; *PP*, 60-89; R, 661-71; RTD, 184-87.
[25] "The Naturalistic Fallacy," *Mind* XLVIII (1939), p. 474.
[26] Especially the current state of logic illustrates this point. At present a Babel-like confusion reigns in regard to the analytic-synthetic distinction. Some under the influence of Quine and White are questioning the very division itself. For the assault of the distinction: Quine, *From a Logical Point of View* (1953); N. Goodman, "On Likeness of Meaning," *Analysis* X (1950); M. White, "The Analytic and the Synthetic: An Untenable Dualism," *Semantics and Language* (ed. Linsky). For discussion and defense: H. P. Grice and P. F. Strawson, "In Defense of a Dogma," *PR* LXV (1956); Hofstadter, "Myth of White," *JP* LI (1954). Cf. also, pp. 176-78.
[27] As A. White has argued, it is illegitimate to portray Moore as the first "Ordinary Language" philosopher. He did not argue from "it is correct English" to "it is therefore true." Cf. White, *op. cit.* pp. 5-8. Also N. Malcolm, "Moore and Ordinary Language," *PGEM* and "Defending Common Sense," *PR* LVIII (1949); and V. C. Chappell, "Malcolm on Moore," *Mind* LXX (1961), p. 417. Whereas Moore generally argued

viously true" (*PS*, 289), is the every-day, every-man way of looking at things. There are certain beliefs, those of common sense, "which we all commonly assume to be true about the Universe, and which we are sure that we know to be true about it."[28] Moore begins his enumeration by noting that "we certainly believe that there are in the Universe enormous numbers of material objects" (our bodies, the bodies of others, animals, plants, inanimate objects, cultural objects, the earth itself, Universe, sun, moon and stars, etc.). "We believe that we men, besides having bodies, also have *minds* . . . that we perform certain mental acts or acts of consciousness" (*SMPP*, 2-4).

For Moore, it is not so much common sense as "good judgment" but as "common knowledge or belief." He has a healthy respect for the "views of Common Sense" which he believes to be "'in certain fundamental features' wholly true." It is a view "which every or very nearly every sane adult, who has the use of all his senses, believes or knows" (*CPB*, 280).[29] In so believing, Moore considers himself justified in bypassing the question of *truth* and *meaning* (on a first or basic level). The truth of such propositions, if they are those of common sense, is more or less certain (absolute certainty on such matters is excluded in any case) and their every-day, ordinary *meaning* is well-known (otherwise such beliefs would not be common sense beliefs). Such statements have a peculiar self-authenticating character which makes it strange and even improper to question their validity.

Moore is "not at all sceptical as to the *truth* of such propositions." He is sceptical about their analysis. There is a compelling need to avoid the prevalent error of confusing "the question whether we understood its meaning (which we all certainly do) with the entirely different question whether we *know what it means,* in the sense that we are able to give a *correct analysis* of its meaning" (*PP*, 37).[30] Not doubting the meaning or truth of common sense beliefs, he in turn was able to appeal to such deliverances both in support and in refutation of suggested analyses. These common sense beliefs acquire a certain normative status and function insofar as the touchstone of truth. Moore concludes his *Principia Ethica* with the prayer that the book "will not appear so strange, I venture to hope and believe . . . to Common Sense" (224). Habitually Moore

that it is wrong to question the beliefs of common sense *because they are known*, some of his followers tend to argue as if challenging them is wrong because it conflicts with *ordinary usage*.

[28] See *LP* (174ff.) where Moore points out that "presupposed," although still not the proper word, is more correct than "assumed." Cf. also *PP*, 42ff. and *CPB*, 280.

[29] Although his appeal to common sense becomes more pronounced after his 1925 essay "A Defense of Common Sense" (*PP*, 32-60), already in 1898 Moore had a high regard for "the common point of view" (F, 194, 204; Cf. also NJ, 192; I, 103).

[30] Thus in keeping with Moore's 1942 confession that the "main stimulus to philosophizing" has not been "the world or the sciences" but what "other philosophers have said about the world or the sciences" ("Autobiography," *PGEM*, 14).

argues that his opponent's view denies certain matters and that in "doing so they do flatly contradict Common Sense" (*SMPP*, 113; cf. *PS*, 288). Whereas such contradictions are sufficient reason to reject a theory, (e.g. *SMPP*, 2ff., 21-22, 138-39, 150 passim; *LP*, 89; *E*, 127) agreement is likewise a strong presumption in favor of a certain theory (e.g. *SMPP*, 156, 345; *E*, 153). At times common sense takes "no view," it simply does not raise the question. But, even then, it is usually possible to judge between the contesting theories. "All that we can say is, I think, that some of these views *would* appear more natural — less paradoxical than others — to any plain man who could understand the question" (*LP*, 88).

Moore's usual approach involves asking what a particular theory means when translated into the concrete. More often than not, the theory in its concrete form loses "all its plausibility." Moreover this translation-into-the-concrete method points out to the philosopher that he has been advocating something which is "utterly different from what we believe in common life, and also very difficult to believe even now when we try to consider it philosophically" (*SMPP*, 135). A philosopher in such instances must "believe ever so many propositions which contradict, what he himself constantly believes and cannot help believing in ordinary life" (*SMPP*, 149-50). In 1925 Moore boldly generalized:

All philosophers, without exception, have agreed with me in holding . . . that the "Common Sense view of the world" is, in certain fundamental features, *wholly* true... and that the real difference . . . is only a difference between those philosophers, who have *also* views inconsistent with these features in the "Common Sense view of the world, "and those who have not." (*PP*, 44)

In spite of the prominent role given to common sense beliefs, Moore does not claim that such statements are always true and never false. Indeed, they *may* be false, and some certainly *are*.[31] One cannot prove their truth (*PE*, 75; *SMPP*, 176, 191) and may have to question it (*PS*, 52ff.). The point is that we all simply *assume* them to be true (*SMPP*, 2, 27, 156). One could even put it stronger and say that no one can refuse to believe them. Just these features of *universal* and *compulsive* acceptance are important criteria by which to

---

[31] Moore cannot and does not deny that the every-day view of the Universe has changed, and considerably at that, throughout the ages. In an attempt to minimize the fact that we "*now* believe that these primitive views about the material Universe were certainly wrong," he lays the stress on the equally undeniable fact that men "have always believed in the existence of a great many material objects" (*SMPP*, 3). He also realizes that in bygone times "most men believed that acts of Consciousness *were* attached to logs of wood and stones" (*SMPP*, 8). But even then, it was believed that at many places there were no acts of consciousness going on. The difference today is only that we believe in still fewer spots in which acts of consciousness take place.

ascertain whether certain views belong to common sense or not.[32] However, the ultimate reason for holding common sense statements to be true is simply that they are seen to be *self-evident* (*SMPP*, 157; *PP*, 32-60). As logical inference can no longer help, it is a matter for inspection or intuition.

Inspection

Prior to concluding our discussion of common sense, it is necessary to give separate treatment to inspection. Not only is inspection the last court of appeal in regard to common sense beliefs, it also plays this role in ethics and in analysis in general. In the last analysis every situation and every debate is illuminated and resolved for Moore by "actual inspection." For every argument is finally whittled down to a stage where further argumentation is simply impossible. "There is no conclusive argument in favor of either. It is simply a matter of inspection" (*SMPP*, 357). This is a constantly recurring refrain in Moore's writings. When he is unable to decide whether the suggested definition of truth and falsehood is indeed correct, he intones: "This is a question which can only be settled by actual inspection." Not only does he advise one to bring "natural objects" before the mind's eye, he also admonishes one to inspect the correspondence relation which characterizes truth.

The essential point is to concentrate upon the relation *itself*: to hold it before your mind, in the sense in which when I name the colour 'vermilion', you can hold before your mind the colour that I mean. If you are not acquainted with this relation in the same sort of way as you are acquainted with the colour vermilion, no amount of words will serve to explain what it is, any more than you could explain what vermilion is like to a man born blind. (*SMPP*, 279)

Inspection may be employed in order to support certain analyses as in the case of truth (*PE*, 124), but more often as evidence against analyses as in the case of Bradley's view of reality (*SMPP*, 233), of certain views of truth (*SMPP*, 262-63), of universals (*SMPP*, 351), of right and good (*E*, 104, 112, 147). Often he admonishes his readers to look carefully and *see* whether one notion that you have before your mind is no different from another notion that you had before your mind previously. Sometimes, having left the matter to inspection, even Moore has doubts as to what he sees (*SMPP*, 278). At times he rationalizes that one can see the answer but be unable to express it in words (*SMPP*, 109, 252, 296: *PS*, 260).

In defending the existence of material objects, Moore raises his two hands (*PP*, 146ff.) or simply exclaims: "I *do* know that this pencil exists." These proofs he argues are conclusive in the sense that they are as "strong and good .... as any that could be used." In the final stage one must inevitably appeal

[32] Cf. White, *op. cit.*, pp. 11-20 for a discussion of the criteria of common sense.

to a proposition "*without* knowing any other proposition whatever from which it follows." Failure to do this results in an *ad infinitum* regress. If we ever want to know anything, we must begin with something we know *immediately* without inference. Moore names this knowing of at least one proposition to be true without knowing any other from which it is derived "*immediate knowledge*" (*SMPP*, 119-23, cf. 90).[33] In a later series of lectures he allowed that it seemed to him

perfectly evident that if we're to have reasoned knowledge of anything, we must have unreasoned knowledge of some things. So that to say that such props. were matters of Faith, *not* of Reason, wouldn't necessarily exclude their being known. (*LP*, 47; cf. 149)

Although Moore established that there are ultimate propositions (or at least that there is a point in such argument beyond which logic cannot go), he is unable to show that a certain proposition which strikes one as self-evident is in *fact* self-evident. He concludes that whereas it is possible to *show* that a statement is ultimate, it is impossible to prove whether it is in itself true or false (*PE*, 75, 145; *SMPP*, 191-92). However this lack of proof should not lead to doubt. For no position can appeal to a final proof, and the common sense view is at least as reasonable as any other. Stronger than that: disproving common sense statements must finally rest on premises less certain than the statements to be refuted. Moreover everyone agrees that these beliefs are true, and it is this universal agreement, not argument, which is our concern in the finale. At a certain point in the last lap one advances beyond the stage of proof and is concerned only with common beliefs and agreement or consensus.

This is true, argues Moore, for statements of common sense as well as for the laws of logic (*PE*, 76). We agree that they are true, we cannot prove it. At the same time he is quick to note that one becomes entangled in inconsistencies if he denies certain beliefs. Demonstrating such logical foibles constitutes *indirect* proof of the statements and is capable of convincing the intellect to give assent to them as being true. And all this, Moore is confident, is sufficient warrant to act with certainty. Seeing that a final universally valid proof is impossible, one must employ his energies to discover good reasons for *holding* a certain view. Agreement on this matter is not everything, but it has shown itself to be sufficient. Thus the passion with which Moore marshalls considerations designed to convince the intellect that his view of the matter deserves

---

[33] "Immediate knowledge" is one form of "knowledge proper." Knowledge proper involves a) direct apprehension of proposition, b) belief in the proposition, c) proposition must be in itself true, d) "and also some fourth condition" (*SMPP*, 123, 81 ff.). Immediate knowledge stands over against mediate knowledge (knowing a proposition "because you know some other from which it follows").

approbation. If the considerations are set in proper array, then everyone will *obviously see* that his answer is (to be considered) true.

Common Sense and Science

Although one can never know whether the propositions he holds are true in themselves, he can rest assured because the beliefs of common sense are so universally accepted that one can proceed *as if* he knew them to be true in themselves. But in the same context in which Moore has dismissed theories because they clash with common sense beliefs, he rejects a theory which agrees with the common sense view (*SMPP*, 137). In regard to sense-data he is willing to discount the reports of common sense when faced with the givens of scientific investigation by means of the microscope (*SMPP*, 146ff.). Even though common sense affirms that we "see trees, houses, and the sun and moon," he chooses to disregard the normative character of such beliefs and affirms "all that we in fact directly perceive are sense-data, which are not identical with any parts of these objects" (*SMPP*, 241).[34]

Again, whereas in regard to certain questions (such as God's existence[35]) he declares common sense impartial, he confidently affirms that common sense has a worked-out theory in other instances, for example in the relation of mind and matter: "every state of consciousness is *accompanied* by some state of the brain, and that each of these accompanying brain-states is caused by and does cause some other brain-state or nerve-state." It is this "theory which is, I think, the one now commonly held, and which is, in fact, the one which I myself suppose to be true" (*SMPP*, 159-60).[36] Thus, sometimes the common sense view is to be rejected, sometimes common sense has no view, other times it has a most intricate view, or again more than one view.

How is Moore able to judge when and when not to break with the utterances of common sense? Perhaps when they conflict with this theory? But it is just *his* theory which is the common sense view. Or is there a certain view of reality

---

[34] Moore devoted much of his philosophic effort to detailed painstaking discussion of sense-data (a term which he invented) and perception. Perceptual statements are also ultimates which cannot be proven true or false.

[35] The existence or the non-existence of God places Moore before a difficult choice. Today, Moore admits, it is hard to determine whether the majority believe or disbelieve in God's existence. His conclusion: "It is fairest to say, that Common Sense has *no* view in the question" (*SMPP*, 17; cf. *LP*, 174). For Moore's answer to the question "ought we to believe in God?", cf. "The Value of Religion," *Intern. Journal of Ethics* XII, pp. 81-98. Moore concludes: "We might perhaps with advantage worship the real creature a little more, and his hypothetical Creator a good deal less."

[36] Moore rejects occasionalism, epiphenomenalism and parallelism because the connection mind-body is too loose. For him every change in mind is accompanied by — absolutely simultaneously — definite change in brain-matter, and vice versa.

which he simply girds with the simplicity, and self-evident "gown" of common sense? And here the problem of truth which Moore initially shunted aside returns to haunt him. For analysis does not simply acquiesce with clarifying, in fact, it seldom or ever is able only to do that; rather as it probes deeper it must make decisions of truth of at least two kinds. It must referee between dissonant views all claiming the favour of common sense, and it must make decisions in regard to problems about which common sense has no, or at best, a blurred, vague opinion. How does analysis decide? By what criteria? After distinguishing carefully all he can do is leave the result up to inspection. What inspection decides depends entirely on what extra-logical position Moore has adopted as his own.

By clothing his theory in the gown of common sense, or perhaps better, by palming off his theory as the common sense view, Moore seeks to win for it the unquestionable authority which everyday experience carries with it (at the same time avoiding the obligation to give a scientific accounting of his position). But in that the views of common sense are generally naive, vague and scanty when measured by the standards of scientific thought, it is impossible to treat them as scientific statements *par excellence*. That is to say, as soon as Moore begins theorizing, the question of *theoretic* truth becomes pressing. Although he rightly sensed the difference between the scientific and non-scientific, giving (again) rightly the priority to the latter, he nevertheless continually confused the two. Just in order to serve the non-scientific, science must operate *theoretically*; that is, it must operate subject to the rules of theoretic thought and not those of common sense. The every-day way of looking at things leaves reality intact (it is not as Moore claimed the "theory of representative perception" *PP*, 55); a scientific theory *about* reality involves analysis and synthesis, abstraction and generalization.

Failure to recognize this indispensable distinction between the theoretical and non-theoretical, in fact attempting to employ non-theoretical views as normative for scientific work, Moore embroils himself in problems on every hand. Thus, faced with scientific givens by use of the microscope etc., he feels forced to introduce technical constructs termed sense-data and consequently breaks his own rule that an analysis cannot be right if it contradicts the truth of what it sets out to analyze; in this case denying that we really see trees, houses, etc. as common sense testifies. He has failed to distinguish the essential difference between normal sense perception and scientific perception, perception opened up under the leading of theoretical thought.

(Subjective) Certainty and (Objective) Truth

Although Moore on the one hand treats inspection as a technique of analysis on a par with division-analysis, on the other hand he is keenly aware that more is involved. Inspection is the *ultimate* appeal and at this point extra-logical considerations play a decisive role. In some instances, as we have seen, he has employed the terms "immediate knowledge" and "unreasoned knowledge" where we have come to expect him to talk of intuition or inspection. There is no significant difference in meaning.[37] All these terms are employed to deal with ultimate situations; when logical inference and proof are no longer possible. Even though — as the examples presented above indicate — inspection is called in for its verdict in situations significantly and essentially different from both everyday sense perception and natural scientific observation, Moore creates the impression that the activities are basically similar (e.g. *PS*, 25; *PE*, 16; *SMPP*, 233).[38] On the one hand, he is well aware that some kind of "immediate knowledge" or "intuition" is required both in regard to common sense and scientific analysis. As we will have opportunity to see, this is especially true for Moore with his ontology and concomitant theory of meaning. However, fearing the subjective connotations (an esoteric faculty!) which the term intuition arouses, he conceives of intuition as inspection with all its overtones of sense perception. Intuition becomes extra-sensory perception, sense perception directed at the non-empirical. Actually, since he conceives of "seeing as an act of consciousness which we can all of us directly observe as happening in our own minds" (*SMPP*, 29), intuition becomes introspection, the natural look turned inward (cf. *PS*, 26; *SMPP*, 244).[39]

[37] Moore, fully in agreement, describes Hume's view; "*intuitive* knowledge is the sort of knowledge you may have of a proposition, when, as soon as you really understand what the proposition means, you can *see* that it is true" (*SMPP*, 90). "Immediate knowledge," Moore recognizes, is some times called "direct apprehension." For differences, cf. *SMPP*, 123.

When "we are said to perceive *that* so and so is the case, i.e. to perceive *not* a thing, but a fact or truth," then "'perceive' does entail 'know'" (*SMPP*, 46, 77).

In his recent book, *Second Thoughts in Moral Philosophy*, A. C. Ewing gives notice that for him the terms "intuition" and "direct cognition" are interchangeable and equivalent (p. 66). In an earlier contribution to *British Philosophy in Mid-Century* (ed. C. A. Mace), he suggests substituting "'practical reason' or 'practical judgment' instead of intuition" (p. 94).

[38] Moore maintains that in addition to the direct apprehension of sense-data and images we have "direct apprehension of a proposition" (*SMPP*, 67-71, 74), as well as of "our acts of consciousness" (*SMPP*, 49, 111). Likewise "the objection to the theory" that there is a universal property "whiteness" is a failure in "perceiving" it clearly (*SMPP*, 351, 361). Or again, we "can perhaps distinguish the universal in question: that we can hold the number two before our minds, and see what it is, and *that* it is". And importantly, he adds, "in almost the *same way* as we can do this with any particular *sense-datum* that we are *directly perceiving*" (*SMPP*, 366, Italics added).

[39] It is important not to identify introspection and intuition (as for example, Ryle, *The Concept of the Mind*, 1949). For then one is led (wrongly) to reject intuition because there is no such thing as a natural scientific method of introspection.

Although Moore is on guard to avoid giving self-evidence, inspection and truth a psychological twist (*PE*, 143-44), within the confines of this position he cannot avoid so doing for the simple reason that human subjectivity (which, when not ensconced in formal logic, is immediately psychological for Moore), to say it softly, is always present. Self-evident means in the strictest sense "true *by itself* alone; that it is not an inference from some proposition other than *itself*" (*PE*, 143). In this proper sense one can never know (logically) that anything is ultimately true. At best one can say that he sees it as self-evident, that it urges itself upon him *self-evidently*. But self-evident is here used in a derivative, weakened sense. Yet this is the only sense in which it can play a real role in human life. Thus, Moore grants that he does not "know exactly how to set about arguing that they are self-evident." All one can do is distinguish and consider carefully and "then to see whether it does not seem as if they *must* be true" (*SMPP*, 191). The same situation obtains in regard to "being true." What one *holds true* or claims to know as true need not *be true*. But unless the former weakened sense is employed, one can only say "what is true is true and that is the end of the matter."

However, these secondary uses themselves will lose all meaning unless they can lean on or appeal to something which is known to be in itself, self-evident and true. Which is to say that in spite of his theory, Moore depends (at least initially) on intuitive certainty as to the truth in itself or *universal validity* of certain concepts and propositions. Thus, his ethical enterprise rests on the certain intuition of the universal validity of "goodness." But, and this holds for Moore's philosophy as a whole, his position never allows him the room to declare such an intuition to be more than an indication that one has *adequate* and *good* reasons for holding a certain position. In the ethical case, he must claim that "good is good" is a result of logical argument. (That he does finally appeal to inspection to "back up" his logical argument only confirms the present analysis. And even then, Moore appeals to inspection at the *end* of the argument). Nevertheless – his theory not withstanding – without being able to count on the givens of intuition at the *beginning* of his ethical enterprise, there would have been no ethics. His difficulty arises when, subsequent to initial pre-theoretical intuitions, he theoretically isolates certain concepts such as truth, beauty and goodness in order to guarantee their objectivity or intrinsicness. But in so doing, he makes it impossible for human subjectivity to draw on them. He attempts to save the situation by touting the views of common sense as trustworthy and true. However, in the last analysis he must admit that there is no infallible "warrant of truth" (*PE*, 76). Although common sense is the *only* available guide, it is not *sure* (i.e. infallible, objective, universally valid). At the same time, it does offer one subjective certainty ("meaning by 'certain', not merely true or probably true, but *known* to be so") (*SMPP*, 121).

To point up the dialectic again: Even inspection can be myopic, even intuition brings with it no proof of truth itself. Although the ultimate statements of common sense defy proof or disproof, they can rightly be claimed to be *known* as true. They "are much more certain than any premiss which could be used to prove that they are false; and also much more certain than any other premiss which could be used to prove that they are true" (*SMPP*, 125). But, again, how does one know that they are more certain than other premises? There would seem to be only one possibility — but in that it is an impossibility for Moore, it points to a basic antinomy in his position — an intuition which prehends *sure* knowledge of that which is true in itself.

ONTOLOGY AND MEANING

Theory of Meaning

In order to bring together in clearer focus all the aspects of Moore's philosophy which we have thus far discussed, we can do no better than examine his theory of meaning. Moore held more or less consistently throughout his life that the meaning of an expression is identical with the *concept* (or proposition) for which it stands. The function of words is to *name* something, to describe concepts standing behind to which the words point. Good is thus the "object or idea which I hold . . . that the word is generally used to stand for" (*PE*, 6).

This view of meaning as something objectively subsistent radically colors Moore's view of analysis. A person analyzing a concept or an idea is stooped over peering intently at something behind the words which he holds before his mind's eye (*PE*, preface; *SMPP*, ch. XII *passim*) or even in his mind (*SMPP*, 29,52). He regards these properties, notions or concepts, as a special sort of object brought up before the mind when the word denoting it is uttered. It is as if there is a mysterious subterranean underworld of concepts which take turns being called up by the stimulus of a word. It is about these notions or concepts which Moore is concerned (*SMPP*, 118). His preoccupation is with "the kind of idea which words express" (*PS*, 135), his first question is "what is the property which we denote by the word?" (*SMPP*, 300)

In brief, Moore is interested in the "'meaning' in the sense of *what is meant*; for in fact the thing I want to talk about *is* the object or property or notion or idea which is conveyed or meant by the word . . . . and is in that sense, its meaning." He is quite aware that it is unusual to call the same thing both an "object" and a "concept." But regardless of the fact that he considers it more natural to designate what he intends with the words "notion," "idea," "conception," he wishes to erase any possible misunderstanding that the something conceived "cannot *be* at all except in a mind" and thus also terms a notion an "object." Concepts are objective extra-mental, mind-independent. Nevertheless, since talk of "object" may lead one mistakenly to think that he was referring to "objects or things which *are* real," he considers it preferable to talk about "a notion or idea or conception" (*SMPP*, 217-18).[40]

In addition to "concepts" which stand behind words, Moore has another "entity" which stands behind sentences — "propositions." "A proposition is here to be understood, not as anything subjective — an assertion or an affirmation of something — but as the combination of concepts which is affirmed" (NJ, 183). A proposition is not a collection of *words* or a sentence, but what such a collection of words expresses, "what these words mean" (*SMPP*, 57, 72). "It is a name for what is before your mind, when you not only hear or read but *understand* a sentence" (*SMPP*, 259). He even divides the contents of the universe ("absolutely everything there is at all") into propositions and things which are not propositions (minds and material objects). "The sort of thing that I mean by proposition is certainly one of the things that *is*" (*SMPP*, 56, 296 ff.).

In the *Baldwin Dictionary* article of 1902 on Truth and Falsity, Moore feels called upon to refute the "generally held" view that "the proposition is a *mental* copy of the reality, or an 'idea.'" And this erroneous view "seems to be solely due to the almost universal error, whereby the *object* of a belief or idea is regarded as the attribute or content of such belief or idea." That is to say: the "object" is considered to be a creation of mind. It is just this mind-enthronement in vogue since Kant which he disputes.

Even after this slight acquaintance with Moore's theory of meaning, one can more meaningfully follow him when he writes: "To define a concept is the same thing as to give an analysis of it; but to define a word is neither the same thing as to give an analysis of that word, nor the same thing as to give an analysis of any concept" (R, 665). However, to win more insight into the ins-and-outs of his position, we must turn to his highly significant paper of 1899 "The Nature of Judgment."[41] In this essay in which he first announced his rejection of Bradley's neo-Idealism, he in the same breath set forth his ontology. And, although he was gradually induced to reject certain features of his 1899 position, or at least to allow it to lie fallow, he never overthrew, abandoned or gave up

[40] That is to say, as we shall see, Moore distinguishes between *objects or things* which have or are composed of certain properties or concepts and the *properties or concepts* themselves. This being the case we shall employ "object" exclusively as a synonym for "things."

[41] J. A. Passmore has performed a real service in beginning his exposition of Moore by treating this often-neglected article. Cf. Passmore, *A Hundred Years of Philosophy* (1957). Cf. also H. Hochberg, "Moore's Ontology and Non-natural Properties," *Review Of Metaphysics* XV (1962), pp. 365-93; D. Lewis, "Moore's Realism," in *Moore and Ryle: Two Ontologists* (1965) and their philosophic mentor Gustav Bergmann, "Inclusion, Exemplification, and Inherence in G. E. Moore," *Logic and Reality* (1964). Also relevant is J. O. Nelson, "Mr. Hochberg on Moore: Some Corrections," *Review of Metaphysics* XVI (1962), pp. 119-32.

the "objectivist" spirit which it breathed. He confessed that it was always this spirit which motivated and drove him: "the meaning of an idea was not anything 'cut off' from it [mind], but something wholly independent of mind" (*PGEM*, 22). Indeed, there is little positive evidence that he ever abandoned the basic ontological pattern there sketched. In any case the imprint of this position is indelibly stamped on all of Moore's publications.[42] And there is no doubt — in our study of particular importance — that he wrote *Principia Ethica* from within the 1899 perspective.

Being and Existence

A judgment is not à la Locke simply about subjective "ideas," neither is à la Bradley an idea itself, as psychic phenomenon, a constituent of our judgments. Rather judgments are about what "ideas" mean, what they point to; they are composed of "concepts" or "logical ideas." Ideas are not to be considered as exclusively states of the mind or as contents in the mind, or as productions of the action of minds. An idea is a "universal meaning" (to employ Bradley's phrase), a "concept," a "logical idea"; that is to say, concepts or ideas are neither mental facts nor mental acts, but the "possible objects of thought." As such they have *being* and *are* something, it is indifferent to their nature whether they are *in fact* thought of or not.

Concepts are neither words nor subjective designations, rather they are "immutably what they are," "incapable of change," "irreducible to anything else," "the only objects of knowledge"; in short, the "ultimate" building-blocks of the universe" (NJ, 178-82, 192).[43]

Thus, both subjective ideas and objective things can be "composed of nothing but concepts." A proposition "is a synthesis of concepts . . . together with a specific relation between them." Further, since "existence is itself a concept," an "existent is seen to be nothing but a concept or a complex of concepts standing in a unique relation to the concept of existence." Indeed, it seems necessary "to regard the world as formed of concepts" (NJ, 180-83). Concepts, or as Moore subsequently refers to them, "Platonic ideas," "universals,"

[42] The lack of attention to Moore's early articles is no doubt partly due to his own decision to leave them lie in 1922 (when faced with the task of selecting essays for publication in *PS*). But although in 1942 he called his 1898 article on "Freedom" "absolutely worthless" and his *Baldwin Dictionary* articles of 1902 "extraordinarily crude," he judges that his article on "Judgment," apart from many confusions, revealed the "beginning . . . of certain tendencies in me which have led some people to call me a 'Realist' and was also the beginning of a breakaway from a belief in Bradley's philosophy . . . I think there was probably some good in it" (*PGEM*, 21-22).
[43] In this way Moore considers the "material diversity of things, which is generally taken as a starting point" as derived and "the identity of the concept, in several different things . . . as the starting point" (NJ, 182).

"general ideas," "abstractions" (I, 114; *SMPP*, 302-03, 373) are in principle non-temporal, non-empirical and non-existent.[44] Universals do not "exist" (as for example lions exist), but they certainly "are" (cf. NJ, 181, 186). Likewise, propositions and truths do not occur in time.[45] In contrast to universals; particulars, things, or material objects do *exist*, are *temporal*, and are *real* (PE, 40-41, 110, 118-19; *SMPP*, 11, 373).

Here is the basic contrast in Moore's ontology of the early 1900's: between concepts and objects, between universal concepts which only *are* and particular objects or things which also *exist*. The primary bifurcation in the Universe is between *being* and *existence*. In contrast to Bradley's schema, existence=time =appearance over against *real*=ideal, Moore worked with the schema: existence=time=*real*=particular over against universal=being=is. "Particulars certainly exist, while it is at least doubtful whether any universals do" (I, 115).[46]

Given the basic dualistic ontology, Moore's basic problem is to bring together and meaningfully relate being and reality. Or in other words, what does the process of becoming "existent" and "individual" involve for Moore. In this early period he could be said to deal with this matter in three different, but necessarily interrelated, ways. The opposition of non-existent concepts and existents disappears since complexes of concepts become existents when they stand in a unique relation to the concept of "existence." Secondly, individuation requires that spatial and temporal universals (here, there, then, now) be present in the congeries of concepts. Thirdly, one class of concepts, empirical concepts to be specific, "can exist in an actual part of time" (NJ, 189).[47]

Moore's later changes in or his increasing dissatisfaction with his position can be seen largely as efforts to avoid the problems involved in these solutions. Since in his view existents are *composites* of concepts, in order for the concept of "existence" to endow existence on concept-complexes, it would seem necessary that the concept itself exist. But can a non-existent concept exist? Moore continued to be puzzled by this matter. Finally in 1926 he denied that existence was a concept. Whereas the proposition "some tame tigers don't growl" has a perfectly clear meaning, the grammatically similar "some tame tigers don't exist" is a "queer and puzzling expression." The cause of the problem is that by "pointing and saying 'This *exists*' we should express *no proposition at all* . . .

[44] Nevertheless, all concepts are given in experience (NJ, 189). But our knowledge "is not confined to the things which we can touch and see and feel" (*PE*, 110).
[45] "The truth that something exists, it would seem, never does exist itself, and hence cannot be accurately said to occupy any moment of time" (N, 297). "Propositions do not occur in time" (N, 299).
[46] "I endeavour to show, what I must own appears to me perfectly obvious, that the concept can consistently be described neither as an existent, nor as part of an existent, since it is presupposed in the conception of an existent" (NJ, 181).

'This is a tame tiger and *exists*' would not be tautologous, but meaningless." Conclusion: "exist" in this usage "does not stand for an attribute" (*PP*, 124, 115-26).

More problematic and more telling for his theory is Moore's introduction of empirical concepts, concepts which strangely enough can exist in time. But a simple concept cannot exist. At best an empirical concept would be a complex, including a simple concept, the concept of existence and the relation involved. But does it then differ from a particular object, existent and substantial? In 1903 he seems in fact to employ empirical concepts under the name of natural properties. They are "in themselves substantial and give to the object all the substance it has." Since these properties are "parts" rather than "mere predicates," without them there is no object left, "not even a bare substance." In such instances objects are said to contain their parts analytically (*PE*, 41).

Moore's endeavour to interconnect being and existence in empirical concepts was fostered, it would appear, by an equivocal use of the term substantial. In concluding his 1899 essay, he writes:

[47] Schematically Moore's ontology, his Platonizing Subsistence Theory, could roughly be sketched as follows (for comparison with earlier stage, cf. fn. 5):

BEING ("is")	Concepts or Universals
Non-natural	a. special e.g. goodness, number
	b. relational
Non-temporal	Propositions
Immutable	a. universal truths (facts)
	b. falsehoods
	Imaginary Objects

REALITY ("Exists")	Particulars
Natural	(including Minds)
Temporal	Empirical Concepts
Mutable	True Existential Propositions

Subsequent to certain modifications (re ontic status of falsehoods, concept of existence, etc., cf. fn. 50 and p. 88 ff.), corresponding changes must be made in the schema.

BEING	Universals
	a. natural properties
	b. non-natural
	c. relational
	Facts or Truths

REALITY	Particulars
	(substances plus predicates)

A concept is not in any intelligible sense an 'adjective', as if there were something more substantive, more ultimate than it. For we must, if we are to be consistent, describe what appears to be most substantive as no more than a collection of such supposed adjectives: and thus, in the end, the concept turns out to be the only substantive or subject, and no one concept either more or less an adjective than any other. . . . The nature of judgment is . . . less ultimate only than the nature of its constituents — the nature of the concept or logical idea. (NJ, 192-93)

Earlier in the same essay and even more clearly, as we have just seen, in *Principia Ethica*, he employed substantive to mean not "ultimate" constituent but something of flesh and blood, materially real. Temporal objects are composed of substantial (read: corporeal, quidditive) concepts. Simultaneously these concepts are substantial in the sense of being the simplest elements into which such objects can be decomposed and in this sense the ultimate building-blocks of the Universe.

The Universal-Particular Relation

Translated into other terms, Moore's struggle is with the universal-particular relation. When two things share the same predicate, does one speak of one or two predicates? This is essentially, Moore recounts, also Plato's problem (cf. I, 106). Are ideas *in* things (thus same idea in more than one place at same time)? Are things rather copies of ideas (cf. *SMPP*, 361)? Or do they "participate" in ideas?

In 1901 Moore argued that the universal differs only *numerically* but not *conceptually* from the particular. Universals may have only one or even no particular, but every particular has a universal. The difference between a universal and a particular is the fact that they belong to *different* classes. Nevertheless, "this red and that red do exist, but [it is] very doubtful whether redness itself does" (I, 115). In 1910-11 he renewed the search for so-called natural universals such as whiteness or redness. Can one empirically see such universals or does one only espy white and red patches? Is whiteness "in," does it "belong" to white patches (e.g. *SMPP*, 349)? Moore wavers. Finally, although far from convinced, he decides that the universal cannot be discerned. However, in a 1953 correction he retracts his view that one cannot see the universal color (*SMPP*, 375 ff.). In 1923 he had also argued that the characteristics of particular things are universal and not particular.[48] In this later period having rejected the idea that properties are substantial "parts,"[49] having

[48] "Are the Characteristics of Particular Things Universal or Particular?" *PASS* III (1923). Cf. also "Is the 'Concrete Universal' the True Type of Universality?" *PAS* XX (1920).
[49] Cf. R, 581-82 and Lewy, *op. cit.*, p. 254.

denied that existence is a concept, he seems to have accepted the notion of individual existent *substances* as the bearers of universal properties.[50]

Complications

Although Moore never explicitly gave up his concept theory of meaning (indeed one could better say that he always remained faithful to it), the fact remains that it continually caused him problems. Sometimes one word (e.g. "fire") expresses a proposition, at other times, a whole sentence (an imperative) does not. Moore revised his definition of a proposition slightly: that what is "*commonly* expressed by a whole sentence" (*SMPP*, 61). He faced a similar, more vexing situation with concepts. In 1944 he recognized certain examples in which several words together only expressed one concept (RTD, 184, 196, 211). In fact, in regard to both propositions and concepts, he never furnished criteria by which to determine the number of propositions or concepts respectively present in a number of words.

But there were other and more serious complications. Do the fictitious objects named in sentences such as centaurs, chimeras, and griffins have existence, or in any case, being? According to his theory of meaning they must have some kind of reality. However, they do not have the *existence* which lions have, or the same *being* as universals. But it does seem as if they *are* something and not nothing. In spite of this presumption, and in contrast with his over-all theory, Moore concludes provisionally (after drawn-out discussions) that fictitious objects do not belong to the Universe and are not *named* (*SMPP*, 212ff., 234ff.; cf. *PP*, 102ff.; *PS*, 211ff.; *LP*, 20ff.).

Another exception Moore discovered in connection with his analysis of "time" (*PS*, 196ff. esp. 212). In this case he once again chooses against his theory by admitting that it is probable that the words "real" and "unreal" do not stand for any conception whatever. In 1926 he even doubted his view of number. "I think *perhaps* the true view is that nothing is *the* number 2 & that nothing is *a number*: nay more that 'is a number' does not stand for any property whatever" (*CPB*, 90).

In his ethics Moore ran into a snag of an analogous kind. Under the influence of Stevenson he acknowledged that he

was inclined to think that "right" in all ethical uses, and, of course, "wrong," "ought," "duty" also are, in this more radical sense, not the names of characteristics at all, that

[50] This hypothesis appears to be supported by the fact that in 1911 Moore points out that "being" and "existence" are, strictly speaking, no longer to be seen as different properties or predicates. The difference intended in the distinction is due rather to the character differences of the objects or things to which these predicates are ascribed (cf. *SMPP*, 300). No longer do the properties compose the objects, but substances bear properties.

they have merely "emotive meaning" and no "cognitive meaning" at all: and, if this is true of them, it must also be true of "good," in the sense I have been most concerned with. (R, 554)

However, he immediately added that he was also "inclined" to hold to his view that good is a concept and for good reasons. He concludes by leaning in the direction of his old view. From Blanshard and Ewing we learn that in 1950 and even more in 1955 he was "inclined to think his earlier view the right one."[51] In this instance, an important one for our purposes, it appears that Moore's theory of meaning won out — but not before it tottered. In all these cases, as well as in the analysis of false beliefs (which we will soon discuss), Moore's conclusion is the selfsame: "This fact that single words and phrases which we use will constantly seem to be names for something, when in fact they are not names for anything at all, is what seems to me to create the whole difficulty" (*SMPP*, 290, cf. 264-65).

False Beliefs and the Nature of Truth

The obstacles over which Moore stumbled in the previously described instances became insurmountable in his analysis of false beliefs. He began lecturing in the winter of 1910 with one view of belief and ended the series of lectures (later published in *Some Main Problems of Philosophy*) by rejecting this analysis. Moore distinguished the act of belief from the object of belief,[52] a proposition expressed or named by the sentence employed. What then is the difference between true and false beliefs? In both cases there are "propositions," the only difference is that the true proposition has an additional property, that of being "true." In 1910 he depicted this earlier theory as follows:

In the case of every belief, true or false, there is a proposition which is what is believed, and which certainly is. But the difference between a true and a false belief it says, consists simply in this, that where the belief is true the proposition, which is believed, besides the fact that it *is* or 'has being' also has another simple unanalysable property which may be called 'truth.' ... The propositions which don't possess it, and which therefore we call false, *are* or 'have being' — just as much as those which *do*: only they just have *not* got this additional property of being 'true.' (*SMPP*, 261)

This theory, especially prominent in Moore's essay of 1899, was most influential in the early 1900's. "Truth, however, would certainly seem to involve at least two

---

[51] Blanshard, *Reason and Goodness* (1962), p. 269. Ewing, "G. E. Moore," *Mind* LXXI (1962), p. 251.
[52] The act of belief or disbelief differs *only* from the act of understanding in that we also have an *attitude* towards the proposition which is called belief (*SMPP*, 60, 258).

terms, and some relation between them; falsehood involves the same; and hence it would seem to remain, that we regard truth and falsehood as properties of certain concepts, together with their relations — a whole to which we give the name of proposition."[53] Two distinct relations and their respective unanalyzable properties are involved. "What kind of relation makes a proposition true, what false, cannot be further defined, but must be immediately recognised ... like red or two" (NJ, 180-81). In his *Baldwin Dictionary* article on Truth and Falsity he affirmed a similar view. "*Falsehood*, however, or *falsity*, and not error, is used to denote that property of a false proposition in virtue of possessing which it is called an error." Russell, following Moore's lead, gave the theory fame (or infamy) by comparing the difference of truth and falsehood to the difference between red and white roses.[54] Falsehood had, it appeared, equal logical and thus ontological status with truth. A judgment is "equally necessary whether it be true or false" (NJ, 192).[55]

In 1907 Moore defended this view over against the attacks of Joachim,[56] but in 1911 he is led to introduce severe strictures. There must, he adjures, be more to the truth-falsehood distinction than this view allows. Surely when we assert that a belief is true we mean more than simply that a certain proposition we believe has the unanalysable property of "truth." Surely it belongs to the very nature of a false belief that what it asserts is *not*. How can one maintain that such false propositions *are*? Moore can no longer and exclaims: "there simply are no such things as *propositions*" (*SMPP*, 265, 309). Once again, and in regard to this important case, he abandons the clear lines of his theory of meaning. He now turns to the "correspondence" theory of truth.[57] "'To say that this belief is true is to say that there is in the Universe *a* fact to which it corresponds; and that to say that it is false is to say that there is *not*

---

[53] Whereas concepts cannot, propositions can be true or false (*SMPP*, 62; *LP*, 133). Propositions can be true even if there are no sentences (*CPB*, 378).

[54] "Some p's are true and some false, just as some roses are red and some white" ("Meinong's Theory of Complexes and Assumptions," *Mind* XIII, 1904, p. 523). And on falsehood: "And as regards being, false propositions are on exactly the same level, since to be false a proposition must already be" (*Principles of Mathematics*, p. 450).

[55] Falsehood was not for Moore, as George Pitcher affirms, "mere absence of truth . . . mere negation or deficiency" (*Truth*, p. 3).

[56] Joachim attacked the theory of Russell-Moore in 1906 with the publication of *The Nature of Truth*. In the same year Russell reviewed the book (*Mind* XV, p. 528 ff.). In 1907 Moore added a note (*Mind* XVI, pp. 229-35), which in turn was answered by Joachim (*Mind* XVI, pp. 410-15).

[57] Throughout his defense of the correspondence theory, Moore is zealous to set his views off against the pragmatists (*SMPP*, 284 ff.; "William James' 'Pragmatism'," *PS*, 97 ff.; *LP*, 132 ff., 143, 147 ff.) and that of the idealists (*SMPP*, 284 ff.; *LP*, 132 ff., 143). In 1902 Moore had refuted the "coherence" and the "correspondence" theories of truth (cf. *Baldwin Dictionary* article on "Truth").

in the Universe any fact to which it corresponds'" (*SMPP*, 277, 255, 267; *CPB*, 231; *LP*, 132-49).[58]

Facts and Propositions

Moore's adoption of the correspondence theory of truth was not without its repercussions. One of the most important was the changed situation in regard to "propositions." In his early position propositions were particularly prominent, everything revolved around them; after 1911 the attention shifts to facts (to which propositions must correspond).[59] Prior to 1911 propositions which also had the property of truth were facts. Moore does not state this explicitly, but the implication of his words is obvious. "For, in order that a fact may be made the basis of an argument, it must first be put in the form of a proposition, and moreover, this proposition must be supposed true ... the nature of a true proposition is the ultimate *datum*" (NJ, 181).[60]

Suddenly in his Morley lectures, Moore is struck by the all-overshadowing importance of that which *is* in contrast to that which *is not*. The question of truth and falsity cannot simply be a matter of having just another property. Thus, in denying the existence of propositions, he is admitting that he had given them previously too much attention. Facts have captured his fancy (and facts not as another word for propositions, but as that with which propositions must correspond to be true).

A prop. is true if & only if there is some fact wh. directly verifies it, & false if & only if there is some fact wh. directly negates it. And the relation of the prop. in each case to the fact is *necessary*, not accidental: that *prop. couldn't* have been verified or negated by any *other* than this one. (*LP*, 142)

Formerly, when the question of truth was in the background, Moore ascribed *being* to fictions as well as to facts. Whatever was named, enjoyed *being*, be it of first (lions), second (universals, properties) or third (centaurs) degree. Fictions and falsehoods stood on the same side of the major line as facts,

---

[58] He now distinguishes "true" and "truth"; the former being the the relation of correspondence between an act of belief and a fact, the latter is just another word for "fact" (*SMPP*, 297). Whereas an act of belief can be true, it cannot be a truth. However, the fact that a proposition is true is a truth (*SMPP*, 250; *CPB*, 3).

[59] As Moore pointed out in his 1953 Preface to *SMPP*, his denial of propositions must not be taken too literally. All he intended was the repudiation of a certain analysis of false beliefs. Propositions still are. But now they need be distinguished precisely from facts. *Cf.* "Facts and Propositions," *PP*; "Propositions and Truth," *LP*; *CPB*, 313, 330.

[60] Russell was more direct: "A fact appears to be merely a true proposition, so that what seemed a significant assertion becomes a tautology" (*Mind* XIII, p. 523).

propositions and concepts (as over against particulars which are real and exist); in the later position facts and universals stand alongside of particulars (as things which *are*) over against griffins, centaurs and falsehoods (as things which are *not*). Moore summarizes his new position on the last pages of *Some Main Problems of Philosophy*:

The really fundamental and important . . . distinction [is] that between the things which do have *being*, and those which simply have not got it. . . . It is this distinction, as we saw, which is at the bottom of the distinction between truth and falsehood. . . . And it is, I think, this fundamental distinction which is overlooked by those who talk as if universals, because mere abstractions, were therefore pure fictions and something negligible. Those who talk in this way do, I think, really mean to degrade universals to the levels of griffins and chimaeras; . . . If you fix clearly in your mind the sense in which there certainly are no such things as griffins and chimaeras, that seems to me to give the sense in which it is important to enquire whether there are such things as universals or not. And if you do fix this sense clearly, it seems to me quite plain that there *are* such things, that universals are not in any way to be classed with griffins and chimaeras: that, on the contrary, there is *the* most fundamental difference in the Universe between the two, a difference ever so much more important than that which separates universals from particulars. (372-73)

Now, although he no longer faces the unpleasant task of assigning false beliefs or fictions *being*, Moore was not out of the woods. After all, even though fictions *are not*, they are. And as he could not simply call them creations of the human mind (too subjectivistic!), he was stymied. He was well aware of his predicament. Even though he has been induced to allow certain exceptions to his theory of meaning, he still retains his "objectivistic" slant and as such there is an inherent bent in his philosophy to grant everything some kind of extra-mental being. Thus there always remains the conjecture that it is impossible to deprive false beliefs of all being. "A thought of a centaur" is obviously not to be confused with a "centaur." Yet if a centaur is neither mental, nor something which is (has being and is thus a fact), what is it? Moore is unsure. On the one hand, he is certain that the "proposition" believed in a false belief is "something," we can talk about "it," discuss "it," etc.; on the other hand, it is incontrovertible that this "it" is, in an important sense, "not."

Another facet of the situation comes to light when we examine the relationship of facts and propositions in Moore's later position. A number of disturbing features strike one at once. Although he was induced by the embarrassment of granting false beliefs equal status with true beliefs to adopt another theory, the problem of "falsity" is far from solved. In 1927 he is sure that "on any view, there certainly are negative *facts*. It certainly is a fact, for instance, that King George is not at this moment in this room; or that the earth is not larger than the sun" (*PP*, 86). "Falsity" remains something positive. "False" does not equal "not true." It is "quite plain that 'false' is a positive conception;

i.e. that there's a positive relation such that we're saying: has this positive relation to some fact" (*LP*, 147).[61]

Another disturbing aspect — adding to the presumption that the same problems re-appear in the new theory, but then clustered around "facts" rather than "propositions" — is the fact that the same warning is given in relation to facts as was previously uttered in regard to propositions. "I never mean only a form of words, but *always* only the kind of thing which certain forms of words express" (*SMPP*, 307, compare with 57, 72, 258-59; *PP*, 103; *LP*, 135 ff., 142; *CPB*, 375). Further, he defines facts as a class of entities which "we can only express by a clause beginning with 'that' or by a corresponding verbal noun" (*SMPP*, 296). This too formerly applied to propositions, and presumably still holds for them.

What are facts for Moore? On the one hand, despite the points just raised, it is clear that facts and propositions are to be distinguished. On the other hand, it is well to note that he also discerns a difference between a fact such as "that a lion does exist" and the "lion itself," between "the fact that twice two are four" and the "number two itself." Whereas the "existence of lions is a fact, the lions themselves are not facts." Facts *are*, particulars *exist* — after all, it is ridiculous to assert "that the fact that lions exist, *itself* exists" (*SMPP*, 296-301). Or as spiritedly put by Strawson, "The facts (situation, state of affairs) cannot, like the chessboard-and-pieces have coffee spilled on them or be upset by a careless hand.[62] Moore is not oblivious to the snags. He senses that his use of facts is not shared by the majority of mankind. Thus, he suggests speaking of "truths" in place of "facts." But this too, he is quick to realize, has its shadow-side. Truths might be confused with true beliefs or true propositions (if the latter exist at all).[63]

In spite of all his attempts to lift the fog, it refuses to dispel. On the one hand, the relation of "fact" and "proposition" as well as the nature itself of "facts" and "propositions" remains in the dark. On the other side, the relation of "facts" and "particulars" is far from cloud-less. Beliefs are only true when

---

[61] At the same time Moore (at least in "The Conception of Reality") endeavours to avoid dealing with these negative facts as if they genuinely enjoyed being. "What 'Unicorns are *unreal*' means is that the property of being a unicorn belongs to *nothing*" (*PS*, 212). Such a negative fact is to be interpreted not as referring to (the existence of) unicorns and then denying their existence, but rather, it refers to all existent, actual objects and denies that *they* have the properties of being a unicorn. In this way Moore maintains "negative facts" without being forced to introduce the concomitant "negative existents."

[62] Strawson, "Truth" in *Truth* (ed. Pitcher, 1964), p. 41.

[63] It is instructive to recall that Moore had earlier employed the danger of confusion as a solid argument against his previous analysis of false beliefs. That analysis had entailed the existence of *two* different facts going by the same name (cf. *SMPP*, 260). But now we learn that the new analysis faces a similar danger.

90

they correspond to facts, but facts themselves depend on some relationship to particulars, e.g. "the fact that lions exist" relates in some unexplained way to the "lions themselves." But, what is the connection between "facts" (which *are*) and "particulars" (which *exist*)?[64]

Ethical Propositions

The importance of these later developments for our ethical discussion lies largely in the fact that both "truth" and "goodness" were originally unanalysable qualities. Qualities which were affixed unpredictably, erratically, in hit or miss fashion — at least so it seemed — "on the backs" of objects or propositions. This was too easy a solution for the problem of truth, and so, in 1911 Moore explicitly rejected his old theory of truth and adopted a correspondence theory. There has been no such public announcement in regard to "goodness." But, closely examined, is not Moore's emphasis in "The Conception of Intrinsic Value" (written between 1914-17, thus it "clicks" chronologically) that goodness is supervenient, dependent on the presence of intrinsic natural properties, indicative of a similar shift? Neither "truth" nor "goodness" hover about the world, descending capriciously who knows when; they have a predictable, invariable connection to reality — see here the relevance of his search for the kind of "necessity" involved in the fact-value relation. Thus, whereas in the *Principia Ethica* he stressed that "goodness" was autonomous and absolute, he later concentrated on the relation of "necessity" in force between fact and value.

What does this mean for *Principia's* self-evident propositions? If the truth of a proposition is no longer self-evident, but must be tested in relation to the facts, is not Moore obliged to follow the same policy in regard to such ethical propositions? Must they not also be tested on the "facts"? But on which facts? On ethical facts? But ethical facts, e.g. that natural objects bear the quality of goodness, must themselves be checked out on natural facts. However, if in such cases logical verification is possible, Moore has pulled the rug from under his own feet and landed in Naturalism. Either the logical evidence in regard to self-evident propositions only *provides* reasons for *holding* them to be self-evident — in which case intuition is required and one must speak of synthetic a priori — or one can employ the good-making characteristics as criteria in order to determine which propositions are self-evident in themselves — in which case logic is all-sufficient and analytic necessity is the order of the day. Moore never adopted the latter alternative. The propositions remain

[64] The question here mentioned (nature of "facts," "propositions," their interrelations, their relations to particulars, etc.) are among the most vexing and bothersome questions facing linguistic analysis. The debate has been advanced since the work of Moore, but it cannot be said that a solution is nearer.

self-evident (although *afterwards*, we can say of a good X, that it was good *because* of A. B, C), but whether they are *in themselves* true remains an unknown.

Our incursion for ethical purposes into the philosophical undergrowth has been completed. And it has been a rewarding search. We have been able to track down Moore's ethical doctrines to their philosophic roots. Moore's ethics, we have found, is firmly placed on a philosophic foundation, and it has turned out to be an edifice which belongs with, and makes the most out of the possibilities which the foundation affords. His ethical search for the intrinsic good, and for the meaning of "good," corresponds with his philosophic creed that nothing can be constituted by the system to which it belongs. His ethical method of isolation is possible because he believes (in contrast to the British Idealists) that there are relations ("external relations") which do not affect the essence of the thing related. Moore's epigraph to *Principia Ethica* is appropriate, not so much as a capsule summary of his ethical position, but rather as a pithy summation of his philosophic position as a whole.

We have seen how the being-existence bifurcation is reflected in the non-natural/natural distinction. Through an examination of his "concept" theory of meaning, we acquired insight into the function of "self-evident propositions" in his ethics. "Goodness" is indefinable because it is a concept, and concepts are simple independents, the ultimate building-blocks of the universe — behind which you cannot go and over against which an appeal to the facts is ridiculous (cf. NJ, 181). It became clear that his theory of meaning incapsulated his general philosophic position, and that this "objectivistic" stance ruled both his philosophizing and ethicizing. The fact that Moore tenaciously held on to his position, notwithstanding all the exceptions, paradoxes and problems, gave us occasion to realize that he was driven by supra-logical motives. We have seen that the relation logic-intuition is as crucial and as touchy in his philosophy as in his ethics. In both instances, logic, so it seemed, cannot but try to say the last word, a last word which, it turned out, was the part of intuition.

From Moore to the present: history's critique

4

Prior to a discussion of the deeper issues involved in Moore's ethical position, it is revealing as well as rewarding to trace the contours of the ethical landscape from Moore to the present. Revealing in that new positions develop at the point where previous theories are considered vulnerable; each newly-launched view is as such a critique of by-gone views. Rewarding in that the central concerns emerge more clearly when seen in the expansive perspective of history. At the same time, we will be enabled to treat, be it only in main lines, these post-Moorean developments. Thus our objective in this chapter will be two-fold: to unearth the main bones of contention between Moore and his successors, and secondly, to appraise in how far Moore's epigoni have successfully wrestled from under the problems which bettered their "father."

A novel historical movement, even as it builds on the shoulders of tradition, surges forward as a merciless critic of that past. In our case employing sub-sequent developments as a first line of attack has a peculiar appropriateness; for with G. E. Moore a new epoch in moral philosophy was born. His *Principia Ethica* unleashed a veritable flood of publications, slowly at first, only now, some sixty years later, reaching crest proportions. It is not that Moore's positive constructions have been universally received. On the contrary, "intuitionists" are few and far between today. Nevertheless, the whole style of ethicizing (and philosophizing) which has come to be known as Linguistic Analysis finds its source, fountain and adumbration in the work of Moore. Twentieth century moral philosophy cannot be understood apart from him.

Thus far, at least three and perhaps four distinguishable tidal waves (with their innumerable crests, surges and ripples) have reached shore testing, threat-ening, lashing and/or overwhelming Moore's ethical edifice.

THE DEONTOLOGISTIC EMPHASIS

It is perhaps debatable whether one ought to credit the "deontologists" with comprising a full-scale wave in their own right, or whether one must view them

93

as forming the Oxford conjunct of a tidal wave with Moore riding the crest. Although it has become somewhat fashionable to pay respects to Moore and other "intuitionists" in one breath, it remains a point of historical accuracy that much of the critique of the deontologists was directed in the first place towards Moore. In any case it is certain that the small coterie of philosophers at Oxford, H. A. Prichard (1871-1947), W. D. Ross (1877-1940), and E. F. Carritt known as the "deontologists," as well as a number of closely-allied thinkers such as H. W. B. Joseph (1867-1934) at Oxford and C. D. Broad (b. 1807) and A. C. Ewing (b. 1899) at Cambridge stand with Moore as "objectivists" in regard to the question of values[1]. Since in this light the deontologistic critique of Moore takes on an intra-mural character, we will restrict ourselves to a capsule summary of the general position involved, followed by a succinct discussion of the views of Ross and Ewing concerning the fact-value relation.

To the ardent deontologist Moore's (initial) view was virtually a licence for evil-doing. Evil-doing is permissible, it must even be judged right, provided that the resulting evil is so to speak outbalanced by the good consequences. In reaction, the Oxford Group (excluding Joseph) stressed *to deon* (that which is right or binding). Rightness is independent of its productiveness of good, sometimes one is obliged to do B (it is right) even though the performance of A would produce presumably better consequences, that is, more good. Reasons for acting in a certain way are self-evident, immediate and intuitive. For Prichard any talk in moral philosophy of *reasons* for what can only be immediately apprehended, the goodness of states of affairs, the rightness of acts, "rests on a mistake."

Value as Toti-Resultant Property: W. D. Ross

W. D. Ross is the best known, if not the most radical, representative of deontologism. Although he differs with Moore in regard to "rightness," his exposition of the nature of "goodness" is literally a working-out of Moore's views on the subject. Recalling the main theses of Moore's essay "The Conception of Intrinsic Value," he appends the wish "to examine further the way

---

[1] H. A. Prichard's classic "Does Moral Philosophy Rest on a Mistake?" (1912) inaugurated, as it were, the movement. After Prichard's death, this along with other important articles was published under the title *Moral Obligation* (1949). The most worked-out statement of the position is found in W. D. Ross' *The Right and the Good* (1930) and *The Foundations of Ethics* (1939). A third key member was E. F. Carritt, *Theory of Morals* (1928), *Ethical and Political Thinking* (1947). Also significant are: H. W. B. Joseph, *Some Main Problems in Ethics* (1931); C. D. Broad, *Five Types of Ethical Theory* (1930); A. C. Ewing, *The Definition of Good* (1947), *Second Thoughts in Moral Philosophy* (1959). For a critical study of deontologism, see Oliver A. Johnson, *Rightness and Goodness* (1959).

in which the goodness of a thing depends on its intrinsic nature" (116).[2] This is, we recall, Moore's central theme in the essay concerned, a thesis which he could not clarify or explain to his own (or to our) satisfaction. It is thus of importance to consider Ross' exposition.

Neither "factual" nor "causal" necessity can characterize the fact-value relation. So far Ross agrees with Moore. He also admits to sharing Moore's misgivings as to whether one can call it "logical" necessity. Moore faced *two* problems, we remember, at this point. The first concerns the nature of the "necessity" involved. He is far from clear how it can be deduced from any logical law that, if a given patch of color is yellow, any patch exactly alike must also be yellow (or that if A is beautiful, anything exactly like A must also be beautiful). Secondly, he is at a loss as to how to differentiate between "yellow" and "beautiful" (or "good") as predicates. Ross endeavours to solve both problems in one breath.

The necessity that if the intrinsic nature of the two patches is the same their colour (or brightness, or size, or shape) must be the same is analytic; the necessity that their degree of beauty must be the same is synthetic. (120)

Translated: the special kind of necessity involved in the fact-value relation is *synthetic*. The second question is also answered: "yellow" differs from "beautiful" because — contrary to Moore's opinion — analytic necessity is involved in the "two patches of yellow" example.

In order to render this difference between natural and non-natural characteristics as conspicious as possible, Ross terms natural qualities such as "yellow" and "hard" *constitutive* or *fundamental* and non-natural qualities such as "beautiful" and "good" *resultant, dependent, consequential*.[3] "Value is a toti-resultant property, based on the whole nature of its possessors. And this is true not only of 'good,' the adjective which expresses intrinsic value, but also of 'right' and 'beautiful'" (122). Having said that, Ross concludes his examination of the fact-value relation.

All that has been said that Moore had not already explicitly asserted (leaving aside Ross' introduction of appropriate terminology) is that the nature of necessity at issue is "synthetic" — and even this, calling to mind Moore's profuse use of the synthetic a priori, is hardly new. Putting aside the matter of novelty, the question remains whether Ross has indeed solved Moore's two

---

[2] Bracketed page numbers in this section refer to Ross' *The Right and the Good*.
[3] The Cambridge philosopher C. D. Broad has introduced a similar terminology, replacing "constitutive" and "resultant" with "ultimate" and "derivative." The non-ethical facts upon which goodness depends are dubbed "good-making" characteristics. See "Is 'Goodness' a Name for a Simple Non-natural Quality?" *PAS* XXXIII (1933-34), and *PGEM*, pp. 57-67.

problems. The matter is not easy, but it is at least doubtful if Ross provided an answer acceptable to Moore.

Ross began by implying that Moore is inconsistent in considering the example of two similar yellow patches as being in the same class as the example of two beautiful objects. He suggests that since Moore instances the fact that "from the proposition with regard to any term that it is red it *follows* that it is coloured" (*PS*, 285) as an example of logical necessity, he must also do this in the case of the two yellow patches. Thus, he is free to claim that *synthetic* necessity is the monopoly of the natural/non-natural relation — presto, both problems have evaporated. However, it would seem doubtful if Ross is justified in reclassifying the two patches of yellow example as evidencing *analyticity* in the Moorean sense. The difficulty is the fact that Ross operates with a "broader" view of analyticity than Moore can allow. Logical or analytic necessity is incontrovertibly involved in "whatever is red is colored," or "whatever is a right-angled triangle must be a triangle" (only *one* whole with its parts is involved); this is not true in the case of the two yellow patches (here there are numerically *two* wholes). With this narrow view of analyticity Moore must insist that synthetic necessity is embroiled not only in the relation of natural and non-natural but also on occasion between natural objects (*two* patches of yellow). This being the case the peculiarity of the fact-value relation is still an unknown factor and Moore remains unable to delineate the difference between "yellow" and "good," except to say that the one is natural and the other non-natural.

Conclusive evidence that Moore would challenge the exclusion of all non-ethical characteristics from the class of consequential attributes is furnished in 1942 when he confesses to "completely agree" with C. D. Broad's conclusion "that it is *impossible to identify the non-natural characteristics of a thing with those among its intrinsic properties which are derivative*" (R, 587). Pleasantness, assuredly a natural characteristic, is a "derivative," or in Rossian terms, a "consequential" attribute just as obviously as "goodness." But if both pleasantness and goodness are derivative properties, then the synthetic necessity which is perhaps involved in the employment of such properties cannot be regarded as the distinguishing mark of the fact-value bifurcation. It is not a *sufficient*, but at best a necessary condition for such a relation. The uniqueness of the natural/non-natural relation and thus the non-natural character of goodness remains to be demonstrated.

Even if Ross were able to justify his broadening of analyticity, he must still legitimatize his claim that analytic necessity is involved in the case of "yellow patches" and not in the case of "beauty." Why, in other words, must we speak of *synthetic* necessity at all? How does the constitutive-resultant distinction authorize the distinction between analytic and synthetic necessity? Earlier it appeared as if his expansion of analyticity rescued him from the acute embarrassment which plagued Moore, now it becomes evident that his manoeuvre boomerangs. When challenged, Moore was able to trot out an argument for his view that synthetic rather than analytic necessity is at stake; namely, that more than one (simple or complex) whole is involved. Ross cannot make this move. If pressed he would presumably appeal to the intrinsic difference between facts and values as sufficient justification. Can one, however, prove the fact-value dichotomy by pointing to the reality of synthetic necessity *and* at the same time corroborate the reality of synthetic a priori by reference to the fact-value distinction? Certainly that is to argue in a circle, begging the very question at issue.

Second Thoughts: A. C. Ewing

In bringing chapter three to a close we wondered out loud, among other things, whether Moore's mature views, in particular the correspondence theory of truth and the supervenience of good, did not threaten to seal the ethical/non-ethical gap — the reality of which break provided the vindication of Moore's thesis that ethics was autonomous. That our musings were not altogether out of order is confirmed by A. C. Ewing's latest volume, *Second Thoughts in Moral Philosophy*.[4] A long-time Cambridge intuitionist, Ewing explains that ethical judgments in order to be true must correspond to reality in the sense that they "must be based on and follow from the empirical nature of what is evaluated as the empirical circumstances of the action." He immediately admits that his "account will give rise to the objection that it implies . . . that ethical conclusions can be derived from non-ethical, factual premises" (47ff., 60). In view of Moore's similar situation, Ewing's reply is instructive. In the best Moorean tradition he first assures his readers that he does not in the least propose that ethical propositions could be *reduced* to merely factual ones or deduced *finally* from the latter. However, as he doubts whether any general ethical principle (said to be required by some to construct a valid syllogism) is possible without a fixed base in the facts of the matter, and as he recognizes, pointing to Dorothy Emmet's brochure *Facts and Obligations*, that "apparently factual premises of an ethical conclusion very commonly already contain a valuational element," he is convinced that "our valuations and judgments of obligation are based on the factual nature of what we value and pronounce obligatory."

Turning to the logic of the matter, Ewing is confident that ethical judgments cannot be established by mere empirical observation. They are necessary. On the other hand, they are certainly not analytic in character. But what kind of necessity? Even though he questions the prejudice that all deductive inference is analytic, and in spite of his acknowledgment that the original intuitionist

[4] In this section bracketed page numbers refer to Ewing's book. The fact that Ewing in this book announces his abandonment of the "goodness-is-a-quality" view does not significantly alter the situation.

position involved synthetic necessity, he pleads for a unique type of necessity which "falls outside the dichotomy, analytic-synthetic. Is it not simply this? If we evaluate A correctly (otherwise than by chance), the evaluation must depend on the nature of A and so could not be different, A being what it is in fact" (70). Such necessity Ewing argues is a bulwark against any form of Naturalism (equating value with some empirical fact). It is impossible to say of empirical facts, as we can say of values, that "they *must* belong to the object to which they are ascribed, its other properties being what they are."

Has Ewing shed new light on the controversial and complex fact-value relation? On the one hand, Ewing is certainly moving in the proper direction when he talks of factual premises containing valuational elements. Moreover, evaluation does depend on the "nature" of A. However, on the other hand, since he still clearly works within the basic fact-value dichotomy, and since he is urging an even "tighter" fact-value relation without analyticity (identity) than Moore did, he is duty-bound to elucidate the nature of the "necessity" involved. At this point it is questionable if there is a tangible advance in the discussion. Here too intuition is called in to ascertain when a certain value is to be ascribed with necessity to a particular factual object. And again the nature of necessity proves irksome. Simultaneously it seems, Ewing claims and disclaims that synthetic necessity is essential to his solution. To ward off the nemesis of Naturalism he requires necessity of a non-analytical, non-causal type; but then, fearing to challenge current logical orthodoxy, at any rate wishing to evade misunderstanding, he comes out for a "novel" kind of necessity. Nevertheless, despite Ewing's allegations, one can only espy what has been traditionally known as synthetic necessity.

THE SHIFT TO EMOTIVISM

The second, and immensely more radical wave of critique, usually christened "emotivism," was unleashed with the publication in 1936 of A. J. Ayer's *Language, Truth and Logic*. Although the conditions necessary for such ferment were established already in 1923 by the discovery of the "emotive" use of words by C. H. Ogden and I.A. Richards,[5] and independently, as well as on a much broader front by the way of philosophizing in vogue in *Der Wiener Kreis*;[6] although the first warnings of impending turbulence had been signalized

---

[5] *The Meaning of Meaning*, p. 125. The relevant quotation graces the frontispiece of C. L. Stevenson's *Ethics and Language*.
[6] Its members included Moritz Schlick (1882-1936), Otto Neurath (1882-1945), Friedrich Waismann (1896-1959), Rudolf Carnap (b. 1891), Viktor Kraft, Herbert Feigl (b. 1902), Gustav Bergmann (b. 1906). Especially Schlick concerned himself with ethics; *Fragen der Ethik* (1930) (E. T. Problems of *Ethics*, 1939). Cf. also Kraft, *Grundlagen einer wissenschaftlicher Wertlehre* (1937).

(faintly) in the 1928 paper of R. B. Braithwaite[7] and (unmistakably) in the 1934 comment of W. H. F. Barnes,[8] the tidal wave itself did not break until 1936. And in that moment ethics as a tillable field of philosophic inquiry was transformed into a quagmire inaccessible to philosophic investigation.

Subsequent to Ayer's *succès de scandale*, philosophy faced a revolting dilemma: abandon ethics as a philosophical enterprise or modify the emotive theory. Reclamation proceedings were immediately begun by the American C. L. Stevenson, first in a series of articles,[9] and in 1944 through publication of *Ethics and Language*. Although Ayer (b. 1910) and Stevenson (b. 1908) are the names to be mentioned in connection with emotivism, nearly every moral philosopher in the Anglo-American world has been affected,[10] be it only temporarily.

The Abolition of Ethics: A. J. Ayer

Ayer's thesis was ruthless in its simplicity. Wielding the logical positivist

[7] "Verbal Ambiguity and Philosophical Analysis," *PAS* XXVIII (1928). In this essay Moore was accused of overlooking the fact that most sentences employing "good" were not propositions at all, but rather vehicles for catharsis, evocation and persuasion. Ironically, in view of the actual course of events, Braithwaite suggested that ethical philosophers ignore the emotive statements and concentrate on the specifically ethical propositions.

[8] "A Suggestion about Value," *Analysis* I (1934). Strictly speaking, he asserted, value judgments "are exclamations of approval."

[9] In 1963 these and other articles were bundled together and published under the title *Facts and Values*.

[10] Wittgenstein's early views on ethics, although closely related to those of Ayer, are in a class by themselves (cf. *Tractatus*, 6,41; 6, 42; 6.421; 6.422). In a lecture presumably delivered in 1929-30, although only published in 1965, Wittgenstein expands on his views. "Ethics, if it is anything, is super-natural and our words will only express facts. ... To write or talk Ethics or Religion was to run against the boundaries of language. This running against the walls of our cage is perfectly, absolutely hopeless. Ethics so far as it springs from the desire to say something about the ultimate meaning of life, the absolute good, the absolute valuable, can be no science, What it does say does not add to our knowledge in any sense. But it is a document of a tendency in the human mind which I personally cannot help respecting deeply and I would not for my life ridicule it" ("A Lecture on Ethics," *PR* LXXIV 1965, pp. 3-12).

Other notable versions of emotivism are contained in B. Russell's *Religion and Science*, ch. 9 (1935); R. Carnap's *Philosophy and Logical Syntax* (1935) and *The Logical Syntax of Language* (1937); and H. Reichenbach's *The Rise of Scientific Philosophy* (1951). Important articles include: A. Kaplan, "Are Moral Judgments Assertions?" *PR* LI (1942); W. H. F. Barnes, "Ethics without Propositions," *PASS* XXII (1948); R. Robinson, "The Emotive Theory of Ethics," *PASS* XXII (1948); J. Harrison, "Can Ethics do without Propositions?" *Mind* LVIX (1950). Cf. also, A. Stroll, *The Emotive Theory of Ethics* (1954). Two Scandanavian works belong here also: A. Hägerström, *Inquiries into the Nature and Law of Morals* (1938) and S. Hollden, *Emotive Propositions* (1954).

inspired verification principle that a "statement is held to be literally meaningful if and only if it is either analytic or empirically verifiable" (*LTL*, 9),[11] he consigns value judgments to the rubric captioned "literally meaningless." They do not fit into either of the meaningful categories. An ethical judgment of the form "stealing is wrong" has "no factual meaning — that is, expresses no proposition which can be either true or false. It is as if I had written 'Stealing money!!' . . . I am merely expressing certain moral sentiments" (*LTL*, 107). Ethical judgments do not describe anything, be it natural or non-natural.

Traditionally philosophers have treated four classes of statements in their ethical treatises (*LTL*, 103):

1. Propositions which express definitions of ethical terms.
2. Propositions describing the phenomena of moral experience, and their cause.
3. Exhortations to moral virtue.
4. Actual ethical judgments.

But, pontificates Ayer, only class one can justly be regarded as belonging under the umbrella of ethics. Class two belongs to psychology or sociology, class three contains mere ejaculations or commands, and even class four upon examination turns out to be basically evocative and emotive in character. The illusion that ethics has still at least one legitimate pursuit; to wit, class one, is rapidly dispelled with the terse announcement that "ethical concepts are pseudo-concepts and therefore unanalysable" (*LTL*, 112). Ethics, for all interests and purposes, is abrogated, it becomes a "department of psychology and sociology."

Brandishing the same theory of meaning, Ayer wrecks havoc in the domain of metaphysics and theology. All metaphysical as well as all theological statements lack meaning. For, after all, what empirical evidence can be utilized to prove the existence of God pro or con? Obviously none. But neither can such statements be analytic in that they purport to inform us factually about reality; they must be nonsensical. Or in the terms Wittgenstein

---

[11] Advocates of the verification theory of meaning have hit upon hard days. They are still engaged in a struggle to formulate a version of the theory which is not so "strong" that it declares scientific laws to be meaningless along with metaphysics, but, on the other hand, not so "weak" that "metaphysics" creeps in along with the scientific laws. Thus far they have been singularly unsuccessful. Already in the Second Edition of *Language, Truth and Logic* (1946) Ayer had to tone down his thesis. Something need only be verifiable in "principle" in order to qualify as meaningful. Cf. John Wisdom, "Metaphysics and Verification," *Philosophy and Psycho-Analysis*; Morris Lazerowitz, "Strong and Weak Verification" I and II, *Mind* XLVIII (1939) and LIX (1950); J. O. Wisdom, "Metamorpheses of the Verifiability Theory of Meaning," *Mind* LXXII (1963); C. G. Hempel, "Problems and Changes in the Empiricist Criterion of Meaning," *Revue Internationale de Philosophie* (1950).

made fashionable: whereas tautologies and contradictions (analytic statements) are "sinloss" (lack meaning), metaphysical and theological statements are "Unsinn" (nonsense). Misled by our careless use of language, people have for generations seriously believed that the statements of ethics, theology and metaphysics possessed meaningful content.

> In general, the postulation of real non-existent entities results from the superstition, just now referred to, that, to every word or phrase that can be the grammatical subject of a sentence, there must somewhere be a real entity corresponding. (*LTL*, 43)

Not only in relation to "goodness," or "god," or "being," have we been led astray by grammatical forms, this also happens in the case of "true." When one says that the "proposition 'Queen Ann is dead' is true, all that one is saying is that Queen Ann is dead." The word "true" does not stand for a genuine quality or relation, it does not connote anything and is "logically superfluous" (*LTL*, 88).[12]

Ethics Redivivus: *Charles L. Stevenson*

In this no-man's land of ethical devastation Stevenson embarked on his crusade to revive ethics. And to his credit, in subtle, indefatigable, elaborate and somewhat painstaking fashion he has through a series of dykes and canals reclaimed ethics as a field of scientific investigation — all the while sharing Ayer's basic viewpoint. Stevenson's first move was to salvage and rehabilitate what Ayer had already emphasized, but then, pejoratively, as if it were inferior, below par, pseudo, unfit for scientific purposes; that is, the "dynamic" or "emotive" use of language.

---

[12] Perhaps this is the appropriate place to point out that the discussion of the notion of truth has evolved through stages analogous to that of goodness. As related in the previous chapter, Moore and Russell held at one time to a truth-as-unanalyzable-property view. Later, as we have also seen, Moore adopted a version of the Correspondence Theory; as did the early Wittgenstein with his "picture" theory (cf. *Tractatus*, e.g. 4.01; 4.016; 4.021; 4.03; 4.0311; 4.06-4.063). J. L. Austin is a recent reputable defender of a "purified version" (cf. *Philosophical Papers* 1961). However, under the influence of the later Wittgenstein, many philosophers were led to argue that the well-known theories of truth (correspondence, coherence, pragmatic) only lay out the *criteria* for truth and do not furnish the essential *meaning* of truth. Traditional theories have thus been one-sidedly concerned with the *descriptive* use of language. F. P. Ramsey and A. J. Ayer were among the first to stumble on the problems involved. But there too (just as in the case of goodness), still considering the picture-model normative, Ayer, when he ascertained that "true" did not describe, declared it to be "logically superfluous." Since that time others have toned down this "extremism". B. Savery had proposed "The Emotive Theory of Truth (*Mind* LXIV, 1955), and A.R. White the "Truth as Appraisal" theory (*Mind* LXVI, 1957). The foremost critic of (Austin-inspired) correspondence theories, P. F. Strawson has fashioned a Ramsey-type redundancy theory.

101

Broadly speaking, there are two different *purposes* which lead us to use language. On the one hand we use words (as in science) to record, clarify, and communicate *beliefs*. On the other hand we use words to give vent to our feelings (interjections), or to create moods (poetry), or to incite people to actions or attitudes (oratory). The first use of words I shall call "descriptive," the second "dynamic." (*FV*, 18-19)

And both, enthuses Stevenson, are legitimate and valuable. One may not be minimized or cancelled out in favor of the other, they are incomparable; each has its own time and place depending on the *purpose* of the speaker. Thus, we cannot define meaning as "that *to which* people *refer* when they use the sign" (*EL*, 42). This would entail that only the descriptive use of language was meaningful. Ayer fell into that trap. Meaning as a generic notion must be identified in the "psychological" or "pragmatic sense" with the psychological causes and effects which a word "has a *tendency* (causal property, dispositional property) to be connected with" (*FV*, 20). Two species are at home under the genus meaning:

The "descriptive meaning" of a sign is its disposition to affect cognition, provided that the disposition is caused by an elaborate process of conditioning that has attended the sign's use in communication, and provided that the disposition is rendered fixed, at least to a considerable degree, by linguistic rules. (*EL*, 70)

. . . .

The emotive meaning of a word is the power that the word acquires, on account of its history in emotional situations, to evoke or directly express attitudes, as distinct from describing or designating them. (*EL*, 33)

Whereas descriptive meaning is associated with *beliefs* as the products of thinking and supposing, emotive meaning has to do with *attitudes* as the emotional reactions to certain beliefs. As a result one may be entangled either in disagreement in *belief* (as to how matters are to be truthfully described and explained) or in *attitude* (as to how matters are to be favored or disfavored). It is disagreement in attitudes — in purpose, aspirations, wants, preferences, etc. — that has a special place in ethics (*EL*, 13).

In spite of the urgent necessity to distinguish descriptive and emotive meaning, beliefs and attitudes, it must remain a distinguishing and not a separating, for *in concreto* they are inextricably interwoven. Most words have both sorts of meaning. Indeed, "the central problem of ethical analysis — one might almost say 'the' problem — is one of showing in detail how beliefs and attitudes are related" (*EL*, 11). His final answer is brief: the relationship between disagreement in belief and in attitude — one could say of fact and value — is "always factual, never logical" (*EL*, 6).

Depending on the nature of the relationship to descriptive meaning, Stevenson talks of "independent" and "dependent" emotive meaning.

102

To whatever extent emotive meaning is *not* a function of descriptive meaning but either persists without the latter or survives changes in it, let us say that it is "independent." ... On the other hand, to whatever extent emotive meaning is a function of descriptive meaning, changing with it after only a brief "lag," let us say that it is "dependent." (*EL*, 72-73)

Nonmetaphorical interjections have wholly independent emotive meaning; verbal chameleons as "democracy" and "liberty" have both types of meaning.

Corresponding to the two uses of language, Stevenson develops two complementary patterns of analysis as aids in examining ethical disputes. In the First Pattern of Analysis, highlighting emotive meaning, he sets up three working models.

(1) "This is wrong" means *I disapprove of this; do so as well.*

(2) "He ought to do this" means *I disapprove of his leaving this undone; do so as well.*

(3) "This is good" means *I approve of this; do so as well.* (*EL*, 21)

In contrast to Ayer who denied[13] that an ethical judgment described the mood of the speaker (it does not describe at all!), Stevenson analyzes an ethical utterance into an imperative and a clause *describing* the attitudes of the speaker. To the extent that such judgments are descriptive, they are verifiable. However, since the imperative is the essential element involved, the significance of such verification depends on the relation of the descriptive and hortatory elements. And since this relationship is *not* logical, but merely *psychological*, it is highly misleading, as well as of little import, to talk of verification. "*Any* statement about *any* matter of fact which *any* speaker considers likely to alter attitudes may be adduced as a reason for or against an ethical judgment. Whether this reason will in fact support or oppose the judgment will depend on whether the hearer believes it, and upon whether, if he does, it will actually make a difference to his attitudes" (*EL*, 114-15). In ethical disputes one reason, provided it is accepted, is as good as any other. For an ethical theorist "validity" has no logical meaning. "Under the name of 'validity' he will be selecting those inferences to which he is *psychologically disposed* to give assent" (*EL*, 171, italics mine). "Empirically verifiable reasons, when used to support or oppose an ethical judgment, are always related to the judgment psychologically" (*FV*,145).

All this implies that the "rationality" which Ayer banned from ethics, and which Stevenson wished to repatriate, is still an intruder. The specifically ethical is beyond rational discussion, it is more a matter of psychological inducement, of effective provocation, or of irrational manipulation. Nevertheless, argues Stevenson, reasoning does have its place in ethical disputes. It can

[13] Ayer has since confessed that he was guilty of over-simplification. A moral judgment does more than *merely express* feelings, it "expresses the attitude in the sense that it contributes to defining it." Cf. "On the Analysis of Moral Judgments," *Horizon* XX (1949), p. 176.

resolve ethical disagreement if such dissensions are rooted in disagreement in belief as to the *facts* — by the nature of the case accessible to analytic probing. On the other hand, it is necessary to recall that it is disagreement in *attitude* rather than of belief which fundamentally characterizes ethical quarrels. In the last analysis ethical discussion supercedes the rational, it goes beyond the facts to the world of attitudes (values); there one can only threaten, coax, cajole, wheedle, persuade and inveigle[14].

It becomes even clearer that reason is on a short leash in the Second Pattern of Analysis. This pattern which focusses on the descriptive meaning is schematized by Stevenson as follows:

"This is good" has the meaning of "This has the qualities or relations X, Y, Z . . . ," except that "good" has as well a laudatory emotive meaning which permits it to express the speaker's approval, and tends to evoke the approval of the hearer. (*EL*, 207)

Ethical terms possess various as well as numerous descriptive meanings. However, since there is no logical reason for accepting one descriptive meaning above another, "to choose a definition is to plead a cause, so long as the word defined is strongly emotive" (*EL*, 210). To cover this situation, Stevenson coined the phrase "persuasive definition."[15] Definitions of emotive terms are as a rule persuasive in character; one attaches an emotive flag such as good to a descriptive cargo of one's choice with the express purpose of persuading others to do likewise. Emotive words "are prizes which each man seeks to bestow on the qualities of his own choice" (*EL*, 213). Thus, descriptive meanings vary as human preferences vary, *without* a corresponding change in emotive meaning. "Good," for example, retains its aura of emotive approval regardless of whether it is descriptively defined as "pleasure" or as "the will of God." Stevenson's conclusion: since there is *no logical* reason for accepting one descriptive meaning instead of another (it is a normative choice and not a logical necessity), the descriptive meaning of ethical terms is not a sufficient guarantee of the ultimate rationality of ethics.

Moore and Emotivism

At first glance one is only struck by the utter discrepancy between the "objectiv-

---

[14] Stevenson is well aware that his argument stands or falls on the assumption that all ethical disagreement is *not* finally rooted in disagreement in belief. He further confesses that this supposition can neither be proven nor disproven (cf. *EL*, 136ff.; *FV*, 69, 170, 171).

[15] "Persuasive definition" bears for Stevenson the same stigma that the "naturalistic fallacy" carried for Moore. The situation is no longer *open*; victory has been unfairly insured by incapsulating a normative stance in the very definition of terms. "Where-ever Moore would point to a 'naturalistic fallacy," the present writer, throughout the many possible senses which the second pattern recognizes, would point to a persuasive definition" (*EL*. 273).

ism" of Moore and the "subjectivism" of Ayer and Stevenson. And indeed a shift of major proportions has taken place. Nevertheless, there are major points of contact. Both Ayer ("I have learned a great deal from Professor Moore." *LTL*, 32) and Stevenson ("My indebtedness to Moore, here and elsewhere, is a great one." *FV*, 210; cf. *EL*, 272-73) royally acknowledge their debt to Moore. Upon close scrutiny the co-existence of extensive influence and marked variance is not as paradoxical as it sounds. The incongruity results from the wielding of incompatible theories of meaning, the congruity from a common repudiation of "Naturalism." On account of the disparity between Ayer and Stevenson, we must uncouple our treatment of the Moore-Ayer relation from that of Moore-Stevenson.

Moore and Ayer

As we recall, Ayer is committed to the view that a statement is only meaningful if it is analytic, if its "validity depends solely on the definitions of the symbols it contains," or synthetic, if its "validity is determined by the facts of experience" (*LTL*, 78). But what about value judgments? Are they analytic? It would seem certain that they are *not* "entirely devoid of factual content" as are the tautologies of mathematics and logic. They must, then, be synthetic and testable by empirical observation. But, Ayer quickly counters — obviously under the spell of Moore's refutation of Naturalism — ethical concepts cannot be reduced to empirical concepts. Naturalism, whether in the guise of "subjectivism" or "utilitarianism," is discarded as untenable (*LTL*, 104 ff.).

Can Ayer now continue to follow Moore and declare that value judgments are the members of a special third class, called perhaps *synthetic a priori*? By no means, this way of escape was cut off from the moment Ayer under the Vienna influence dictated that the terms "analytic," "a priori," and "necessary" were synonyms (with as antonyms "synthetic," "empirical," and "contingent"). Roped in, so to speak, on all sides, Ayer frantically slashed the Gordian Knot. Ethical judgments do not say anything at all, they pass through the analytic-synthetic net and are thus meaningless evocations of moral sentiment. "Values" do not inhabit any kind of an objective world, whether natural or non-natural. Such judgments do not even describe subjective preferences, they are merely expressive of personal idiosyncracies in a class with ejaculations and interjections. Ethical talk is evicted from the universe of meaningful, that is factual-descriptive discourse.

Since non-natural objects do not exist, ethical judgments cannot describe. Since ethical concepts are pseudo-concepts, any need for an organ such as Moore's "mysterious 'intellectual intuition.'" (*LTL*, 106) capable of apprehending knowledge of values vaporizes. Besides, adds Ayer for good measure, moral intuition is notoriously unreliable, "what seems intuitively certain to one person may seem doubtful, or even false to another."[16]

Moore's celebrated argument that adherence to a non-objectivistic theory renders impossible any debate about questions of value does give Ayer pause, but then only for a moment. His riposte: Moral disputes have nothing to do with a question of values, they are basically questions about logic or questions about empirical fact. "It is because argument fails us when we come to deal with pure questions of value, as distinct from questions of fact, that we finally resort to mere abuse" (*LTL*, 111).

After clearing this hurdle, Ayer is home-free. But at a high cost — the relationship between facts and values which Moore was essaying to capture is severed beyond repair. Facts and values stand over against each other as significant and insignificant, as universally valid and personally preferable, as descriptive truth and uninhibited ejaculation. Not only has all contact been broken, the very possibility of communication has been abolished.

Moore and Stevenson

At this juncture Stevenson steps in, if possible to bridge the break. And he does so as a one-time protegé of Moore. For him Naturalism is also unaccept-able, it refuses to take account of an "added factor" over and above factual concerns. But whereas Moore, unfortunately in Stevenson's mind, "intel-lectualized" this additional factor into an indefinable quality, Stevenson is content to observe that we have to do with "emotive meaning" (*EL*, 271). In a clear parallel, Stevenson envisages "descriptive" and "emotive" meaning where Moore sighted "natural" and "non-natural qualities."

Stevenson's role in the development of ethical theory is best appreciated in relation to his precursors. For a naturalist "X is good" is analytic, for Moore it can only be synthetic; for Ayer it is beyond either classification. The pecu-liarity of Stevenson's view roots in his concern to mollify all the parties con-cerned. With the naturalist he allows that "X is good" is analytic, with Moore he is sure that such a statement involves an extra factor (emotive meaning) and is thus far from "trivial." Finally, since advocating his *analytic-plus* theory is a breakthrough of the usual analytic-synthetic bifurcation, he does justice to Ayer's contention. In view of the foregoing, it is no doubt superfluous, but perhaps on account of its importance advisable, to note that we have uncovered the seductive appeal of Stevenson's emotivism. For one unwilling to treat ethical judgments as trifling tautologies (and thus analytic) and likewise

[16] This criticism, as a well-known refrain, has since been on virtually everyone's lips. For perhaps the most celebrated critique of Intuitionism, cf. P. F. Strawson, "Ethical Intuitionism," *P* XXIV (1949) (Reprinted in Sellars and Hospers, *Readings in Ethical Theory*).

ill at ease considering them either empirical hypotheses (and thus synthetic) or psychosomatic ejaculations (and thus neither), Stevenson's "solution" easily bewitches. On the other hand, it is well to state unequivocally that the conciliatory character of Stevenson's venture is at the same time the source of internal rumblings, strains and stresses. He must simultaneously hold to the *con-* and *dis-*junction of facts and values, in his terms, of descriptive and emotive meaning. The gulf must remain in the last analysis unbridgeable, but it cannot become à la Ayer a yawning chasm swallowing any possibility of contact; a makeshift foot bridge of some sort must be strung up.

This is, to put it mildly, a ticklish business, and even the accomplished skill of the craftsman with all his inventiveness, meticulousness and sophistication is unable to gloss over the basic dissonance. To maintain the gap Stevenson talks of "descriptive" and "emotive" meaning; to provide a semblance of unity he sets them up as two species of the single genus "meaning." The inherent equivocalness of the Stevensonian stance surfaces in short order to any but the most superficial observer. With his analytic-plus view he restores ethics to the ranks of the sciences (the "analytic-" part) even as he insures that ethics is beyond science (the "-plus" aspect). He clears a place for ethics even as he takes precautionary measures to insure that it does not reach the ethical "holy of holies." To call back ethical discourse from the limbo of the irrational where it had been tossed by Ayer, Stevenson stressed the "descriptive" meaning of value judgments. Such utterances could be backed by reasons. Whereupon he immediately adds that the typicalness of ethical judgments lies in their "emotive" meaning. A reason, it turns out, is "valid" only in the sense that it is "effective." A man advises what he advises, he chooses what he chooses, he rejects what he rejects. And that is the end of the matter. The reasons he accepts for his actions are by his very acceptance of them "good" reasons. No argument is possible. From a logical point of view one reason is as good as another.

Thus, Stevenson is unable to conceive of ethical judgments as having a general or universal character;[17] they can only be reports of the feelings or attitudes of one person on one particular occasion. This individual may, without logical contradiction, a moment later change his feelings or attitudes in respect to the same object. A consideration of the Second Pattern of Analysis reveals the same conclusion. Since a persuasive definition depends on a normative decision as to which psychological attitude to adopt, moral reasoning ends up as a clash of irrational attitudes.

Perhaps it is well to show in detail how Stevenson embroils himself in impossible situations. The "major use" of ethical judgments is "not to indicate

---

[17] Stevenson's appeal to the "psychological economy that comes from ordering the objects of his attitudes in some rough sort of classification" (*EL*, 95) cannot make up for this lack of logical generality.

facts but to *create an influence*. Instead of merely describing people's interests they *change* or *intensify* them. They *recommend* an interest in an object, rather than state that the interest already exists" (*FV*, 16).[18] Ethical judgments can according to Stevenson fulfill their function by means of their "dependent" or "independent" emotive meaning.

Dependent emotive meaning is, in brief, the complex of emotional responses called up by the cognitive meaning of a certain term. When the cognitive meaning varies, there is a concomitant variation in the accompanying emotional states. Are attitudes or interests *changed* in such a case? Since in this instance attitudes depend on beliefs as to the facts, only if the beliefs are first modified. But if this does not take place argument can only strengthen or reinforce, and perhaps elicit *already present* attitudes. And since changing *beliefs* is a matter for empirical science, ethics can only claim that this belongs to her competence at the risk of donning the straight-jacket of "Naturalism" − and this is anathema to Stevenson. The only other possible alternative is to give up ethics as a science and take refuge in irrational attitudes − likewise anathema.

Turning to "independent" emotive meaning, the "sheer, direct, emotional impact" of words (*EL*, 139) in which the descriptive meaning is influenced by modifications in emotive meaning, we again query if attitudes can be altered. Undoubtedly words with independent emotive meaning, e.g. interjections, can influence us, but then only, it would appear, in a way analogous to the way one jumps involuntarily at a sonic boom or instinctively starts at a hypodermic injection. Does such influence qualify as "changing attitudes" in Stevenson's sense? Such reactions are at most the expressions of attitudes. In order for words to function as "persuasive tools," Stevenson is forced to fall back on "dependent" emotive meaning. But then one is again faced with the impossible dilemma that we have just set forth. In fact, Stevenson tries to avoid choosing for either Naturalism or complete irrationalism by more or less accepting both. Ethics does not become an empirical science, but "normative ethics draws from the sciences, in order to change attitudes *via* changing people's beliefs" (*FV*, 8).[19] On the other hand, if disagreement is not rooted in belief but in attitude, there is no "*rational* method" of settling it (*FV*, 29). And thus, "normative ethics is more than a science" (*EL*, vii), it "is in part noncognitive." Nevertheless the problems of ethics "are not cut off from reasoning; for . . . we *can make use* of knowledge" (*FV*, 172).

In capsule form the dilemma is this: If emotive meaning is independent, it

---

[18] In Stevenson's later writings (in his own words) "the term 'interest' systematically gives place to the term 'attitude'" (*FV*, 12).
[19] "Psychology will simply be the most *conspicuous* of the sciences involved" (*EL*, 11; cf. also *FV*, 58). But "ethics is not psychology, since psychology does not endeavour to *direct* our interests; it discovers facts about the ways in which interests are or can be directed, but that is quite another matter" (*FV*, 29).

can only *express* or jolt, never alter, the attitudes of people; if emotive meaning is dependent, it can only reinforce not change, attitudes.[20] This dilemma is inherent in Stevenson's position and can be formulated in many ways. If, and this form of the dilemma reveals the inner contradiction perhaps even more clearly, moral disagreement is anchored in disagreement in belief (as it would in the case of "dependent" emotive meaning), moral reasoning is possible — but it is jejune, barren, it could never alter attitudes, it assumes them. But if, and this is the other possibility, moral disagreement is ultimately reduced to disagreement in attitude (as it would in the case of "independent" emotive meaning), moral reasoning is impossible — we are left with irrational persuasion.

Not surprisingly then, Stevenson stresses time after time that the two elements involved are almost always intertwined. As a rule most words have both "dependent" and "independent" emotive meaning, likewise attitudes and beliefs are normally found together. "Emotive and descriptive meaning ... are distinguishable *aspects* of a total situation, not 'parts' of it that can be studied in isolation" (*EL*, 76). Pressed for an explanation of the relation, Stevenson replies, and that is all he can say from his viewpoint, that the connection is *factual*, and *psychological* in nature, but never logical.

This is a revealing as well as disturbing result. It means that for Stevenson ethical science as such never quite emerges. Despite all his efforts, "ethics" falls out into two incongruous parts. On the one side, there is empirical science (with psychology dominant); on the other there is a realm of irrational (ethical) attitudes. Moore's position was not without difficulties. But, as has now become clear, the "emotive" approach is no less burdened. Declaring values subjective or even non-existent has not brought with it the desired solution to the major problems.

THE LINGUISTIC RETREAT: META-ETHICS AT OXFORD AND CAMBRIDGE

In the late 1930's and the 1940's emotivism was grasped as a way out of the unpleasant dilemma: Naturalism or non-naturalism (intuitionism). But it was never a completely satisfying escape — at least to the majority of English ethicists. And emotivism's very ornateness, its involute but comparatively unrewarding argumentation, its seemingly bifarious character only aggravated an already inflammable situation. On this tinder of discontent fell the spark of the later Wittgenstein. The conflagration was instantaneous. Modern meta-ethics, conceived by Moore, delivered by Stevenson, experienced its baptism by

[20] For a detailed discussion of this dilemma, see George C. Kerner, *The Revolution in Ethical Theory*, pp. 52-64. Kerner's book, a helpful and readable introduction to modern meta-ethics, is written from out of a position similar to the Austin of *How To Do Things With Words* (1962).

fire. Today, a decade and a half later, meta-ethics is emerging as a young adolescent.

Especially two articles deserve mention as first initiating a new way of doing ethics; Stuart Hampshire's 1949 essay "Fallacies in Moral Philosophy," and J. O. Urmson's 1950 paper "On Grading." Published in 1950, although completed in 1948, Stephen Toulmin's *An Examination of the Place of Reason in Ethics* was the first book-length attempt searching for a new approach. In 1952 R. M. Hare's The *Language of Morals* appeared on the scene, followed in 1963 by its sequel, *Freedom and Reason*. 1954 witnessed the publication of P. Nowell-Smith's *Ethics*.[21]

Fallacies in Moral Philosophy: Stuart Hampshire

Although Stuart Hampshire (b. 1914) has become somewhat of a solitary thinker in the circles of linguistic analysis, his essay "Fallacies in Moral Philosophy"[22] deserves treatment at this stage because by pointing out the errors of the past, it prepares the way for the "new."

The Hampshire Critique

A major source of previous ethical ills, Hampshire declares, is uncritical acceptance of the post-Kantian thesis that there is an "unbridgeable logical gulf between sentences which express statements of fact and sentences which express judgments of value and particularly moral judgments." This was interpreted to read that value judgments cannot be "based on, or established exclusively by reference to, beliefs about matters of fact" (481). The result: "moral judgments must be ultimate and irrational, . . . they are established by intuition or are not literally significant." On the other hand, assuming — and this was considered by the Oxford dons a most heinous shortcoming — that "all literally significant sentences must correspond to or describe something," they were led to assimilate value judgments and descriptive statements. Thus moral judgments are said to *describe* external facts (naturalists), absolute values (intuitionists), internal feelings (Stevenson). Ayer denied that such judgments described, but just as clearly under the hegemony of the descriptive-

---

[21] Other important books are: Alan Montefiore, *A Modern Introduction to Moral Philosophy* (1958); A. N. Prior, *Logic and the Basis of Ethics* (1949); Paul Edwards, *The Logic of Moral Discourse* (1955); K. Baier, *The Moral Point of View* (1958); B. Mayo, *Ethics and the Moral Life* (1958); Paul Taylor, *Normative Discourse* (1961); A. I. Melden, *Rights and Right Conduct* (1959), *Free Action* (1961); M. G. Singer, *Generalization in Ethics* (1961).
[22] Hampshire, "Fallacies in Moral Philosophy," *Mind* LVIII (1949), pp. 466-82. Subsequent references are identified by bracketed page numbers.

110

model he could only consider the pseudo-judgments meaningless for purposes of knowledge. All this together has led moral philosophers to be obsessed with the question of definitions, with the truth or falsity of moral judgments about actions, in short, with the problems of the "moral *judge* or critic" (467). The concerns of the "moral *agent*" have been notoriously neglected; there is precious little analysis of the "processes of thought by which as moral agents we decide what we ought to do and how we ought to behave" (468). In recent moral philosophy, Hampshire concludes, the "*primary* use of moral judgments (= decisions) is largely or even entirely ignored" (469).

To facilitate the process of bringing moral philosophy back on to the right track, Hampshire offers various positive suggestions. Moral judgments are "not descriptions of, but prescriptions for, actions. Practical judgments, no less than theoretical or descriptive statements, are in the natural sense of the words, literally significant, although they do not in the normal sense describe" (480). Such judgments are not (normally) characterized as true or false, but they may be said to be "rational or irrational, right or wrong" (482). There is, he argues, a "procedure of practical deliberation" with its own logical pattern. That such practical logical patterns are not acknowledged in textbooks is no countervailing argument, so much the worse for the textbooks, they are simply deficient at this point (470ff.). Granted that value judgments are not logically deducible from any set of factual statements — if they were so deducible they would be redundant — "they are established and supported by arguments consisting of factual judgments of a particular range" (473). There are familiar patterns of argument habitually employed outside the sciences which are rational in the sense of being "more or less strictly governed by recognised (though not necessarily formulated) rules of relevance" (471). There is thus a special logic of "moral decisions." An ethical argument moves towards a conclusion in the sense of moving towards *decisions*. Away with the *critic* or spectator *talking about* ethical actions; in with the *actor* or wise man *doing* ethics.

Moore and Hampshire

For our study it is of particular importance to note that, although Hampshire continues to recognize the reality of the fact-value gap, he is out to minimize its importance, and if possible, to construct a solid bridge over the gulf. There is a *split*, but at the same time the cementing element is *logical* in nature. Not, Hampshire submits, the kind of logical connection described in the textbooks, rather the kind of rational procedure employed almost without exception in ordinary life. This search for some special logical connection is reminiscent of Moore. Since, to my knowledge Hampshire has not (as yet) further described the special logic of moral decisions, we will leave the matter until our treatment of Toulmin.

111

Although Hampshire never states it explicitly, the presumption is strong that the problems of modern moral philosophy began with G. E. Moore. And, recalling the far-reaching influence of Moore, it is certainly plausible to detect the first signs of derailment in his work. It is however questionable if he can corroborate his charge that modern ethicists have been obsessed with definitions to the exclusion of interest in the moral agent. It is beyond debate that for Moore, at least, examination of the *meaning* of concepts (complex QI) was preliminary to the proper task of answering the basic questions of ethics (complexes QII and III), what things are good? What ought we to do? This is not of course to deny that Moore became bogged down in the analysis of judgments of complex QI. Insofar, Moore must plead guilty to Hampshire's accusation.

But, looked at in that light, it is worth asking if Hamsphire is able to evade his own critique. According to him the conclusion "expressed in the sentence 'X is the best thing to do in these circumstances', is a pure or primary moral judgment (the solution of a practical problem)" (469). However, is this not itself another to-be-disqualified judgment *about* an action? This judgment by its very nature *as* judgment is one step removed from the actual act, from the actual doing. Rather than playing off critic and actor in the style of Hampshire, is it then not preferable to accept Moore's arrangement of critic advising actor? In his wish to establish a science of ethics, Moore saw no alternative other than to deal with judgments *about* actions and that in logical fashion. For that matter neither do the current practitioners of meta-ethics.

This is, as we have frequently seen, one of the central problems with which ethicists past and present grapple; to wit, the possibility of a scientific ethics. In the name of its subject matter, human activity, Hampshire accuses Moore and company of squeezing the life out of ethics by theoretical definitions. But in emphasizing that judging is a personal activity with a specific intention which constitutes its meaning, Hampshire has difficulty in setting up a scientific ethics and tends toward the opposite extreme.[23] Later we will have opportunity to see that this never resolved, but recurrent, tension between *theory* (of ethics) and ethical activity roots in a general failure to clearly and consistently distinguish pre-theoretical and theoretical thought; full ethical judgments are made by a friend, teacher, mother, etc., abstract theoretical judgments are made by an ethicist.

---

[23] Hampshire has not explicitly expanded on the ethical views presented in the essay which we have examined. In contrast to the majority of analysts, Hampshire's philosophy is as such *ethical* in nature. His abiding passion is the desire to expugn the contrast between *Thought and Action*, knowledge and decision, criticism and practice, nature and freedom, situation and response. As a result the scope and range of his work is much wider than the typical British ethicist; it is also more abstruse and less studied. Cf. *Thought and Action* (1959) and *Freedom of the Individual* (1965).

Hampshire's general plea for more attention to the practical nature of moral judgments has been taken up, and zealously at that, by his contemporaries, among others, Toulmin and Hare. It is not unambiguously clear how Hampshire responds to these later developments. It is feasible to assume that he answers in kind Hare's repudiation of the general tenor of his work.[24] Sharing, as they do, a common lean to pragmatism, his reaction is no doubt much more positive in regard to Toulmin. However, little has been done to this date in establishing a moral philosophy along Hampshirean lines.[25]

"Good" as a Grading Word: J. O. Urmson

Grading

Maintaining that there is no logical difference between "grading" (apples) and "evaluating" (men), Urmson (b. 1915) seeks to clarify the latter activity by treating the former. After examining the grading process in some detail, he sets up "a symbolic instance where X is a specialized label and A, B, and C are the acknowledged natural criteria for its application."[26] Can the current theories, Urmson wonders, explain this situation? He then investigates whether we are to classify "anything which is A, B, C is X" as analytic or synthetic. If analytic, X becomes simply conceptual shorthand for A, B, and C. This would imply that sorting apples into kinds, e.g. MacIntosh, Delicious etc., is no different than grading them according to size, shape, appearance etc. It further involves the absurdity that "X" or "good" would have as many different meanings as different situations in which it is applied. Can the label "Super Fancy" or "good" then be an intuited, non-natural quality supervening on A, B, and C synthetically, but necessarily? It would seem not. "The pointlessness, the impossibility, of maintaining that a thing is X if it is not A B C or denying that it is X if it is A B C makes the answer 'synthetic' equally unplausible" (157). It would simply destroy all communication to deny that an apple possessing all the essential characteristics A, B, and C was good, or to affirm that it was good if it was *not* A, B, and C.

Yet surely to grade an apple "Extra Fancy" is to do more than register your emotional delight or personal attitude towards the apple. Granted that

[24] Hare, "Review of *Freedom of the Individual*," *PR* LXXVI (1967), p. 230ff.
[25] Eric D'Arcy's *Moral Acts* (1963) could perhaps be mentioned.

However, in general the "subject" has been receiving increased attention through the presently rising (after the low ebb consequent to Ryle's exorcising the Cartesian ghost in the machine) fortunes of the so-called "philosophy of the mind." For example, Anscombe, *Intention* (1957).

[26] Urmson, J. O., "On Grading," *Mind* LIX (1950) p. 154; subsequent references to this work are identified by bracketed page numbers (reprinted in *Moral Judgment*, ed. P. W. Taylor).

certain labels may build up a high emotional charge and that this is often exploited, it remains incontrovertible that emotive significance is quite peripheral to the main business of grading. In summary: 1) Although the present theories do not account for the facts, they have grasped each in its own way a part of the truth. Naturalism is correct in stressing the "close connexion" of X and A, B, and C, just as intuitionism rightly rejects an "identity of meaning" and insists on the "different logical character of grading labels and natural descriptions." Naturalism and intuitionism have both grasped the objective character of grading, while emotivists have realized that the intuitionist answer does not adequately make good the fault of Naturalism. 2) The analytic-synthetic distinction is only applicable in relation to descriptive statements. This ought not to have the pejorative implication that value judgments are not up to par — they are simply of a different kind. "To describe is to describe, to grade is to grade, and to express one's feelings is to express one's feelings, and ... none of these is reducible to either of the others" (156). 3) "Good" has only one sense, although its criteria are in every situation different. To call something good is an act, the making of a *choice* in respect to a criterion.

Description and Evaluation

Once again we notice the decisive role which the analytic-synthetic distinction plays in ethics. Urmson discovers that the fact-value relation cannot be analytic (X and A, B, and C are not identical), nor can it be synthetic ("necessity" is involved). Consequently, the distinction only makes sense when applied to descriptive statements. As we recall, facing an analogous situation, intuitionists broke a lance for the possibility of *synthetic a priori*, "difference" and "necessity" in one. However, Urmson's version of the analytic-synthetic distinction — it could be called the latest orthodoxy — does not allow the existence of such a creature. This throws something of a shadow over his disproof of intuitionism. There is no argument involved: synthetic a priori and consequently intuitionism are simply contradictions in terms. By definition of terms necessity is analytic and contingent is synthetic (Kant's criterion of distinction has been rejected as unworkable, "content" is a metaphorical term which one can "load" to suit his purposes). Nevertheless, considering that philosophers of the stature of Frege, Poincaré, Brouwer and Hilbert have in the recent past taken it up for synthetic a priori, is it not *prima facie* just as reasonable to question the validity of the new logical orthodoxy as it is to declare that the analytic-synthetic distinction does not apply to ethical judgments? In any case Urmson and like-minded thinkers, by reason of their views on the logical analytic-synthetic distinction, still face the problem of finding the proper place for reason in ethics. That they concern themselves with this problem is of course sufficient to show that they have come farther than Ayer.

114

The whole complex receives another complication when we realize that the supposed insusceptibility of value judgments to the analytic-synthetic net also plays its role in proving that description and evaluation are *logically* different in character. Here we are threatened by a *petitio principi*. In Urmson's case it is evident that he goes out from the assumption of the logical difference between description and evaluation. Certainly, he points out, sorting out black and white checkers or sorting out apples by kind differs radically from grading apples according to shape, appearance, size, etc. Likewise description and scientific classification are easily distinguished from grading. Further, and perhaps the most convincing argument is Urmson's contention that whereas the name of a kind of apple, say Delicious, is a conceptual shortform analytically identical with its natural criteria, this could only be true in the case of "fancy" or "good" at the cost of the absurdity that "good" would have as many meanings as different situations in which it is employed.

As the description-evaluation dichotomy is one of the guises, *the* guise in modern ethical theory which the fact-value distinction assumes, it is of utmost importance that we examine it more carefully. In so doing we will have to anticipate our later discussion.[27] It is obvious that there are differences between "sorting" and "grading" apples. The issue is whether the processes are *logically* different. Urmson *et al.* answer in the affirmative, this writer begs to demur. The difference it would seem is not in the nature of the activity involved, but only in the "content" and nature of the criteria which regulate the activity. In both cases one operates in relation to criteria; if an apple meets the standards X, Y, Z it belongs to the sort called Delicious, if an apple meets the standards A, B, C it qualifies as belonging to the consignment termed "Extra Fancy." It is true that, depending on the nature of the criteria and the purpose of the operation, the activity involved requires more or less knowledge, more or less ingenuity, more or less concentration, and correspondingly, the possible margin of error ranges from extensive to almost non-existent. Yet in both cases, there is a process of measurement. The same holds true for describing and evaluating. Even if, as is often the case, one immediately recognizes X to be an apple and not a plum or peach, or one perceives that this is rain and not snow, such recognition involves evaluation in reference to a law-structure.

A complication — no doubt often the occasion for talk of the description-evaluation split — is the fact that, whereas one sorts apples according to physical and biotic standards which are realized in the facts *without* human interference, when he grades apples this occurs according to normative standards which themselves require concretization before grading can commence. In the first case certain immediately given physical-biotic properties are employed to

[27] Cf. discussion ch. 7, p. 188 ff.

identify the sort or kind of apple. Human needs and desires are irrelvant at this point. In the second case these human desires are in the center of interest. The physical-biotic properties of apples which satisfy these requirements, e.g. for an eating apple, for an apple fit to present to the teacher, are sought out and made to do duty as norms.

Our point in the foregoing discussion is that, despite the differences in the two instances, valuation is involved in *both* situations — in description as well as evaluation. One must decide not only if X is a good apple, but also, and in the first place, if it is an apple. The above-mentioned complication does not alter this state of affairs. Indeed, this complication arises in regard to the *description* of (and not only in the evaluation of) countless facts: economic facts (money, bank), ethical facts (friend, family), aesthetic facts (novel, painting), etc. Prior to any description of a house or of a family, the norms for houses and families must be specified. In such situations the structure which holds is at the same time norm.

At this juncture it is necessary to warn against assuming that valuation is a subjective psychically qualified process more or less illogical in contrast to description as an objective accounting of the facts. Facts are never to be qualified as "brute," "solid" and "objective" in comparison with "subjective," "individual" and "relative" values. As Hampshire has clearly seen (but unfortunately been unable to oversee all the consequences), "to state the facts is to analyse and interpret the situation."[28]

The fact that, on the one hand, the name MacIntosh and an apple with typical properties are identified, and, on the other hand, that the label "fancy" or "good" is not identical in meaning with an apple of a certain size, shape and appearance may not be read as evidence for the descriptive-evaluative bifurcation.[29] It only draws our attention to the fact that certain words are used to *name* and *identify* things, while other words are employed to signify how well various things live up to standards. Naming words must needs have a limited range of application in order to fulfill their identificatory task; likewise grading words require an open-textured nature in order to function properly. But even here the contrast is far from perfect. MacIntosh is also the name for a raincoat. And "good" always signifies that norms have been fulfilled to a considerable degree.

[28] Hampshire, "Fallacies," *Mind* LVIII, p. 476.
[29] Urmson talks as if there is in the case of descriptive names an analytic identity between name and criteria (and not only between name and the characteristics involved). Is this possible? Can a thing ever be identical with the structure which holds *for* that thing? The neglect of this essential, qualitative distinction between the law-which-holds-for and that-which-is-subject-to-the-law, between norm as *valid-for* and facts as *answering-to* is, as we shall see, a major obstacle blocking the way to future progress in the thicket of problems in which contemporary ethical philosophy is entangled.

To describe is to value, just as to grade is to value. Urmson concedes that grading words are often used descriptively and descriptive words evaluatively. Sometimes, indeed, words have both functions at once. It is even true, he avows, that one at times confines himself to descriptive terms even though his primary intention is clearly evaluational, and at other times one takes grading terms upon his lips although his goal is in the first place descriptive. But why, then, hold so tenaciously to the descriptive-evaluative dichotomy? And when Urmson confesses that the "difference [with describing] lies in the purpose of the grading, not in its external form," his assumption of the *logical* difference appears even more remarkable — and unsupported. Ought one to spot in this situation the hovering ghost of Moore, warning Urmson against the Naturalistic reef?

A last comment on Urmson's article: calling attention to the norms[30] by which one must *choose* (evaluate) marks a real advance in moral philosophy. However, is it sufficient, as Urmson seems to believe, to consider norms essentially subjective fabrications? Is human subjectivity able to confer the required universal validity on such norms? It is with such questions that contemporary moral philosophy ought to be preoccupied.

The Place of Reason in Ethics: Stephen Edelston Toulmin

The "Look and See" Approach

In the midst of divergent views as to the function of "reason" in ethics, Moore had restricted it, Ayer had banished it, Stevenson had failed in efforts to reinstate it, Toulmin launched his pragmatistically tinged *An Examination of the Place of Reason in Ethics*.[31] Unfortunately, laments Toulmin, previous theorists labored under the plausible but woefully mistaken notion that a value judgment had to *refer* to something either in the subject or object if it was to meet the requirements of intellectual respectability. But in ethics "there need be no such property, nor such a 'psychological state'" (42-43). To think so is to harbor illusions which can only result in proverbial wild-goose chases. People in ethical disagreement "contradict each other about — nothing physically or psychologically 'concrete' or 'substantial', but something which, for logical purposes, is quite as solid and important — namely, whether or not there is a good reason for reaching one ethical conclusion rather than another" (57).

[30] Urmson along with most ethicists usually speaks of "criteria" in place of "norms". This often bespeaks an over-exaggeration of the logical. A criterion is a norm, but a norm is not a criterion. That is to say a criterion is a norm looked at from its *logical* side, but a norm is not a criterion, it is much more than logical. In similar fashion, it is more or less taken for granted that "word" and "term" are synonyms. Although a term is a word, a word is not a term. A term is a word approached from its logical aspect, but a word is much more than a (logical) term.

[31] Bracketed page numbers in this section refer to Toulmin's book.

Indeed, for Toulmin, the question of "good reasons" (and not that of "definitions") is pivotal, indispensable and therefore paramount in ethical theory. This dawns on anyone, he believes, who turns to practical moral life — with one proviso. This "anyone" must jettison any preconceived notions as to the form and nature of ethical judgments. In the words of Wittgenstein, "*look and see . . . don't think.*"[32] And the same advice serves one well when he begins to examine the logic at work in moral reasoning. "Abandoning most of our intellectual machinery and presuppositions" (64), we will not be blinded by any preconceived notion as to the nature of reasoning, e.g. that logic is "inductive," or "deductive," sentences must be "descriptive" etc., rather we will be led by the "familiar, unquestionable facts of usage." No longer shackled by any desire for ethical theories, we will covet only a "*descriptive* account of our ethical concepts," a "language-map" (194). Then, and only then, one discovers that speech is no single-purpose tool, but, like a Boy Scout's knife, is multifunctional.

Likewise, there is an intimate, inseparable relation between the logic of a mode of reasoning and the purpose which such a mode serves. And thus one soon realizes the folly as well as the impossibility of insisting (as did Moore and Stevenson) that the mode of reasoning appropriate in one mode, say the descriptive mode of the natural sciences, is valid for all the other modes.

Rather, we must expect that every mode of reasoning, every type of sentence, and (if one is particular) every single sentence will have its own logical criteria, to be discovered by examining its individual, peculiar uses. (83)

The repercussions for ethics are obvious and far-reaching. No longer may ethical arguments be forced into the Procrustean bedstead of deductive or inductive logic before they can be blessed as valid or branded as invalid. Moral reasoning claims its own peculiar mode of inference "by which we pass from factual reasons to an ethical conclusion — what we might naturally call 'evaluative' inference" (38; cf. 4, 55 ff.). Intimately connected with its own logic, the function of ethics is the "harmonious satisfaction of desires and interests" (223; cf. 137, 160, 166, 170). An ethical judgment is in the last analysis justified when it is supported by "good reasons," and it is backed by "good reasons" when it passes the "test of general fecundity."

Evaluative Inference

Even as Stevenson's view was in effect a rebound from the extremism of Ayer, Toulmin's position is even a stronger ricochet in the direction of Moore. Moore envisioned an unconditional, though not analytic, connection between facts and values. Toulmin suggests an "evaluative inference," neither merely

[32] Wittgenstein, *Philosophical Investigations*, par. 66.

118

deductive nor inductive, from factual statements to value judgments. Both Moore and Toulmin require an element of necessity and entailment which, speaking broadly, is logical, but which cannot be accounted for in the current logical orthodoxy. Besides, even as Moore concluded that the "goodness" of X depended on the natural intrinsic characteristics of X, so Toulmin considers that the truth and validity of an ethical judgment depends on its relation to factual statements.

Admittedly there remains the difference that Moore is an "objectivist" (values are!) and Toulmin is a "subjectivist" (values an sich are non-existent). However, as we have already noted, all the complexities which hounded Moore in the objective fact-objective value relation return to rankle Toulmin (not to speak of Ayer, Stevenson, Hampshire, Urmson, Hare *et al.*) as he examines the relation between *objective* facts and the *subjective* moral conclusions (the fill-in for "values"). Toulmin argued that the relevance of factual reasons was a *logical* rather than à la Stevenson a psychological matter. It is of importance for our study to determine if Toulmin's gambit is able to deliver what he promises.

Toulmin sees the solution of the problem in a unique form of reasoning: evaluative inference. In simple cases of ethical reasoning, and these are the most numerous, all that one need do in order to verify rightness is to inquire if the proposed action X conforms to the accepted moral practices. Does it comply with the rules of the game? If so, the action is right and the argument justified (144-46).

Has he demonstrated that the connection is logical? Not it would seem unless he is willing to treat the *moral* code as being at the same time a set of *logical* rules. But this seems *prima facie* preposterous. Principles to determine moral right and wrong are of a different kind than those designed to determine valid forms of logical inference.

The identical ambiguity as to whether a principle is moral, logical, or both surfaces again when Toulmin deals with the more complicated or test cases. In a conflict of duties, or when a principle itself or a social practice is at issue, appeal to accepted practices avails little. In such instances in line with the function of ethics as the reconciler of human interests, "the answer to be given will be reached by estimating the probable consequences" (150). If the consequences are (likely) to be good, the principle is declared right and the argument valid.

In the "simple" cases, accepted social and moral practices do double duty as rules of inference, in the more complex instances the logical criterion is the moral and social worth, teleologically calculated, of the principles or practices in question. But can a substantial *moral* principle, in this case ultimately the principle of "general fecundity," serve simultaneously as a principle of *logical* inference?

119

Toulmin with almost a nonchalant air brushes our inquiry aside. Such queries, he implies, arise under the beguiling influence of "philosophical theories of ethics" (190ff.). In lieu of such tendentious and persuasive theorizing, Toulmin complies with Wittgenstein's "look and see" advice and seeks to furnish only a "descriptive account of our ethical concepts." Nevertheless, although not deigning to answer our question directly, his affirmative reply is incontestable. On the one hand, it is indubitable that moral codes and the principle of harmony double for Toulmin as *logical* rules of inference. Each of the "two kinds of moral reasoning" (the simple and complex situations) provides its own "logical criteria" (151; cf. 148, 160). In the context the reference is obviously to, respectively, moral codes and the harmonization principle. If an argument answers to the relevant criteria, "good reasons" have been presented and the argument is *logically valid*. On the other hand, Toulmin identifies the codes as *moral* in nature and is keenly aware of the normative (*a*logical) character of the principle of harmony. Thus, when an argument answers to the relevant criteria, we have "good reasons" to judge that the conclusion is *morally* right and true (41, 52ff., 70ff., 80ff., 160ff.).

It seems impossible to avoid the conclusion that the questions of logical validity and ethical rightness are for Toulmin telescoped into one and the same question. Thus, the concept of "good reasons" is also infected with this built-in ambiguity. If one stresses the substantive "reason," he tends to interpret the phrase "good reasons" as indicating logically valid factual considerations. If, however, he lays the stress on "good," there is a powerful inducement to view the phrase as evidencing weighty ethical considerations. But how does one relate the ethical "good" to the factual "reasons"? Toulmin profits by the convenient, not to say deceptive, ambiguity of his pet phrase "good reasons." But is one to take "good reasons" to mean logically good or morally good? Almost certainly neither, there is rather a strong presumption that one must answer *both*: what is logically good is also morally impeachable, and what is morally good is likewise logically impeachable. If a moral conclusion is supported by "good reasons," the argument is at the same time logically valid and the judgment is morally right.

But is the state of affairs that simple? Toulmin himself is forced to recognize that it is not, with as we shall see disastrous results for his entire position. If it were actually true that a *valid* argument (backed by "good reasons") is by that very reason also true and right, then to assert an ethical conclusion would simply be to assert reasons. And as reasons are *factual* in nature, an ethical conclusion would be factual — values have been usurped by facts and "Naturalism" would be our portion. This Toulmin cannot swallow. "Although factual reasons (R) may be good reasons for an ethical conclusion (E), to assert the conclusion is not just to assert the reasons, or indeed anything of the same logical type as R. It is to declare that one ought to approve of, or pursue, or do something-or-other" (55; cf. 145).

What this means for Toulmin's views becomes clear when we tune in on his closing admonition.

Of course, 'This practice would involve the least conflict of interests attainable under the circumstances' does not *mean* the same as 'This would be the right practice'; nor does 'This way of life would be more harmoniously satisfying' *mean* the same as 'This would be better'. But in each case the first statement is *a good reason* for the second: the 'ethically neutral' fact is *a good reason* for the 'gerundive' moral judgment. If the adoption of the practice would genuinely reduce conflicts of interest, it is a practice *worthy of adoption*, and if the way of life would genuinely lead to deeper and more consistent happiness, it is one *worthy of pursuit*. And this seems so natural and intelligible, when one bears in mind the function of ethical judgements, that, if anyone asks me *why* they are 'good reasons', I can only reply by asking in return, 'What better kinds of reason could you want?' (224)

No one must imagine, Toulmin avows, that to state that a certain practice or judgment answers to the principle of harmony is to say that it is right. Indeed, if Toulmin desires to avoid the accusation of Naturalism, "good reasons" may not be awarded the accolade of moral rightness. However, if there is no equivalence in meaning between "harmoniously satisfying" and "right," how is one to know that a factual reason which is harmoniously satisfying is a "good reason" for a moral judgment? The reason may be good in a *logical* sense, but there is no assurance at all that it is also a good reason in the *moral* sense — and that is what ethics is all about. Toulmin is in a tight spot. Beginning with his "but in each case . . ." phrase, he attempts, almost reneging on his previous admission, to recoup his loss. To say that this is a good reason may not be to say that it is right, but it does nevertheless furnish a warrant worthy of being acted on.

But can he, if pressed, verify this claim? Either *worthy* is synonymous with "good reason," in which case it cannot be heralded as imbued with ethical normativity, or it is synonymous with "right," in which case factual reasons acquire by some sudden unexplained quirk normative ethical validity. In fact, it seems that Toulmin attempts to have his cake and eat it too by trading on the built-in ambiguity which we have signalized. When challenged by a non-naturalist, for example, for deducing moral conclusions from factual reasons, he is able to "prove" his innocence. When faced with his self-appointed task to aid a mankind drowning in moral perplexities, he is able to claim that "harmoniously satisfying" practices are *worthy of pursuit*. Mysteriously, as it were, in this last instance the principle of harmony is wielded as *the* ethical standard; only a moment later under the objection of non-naturalists and all those who want their ethics morally clean to be declared part and parcel of the factual state of affairs.

121

And it is this possibility of eating and at the same time having ethical normativity which explains why Toulmin allows himself the leisure of verbally throwing up his hands, "What better kinds of reasons could you want?" But rather than showing up the stupidity of the querist, the gesture lays bare the devious means which Toulmin must employ to ward off his critics. The questioner is not at all interested in a logical justification of the "good reasons," his concern is for an ethical warrant. Toulmin can only act as if he has provided this by brandishing the principle of harmony as a substantial moral weapon. Only then can he ask, what "better" ethical warrant can you demand. But, doing this, he comes once more in conflict with his confession a few lines earlier that to call a practice harmoniously satisfying is not to say that it is morally right. The dialectic is obvious — as is the antinomy. Depending on the situation, Toulmin denies or affirms the normative character (in an ethical sense) of "good reasons" and the "fecundity principle."

It only remains to probe a little deeper and see how Toulmin hopes to throw up a facade which will gloss over the inner dialectic. In the passage just quoted he provided a solid clue. His position seems "so natural and intelligible, when one bears in mind the function of ethical judgments." This function is, as we have seen repeatedly, "to harmonise the aims and actions of the members of a community" (166). There is no harmful "theorizing" involved in its formulation, it emerges simply from a *description* of the "occasions on which we are prepared to call judgements 'ethical' and decisions 'moral'" (160). Again, "what makes us call a judgement 'ethical' is the fact that it is used to harmonise people's actions" (145). Although this may be regarded as his central thesis, Toulmin does not document it in the usual manner. And rightly according to his view, for it is a simple matter of observable fact accessible to all who look and see. By declaring this principle of harmonization morally neutral, public, and factual, Toulmin aspired to kill two birds with one stone. He can be faithful to the sacred canon of neutrality in science *and* simultaneously he is enabled to keep ethics relevant to life, able to help "everyman in his everyday moral problems." Ingeniously, but not without wrinkles and painful burns, he peddles off his own normative view as if it were a fact to be registered and not a position to be argued.[33] By employing a normative proposal as a pseudo-logical criterion, he is able *by definition* to excommunicate all discordant ethical views. According to Toulmin nothing can be *immoral* in principle, it is either moral or *a*moral. But, as we have seen at length, his manoeuvre boomerangs. If his ethical conclusions are to have any compelling, prescriptive force, he is forced as it were to allow the defrocked value (the harmonization principle), now a pseudo-fact, to once again be

[33] Likewise, R. M. Hare, to name one outstanding ethicist, has argued that Toulmin's principle of harmony is not a morally contentless logical principle, but a full-blooded moral principle. Cf. *Phil. Quarterly* I (1951), p. 372; *LM*, 45-55, and fn. 36.

garbed in the gown of normativity. At the same time he must own up to the fact that this is in conflict with the general tenor of his position based as it is on the "familiar, unquestionable facts of usage" (144).

The Language of Morals: R. M. Hare

The Oxford Professor R. M. Hare defends a position which, following his example, could be christened, "'universal prescriptivism'." It is a "combination ... of universalism (the view that moral judgements are universalizable) and prescriptivism (the view that they are, at any rate typically, prescriptive)" (FR, 16). As the title of his latest book indicates, he sets out to resolve the incompatibility between those who, preserving freedom in morality, deny rationality and those, who stressing the rationality of morals, restrict freedom. In short, he wishes to do in the "antinomy between freedom and reason" (FR, 3). Although he did not neglect the demands of reason, he was more concerned in the *Language of Morals* with the "freedom-pole," with the nature of prescriptivity and commendation. While continuing to retain the prescriptive nature of value judgments, in *Freedom and Reason* he was determined to shore up the foundations of his position by a careful delineation of the place of "reason" in ethics.

Ethics and Logic

Ethics, according to Hare, is "the logical study of the language of morals" (LM, v). But, it must be immediately added, this is not to say that ethics is impractical. On the contrary, it helps "us to think better about moral questions by exposing the logical structure of the language in which this thought is expressed" (FR, v). Moral language, in fact, has as its very purpose the *guidance* of human conduct; it is primarily *prescriptive* in character. As the ordinary imperative sentence is the simplest form of prescriptive language, "the study of imperatives is by far the best introduction to the study of ethics" (LM, 2). Hare accentuates the fact that imperatives are not merely persuasive devices devoid of any similarity with fact-stating indicatives.[34] To bring the resemblances as well as the discrepancies of imperatives and indicatives to the fore, Hare recasts them in terms of what he calls "phrastics" and "neustics." Thus, the

---

[34] In distinction from Stevenson, Hare points out that the "processes of *telling* someone to do something, and *getting* him to do it, are quite distinct, logically, from each other" (LM, 13). In commending or prescribing, to employ Austin's terminology, we have to do with an illocutionary act (a performative), whereas in persuading and influencing we have to do with a perlocutionary act. In the former case the attention is riveted on *what is done in* the act concerned, in the latter what is done *by* the act concerned. Cf. Austin, *How to Do Things With Words*, p. 101 ff; 121.

imperative "Shut the door!" and the indicative "You are going to shut the door" are redrafted as follows:

Your shutting the door in the immediate future, please.

Your shutting the door in the immediate future, yes. (*LM*, 17)

The identical part of each sentence is the "phrastic," it *refers* to what the sentence is about; the second phrase is the "neustic," it indicates what is asserted about the referent. In assenting to an indicative one "nods" his belief in X (referred to in the phrastic); in assenting to an imperative one "nods" his resolve to do X.

The fact that imperatives as well as indicatives have a "phrastic" is for Hare of crucial significance. It means that imperatives — and thus value judgments — can, just as indicatives, contradict each other. Commands too, and not only descriptive sentences "must observe logical rules." Just as we are only sincere in our assent to a statement if we "believe that it is true," we are only sincere in our assent to a command if we "do or resolve to do what the speaker has told us to do" (*LM*, 20).

If, so runs Hare's argument, logical relations are possible in the case of extreme prescriptives such as imperatives, this will certainly be true in the case of other prescriptives such as moral judgments. Concretely, this means for Hare that the end of the arduous search for an "intrinsic" relation of ethics and logic, began by Moore, derailed by Ayer, and taken up anew by Stevenson and Toulmin, is in sight. For that reason he devoted the first third of *Language of Morals* to a discussion of imperatives and logic, and the last two chapters to the relation of imperatives and evaluatives. He concludes that a genuine example of moral reasoning must have "as its end-product an imperative of the form 'Do so-and-so'" (*LM*, 39). Only if value judgments "entail imperatives" are they action-guiding, that is, prescriptive. In such cases the specific value words are eliminated and an explicit imperative is attained (this does not mean, and Hare repeatedly denies, that he wishes to reduce moral judgments to imperatives). Nevertheless, this entailment relation is utilized by Hare as the defining criterion for value judgments themselves. "I ought to do X" qualifies as a value judgment if the speaker recognizes that assent to the judgment entails assent to the command "let me do X" (*LM*, 168-69).

Hare has discovered two rules which govern such logical entailments:

(1) *No indicative conclusion can be validly drawn from a set of premisses which cannot be validly drawn from the indicatives among them alone.*

(2) *No imperative conclusion can be validly drawn from a set of premisses which does not contain at least one imperative.* (*LM*, 28)

In support of rule two, the only one relevant for Hare's purposes, he appeals to the rules of deductive inference which according to him are "analytic" in character (*LM*, 32 ff.). In that deductive inference depends on the meaning of words, a conclusion can only add to what is explicitly or implicitly in the premise "solely on the strength of definitions of terms." It is thus logically excluded that one can move from the factual to the evaluative. In the well known and unambiguous language of Karl Popper:

> Perhaps the simplest and most important point about ethics is purely logical. I mean the impossibility to derive nontautological ethical rules — imperatives; principles of policy; aims; or however one may describe them — from statements of facts. Only if this fundamental logical position is realized can we begin to formulate the real problems of moral philosophy, and to appreciate their difficulty.[35]

For Hare, in contrast to Toulmin who moved, we recall, from factual premises to moral conclusions by means of evaluative inference, a moral conclusion is only valid by the ordinary rules of deductive inference. A moral syllogism contains a general principle of action, a factual minor premise and a particular evaluative conclusion. For purposes of logical argument the general principle is recast in the form of the universal imperative it entails. For example:

Never say what is false.
S is false
∴. Do not say S.[36]

Toulmin, by allowing a logical law (or something posing as a logical law) to decide matters of morals, eliminates the factor of decision. And it is just this factor of decision "which is of the very essence of morals" (*LM*, 54). In every moral argument there comes a point where a decision has to be made whether to act upon the principle or not, and just at this juncture inference leaves one in the lurch; a decision of principle must be taken (*LM*, 65 ff.). Such a decision can of course be justified by reference to probable effects and to more general principles, but in the last analysis such references are inconclusive. Principles are never self-evident, they are generalizations, modified, tightened, invented as mankind sees fit. In the last analysis, "if pressed to justify a decision completely, we have to give a complete specification of the way of life of which it is a part." If one is still not satisfied, "we can only ask him to make up his own mind which way he ought to live; for in the end everything rests upon such a

---

[35] "What can Logic do for Philosophy?", *PASS* XXII (1948), p. 154.
[36] Toulmin, Hare argues, illicitly employs the principle involved as a rule of inference. Such an argument can be schematized as follows: S is false. ∴. Do not say S. Toulmin errs because in employing a moral principle as a special rule of inference, he represents matters of substance as if they were verbal matters. In fact, Toulmin's form of argument is really an enthymeme with its major premise understood.

decision of principle." If he does not accept our way of life, then "let him accept some other, and try to live by it. The sting is in the last clause" (*LM*, 69).

Thus, even though principles are indispensable if one would support his decisions by reasons, the principles themselves depend upon prior "decisions of principle." Hare, however, does not consider such a process arbitrary. "Such a decision would be the most well-founded of decisions, because it would be based upon a consideration of everything upon which it could possibly be founded" (*LM*, 69). Nevertheless, his views at this point were greeted with the hue and cry of disbelief. So much so it seems that Hare in *Freedom and Reason* determines to divert the floodlights from decisions of principle and to retrain them on the reasoning process operating in such acts of choice.

Once engaged in such investigations, he confesses that perhaps moral reasoning is not "'straight-line' or 'linear' reasoning from premises to conclusion" (*FR*, 87). Rather, in the spirit of Popper's theory as laid out in *The Logic of Scientific Discovery*, Hare envisions the process as a "kind of *exploration*, or looking for hypotheses which will stand up to the test of experiment" (*FR*, 88). This does not mean that Hare replaces "deductive" inference with "induction." On the contrary, the inferences involved remain deductive, "from the truth of certain observations to the falsity of a hypothesis" (never to the *truth* of a hypothesis).[37] In one sentence, ethical reasoning involves reconnaissance: having the *facts* at his disposal, armed with the weapons of empathy and *imagination*, one investigates what singular prescriptions, formed on the basis of his *inclinations*, he is willing both to commit himself to (prescriptivity) and willing to universalize for others (universalizability) (*FR*, ch. 6).

"Good" as a Commending Word

Having examined the simplest form of prescriptives, the imperative, Hare

[37] Hare accepts Popper's contention that "in science there are no inferences other than deductive" (*FR*, 87). Cf. Popper's *The Logic of Scientific Discovery*. According to Popper the archenemy of inductivism, "falsification," or rather the lack of it, is the criterion by which one judges whether a theory is scientific or not. One does not move from particular truths to general truths; thus, supposedly, verifying the truth of a theory. Rather one *tests* the particular statements deductively entailed by a scientific hypothesis: if they survive repeated testings, the theory is *not* false; it is, so to speak, corroborated (but one can never say that it is true!). A good theory is one which has withstood insistent efforts to falsify it. Popper's thesis has received wide acclaim, and not only in philosophical circles. Anthony Flew, to cite an interesting case, has wielded the "falsification" principle in his efforts to undermine belief in the existence of God. Since belief in God is consonant with every possible empirical fact, it is not open to "falsification." Thus, in that God-belief explains everything, in reality it explains *nothing*. A scientific theory must be incompatible with *some* observations to explain *any* observation. Cf. Anthony Flew, *New Essays in Philosophical Theology*, p. 96ff.

applies what he has learned to the more complex logical behaviour of value words, in particular, "good," "right," and "ought." Value terms, he avers, have "a special function in language, that of commending" (*LM*, 91). Naturalism is to be rejected because it defines value words in terms of factual words which do not *commend*. And obviously, if that is true, we are deprived of the means of performing the very function which is unique to value terms. To judge that a strawberry is good because it is sweet is not to assert, as the naturalists would have it, that a strawberry is "sweet" because it is "sweet." It is clear that Hare sides with Moore. There is no movement from factual statements to value judgments, or more technically, there is no relation of entailment between the criteria (good-making characteristics) and "good."

In distinction from descriptive terms such as "red," whose meaning is identical with their criteria of application, the meaning of value terms is not co-extensive with the criteria of application. As Urmson had already declared, "good" can be applied correctly to any number of different objects. Value terms in addition to having *descriptive* meaning (determined by criteria of application) also have *prescriptive* meaning (consisting in their commendatory function). Although prescriptive meaning is *primary* in such full-blooded value words as "good," in other cases, such as "tidy," or "industrious," it is secondary to the descriptive meaning. In a similar way, although "ought" may be employed in statements of sociological and psychological fact ("I have a feeling that I ought to do X"), its primary use is evaluative ("I ought to do X") (*LM*, 167 ff.).

But what — shades of Moore and Stevenson — is the nature of the connection between the descriptive and evaluative elements? Hare is not sure: the relation is not one of entailment or of identity of meaning, although it "seems to be some close logical connexion" (*LM*, 111; cf. 145 and *FR*, 53-54). Hare's readers are never let in on the secret. All one learns is that the connection of factual (good-making characteristics) and moral judgments occurs indirectly, as it were, via standards or principles of choosing. Only then can there be talk of entailment. As Hare explains:

A statement of the characteristics of the man (the minor or factual premiss) *together with* a specification of a standard for judging men morally (the major premiss), entails a moral judgement upon him. (*LM*, 145-46)

In effect, the situation is almost a carbon-copy of Moore's. The evaluative terms such as "good," "right," and "ought" have a supervenient character. Objects and actions cannot differ with respect to their "goodness" etc. if they are in all other respects exactly alike. The descriptive characteristics are the *necessary* but not *sufficient* condition for the correct employment of a value term. And the exact nature of the relation remains obscure.

Although Hare had not ignored the dissimilarities between imperatives and value terms in *The Language of Morals*, the emphasis was one-sidedly on the similarities. To restore the balance he wrote *Freedom and Reason*. In contrast to an imperative a moral judgment appeals to general principles. It implies that everyone (in the same circumstances) ought to issue the same judgment, or, as the case may be, execute the action prescribed (*LM*, 175-79). In *Freedom and Reason* he dubs this feature of value judgments; viz., that they contain descriptive meaning, "universalizability."[38] On account of it "we can speak of moral thought as rational (to universalize is to give the reason)" (*FR*, 4).

A judgment is universalizable when "it commits the speaker to the further proposition that anything exactly like the subject of the first judgement, or like it in the relevant respects, possesses the property attributed to it in the first judgement" (*FR*, 12). Thus, anyone who judges that "X is a good man" is committed to the view that some man who was exactly like X, or like him in the relevant aspects, would also be "good." Or in respect to actions, "if a person says 'I ought to act in a certain way, but nobody else ought to act in that way in relevantly similar circumstances', then, on my thesis, he is abusing the word 'ought'; he is implicitly contradicting himself" (*FR*, 32). Only by being universalizable do value judgments escape arbitrariness.

Universalizability is "a logical thesis and not a substantive moral principle" (*FR*, 34; cf. 89, 97ff., 195ff.). In Hare's view "there is absolutely no content for a moral prescription that is ruled out by logic or by the definition of terms" (*FR*, 195). And "thus ethics, the study of the logical properties of the moral words, remains morally neutral (its conclusions neither are substantial moral judgements, nor entail them, even in conjunction with factual premises)" (*FR*, 97).

Notwithstanding this neutrality "ethics (i.e. the logic of moral language) is an immensely powerful engine for producing moral agreement." If people can be persuaded to employ moral words in the same way (read: in the same way as Hare), "the other possible sources of disagreement are all eliminable."

---

[38] Value judgments are universalizable — in contrast to imperatives — because of their descriptive meaning (*FR*, 15, 30, 36, *passim*). The question arises if this squares with his earlier contention that imperatives (as well as indicatives) possess "phrastics." For a "phrastic" contains *descriptive* meaning. Should not imperatives, at least in principle, be universalizable? Hare apparently thought so in *LM*, where on the basis of the "phrastic" he built an "enriched" or universal imperative. However in *FR* there is no mention of phrastics. Perhaps he spied the discrepancy and dropped this part of his theory. But then he requires another way to demonstrate the similarity of imperatives and evaluatives.

Interesting in this connection is Kerner's related contention that Hare could have avoided the descriptive-evaluative dichotomy if he would have employed the phrastic-neustic distinction throughout his theorizing (cf. Kerner, *Revolution*, pp. 142-52).

These sources are the other three ingredients in a moral argument besides logic: facts, inclinations and imagination (*FR*, 93-94). Well now, argues Hare, the facts are often ascertainable, people's inclinations tend to be the same, and imagination can be cultivated. All that is now necessary, seeing that agreement in use of moral words is already present, "is to think clearly, and so make it evident." Ethics bears upon moral questions in that it "makes logically impossible certain combinations of moral and other prescriptions" (*FR*, 97-98).

There is one loophole. Inclinations are not *always* the same. Still this is not an insurmountable obstacle — anyway in most, say ninety-nine percent of the cases. Usually in the spirit of "utilitarianism" a compromise solution can be reached whereby both parties declare themselves willing to take into consideration the interests and desires of other people. Once it is this far, a detailed compromise agreeable to all is in sight (*FR*, ch. 7). There are however, Hare concedes, rare individuals who, obsessed with certain ideals, will not yield ground and accept a compromise. Fortunately, he hastens to add, their number is almost negligible. They must be willing to endure evils similar to those they propose to inflict on others. Only a handful will pass this test. "How many Nazis were prepared themselves to die in concentration camps, if, by some miracle, this resulted in the Jews vanishing into thin air?" (*FR*, 197)

There will, sighs Hare, always be some fanatics. Their presence is disturbing as well as distressing. But it is the "price we have to pay for our freedom" (*FR*, 111). Either we risk fanaticism and retain our freedom, or we gain security at the cost of our freedom.

R. M. Hare and G. E. Moore

Perhaps we can best approach Hare's formidable position by investigating his relationship to Moore. It has become clear from our (unavoidably long) summary of Hare's views that he stands remarkably close to Moore on many issues. Adopting Moore's anti-naturalist stance as his own he endeavours to shore up the foundations of the open-question argument by casting it in a linguo-logical form. Naturalist theories "leave out the prescriptive or commendatory element in value-judgements, by seeking to make them derivable from statements of fact" (*LM*, 82).

To expose this fallacy Hare offers his variation of Moore's open-question. If someone claims to have derived a value judgment from a set of facts so that V (a value word) is reputed to mean the same as C (a conjunction of descriptive properties), a check must be instigated to insure that no "covertly evaluative" expressions hide away among the members of C. In most cases this will indeed be the case, terms such as "normal," "natural," "satisfying," "fundamental human needs" have been ensconced in C. In the few remaining cases the supporter must be queried if he "ever wishes to commend anything for being C."

An affirmative answer is excluded because any notion of commending is by definition alien to C. A negative answer is also impossible because to commend a thing for being C is the whole reason why he proposes his theory (*LM*, 92-93).

When we call to memory our earlier detailed discussion of the open-question argument, it is soon evident that Hare's revision is as impotent as Moore's argument to confute a resolute opponent.

Value-terms have a special function in language, that of commending; and so they plainly cannot be defined in terms of other words which themselves do not perform this function; for if this is done, we are deprived of a means of performing the function. (*LM*, 91)

Hare's argument is a lethal weapon for unmasking naturalists only when one is already a convinced prescriptivist. To a naturalist or anyone whose very concern is the obliteration of the evaluative-descriptive bifurcation, his argument (and for that matter, his entire position) begs the point at issue.

Hare himself recognizes that he makes the distinction "in effect, true by definition" (*FR*, 27; cf. also *LM*, 168). Operating with the conceptual scheme that he does, he has little choice if he wishes to maintain his fundamental stance. Behind his view, rather at the base of his position is the same widely-held view of the analytic-synthetic which we have already met in the work of Ayer, and Urmson. "Analytic," "necessity," "a priori" fall on one side of the fence, and "synthetic," "contingent," "empirical" on the other. An analytic proposition is one whose truth or falsity depends on the meaning of one or more of the words it contains, while the truth or falsity of a synthetic proposition depends on the facts to which the proposition refers. Simply stated Hare wishes to insure the rationality of ethical science, and in his view this necessitates talk of logical inference which is analytic in character; the result is a number of propositions in ethics which are true by definition.

Hare is well aware of the significance of the analytic-synthetic distinction for his ethicizing. In his British Academy lecture of 1963 he underlines the fact that the problem concerning the "distinction between description and evaluation ... is very like that concerning the distinction between analytic and synthetic (indeed, it is an offshoot of that problem)."[39] He does not discuss the merits of the distinction (it "is outside the scope of this book." *LM*, 42; cf. 83) even though he realizes that it is "still a matter under dispute." Lack of complete clarity on the matter must not bar use of this essential philosophical tool.

Indeed, certain advantages accrue to a user of this schema. He need not, in fact cannot, consider whether moral principles can be self-evident in the trend of Moore. It is excluded by definition that such Janus-faced creatures can

[39] "Descriptivism," *The Proceedings of the British Academy* XLIX (1963), pp. 115-16; 130.

exist. A self-evident principle, by nature necessary, cannot be synthetic for that is to brand it as contingent. But if it is analytic, it is contentless; impotent to tell one "to do one thing rather than another" (*LM*, 41). And this is obviously contrary to the very nature of a moral principle.

It is not only in certain cases that Hare reaps the harvest of what he has sown. As a result of stipulating that the fact-value dichotomy is true by definition, this partition is worked into the very bones and marrow of his system. This implies that his position, aside from certain adolescent blemishes, has an elemental inwrought integrity. Hare is a master at taking advantage of this situation. When one is foolhardy enough to restrict his siege to details, single features, several facets, Hare's counterattack is studied, predictable and altogether deadly for the opponent. If one presents a countervailing argument, e.g. that "ought" in a certain value judgment is not employed prescriptively, Hare has a ready-made two-pronged reply. Either prescriptivity is covertly present, or no value judgment is involved but a sociological or psychological judgment of fact (cf. *LM*, 167; *FR*, 100, 201). It is simply a matter of definition. Either one accepts his definitions, or one resigns from moral, that is, from evaluative discussion.[40] If one abides by the rules set up by Hare and thus enters the arena of values, he can only disagree with Hare's conclusion at the cost of bearing the mark of a fanatic. With Hare it is double or nothing.

The Fact-Value Nexus

But, despite the shine of many such triumphs, they become tarnished when it strikes one that Hare's apparatus is unable to arrange a solution in the key instances. Not that this has impaired his loyalty to the schema. Thus, just as his predecessors, Hare is baffled as to the precise nature of the descriptive-evaluative relation, It seems to be "some close logical connexion" (*LM*, 111) and that is all we ever learn. A similar problem arises when he wonders in what sense "ought" implies "can." It cannot be "logical entailment. It is a weaker relation" (*FR*, 53, 54). But what exactly?[41] Hare tries to deal with the problem by discussing the relationship of descriptive and evaluative statements. But here too the same maddening situation repeats itself — with a difference.

---

[40] Hare points out that "not all moral judgements are value-judgements" (*FR*, 26-27). Thus, evaluative is the exact word. However, perhaps because he feels one can usually ignore non-evaluative moral judgments, he often discusses as if "evaluative" and "moral" can be employed interchangeably.

[41] Hare is content to point out that it is a relation "analogous to that which Mr. Strawson has claimed to exist between the statement that the King of France is wise, and the statement that there is a King of France. If there is no King of France, then the question whether the King of France is wise does not arise" (*FR*, 54). Cf. P. F. Strawson, "On Referring," *Mind* LIX (1950), p. 330.

There is no need for a Toulmin-like evaluative inference. The ordinary rules of deductive inference suffice (be it by "linear" or "exploratory" reasoning). Yet one may not speak of "entailment" between the facts (minor premise) and the value judgment. This would be (a variation of) Naturalism. If, however, the factual premise is *accompanied by* a major premise, a value judgment follows by entailment. The "key" to the secret has, obviously, to do with the major premise. If the standard involved is merely a generalized factual hypothesis, Hare has trespassed his cardinal rule that no evaluative conclusion may be deduced validly from factual premises. Thus, it is clear that the principle invoked must itself be a universal moral standard. The fact-value contact itself seems to be sparked off in the decision to choose such-and-such a principle. All depends on what standards are called into play, what principles are embraced. If one does not adopt in each instance a certain moral principle, the moral conclusion misfires.

As we have already taken notice, by substituting a type of "exploratory" reasoning à la Popper for the "straight-line" type which he favored in *Language of Morals*, Hare in his latest book hopes to play down the arbitrary ring which this emphasis on decision sounds. He stresses the rationality of the decision-making process which is required before an inclination-based prescriptive can be awarded the status of a moral judgment. Whereas in his earlier work the fact-value nexus appeared more or less irrational, sparked off in a decision of principle, Hare now affirms that a factual state of affairs or human inclinations (actually, certain *facts* about the subject) can only lead to a value judgment by passing through the logical sieve of universalizability. Whereas straight-line reasoning processes too easily fostered the impression that logic comes in only *subsequent* to the decision of principle, and thus after the damage has already been done, exploratory type reasoning provides Hare with the elbow room to argue that logical (i.e. rational) considerations play a decisive role in determining what moral decisions are taken, what commitments are entered upon and thus in bridging the fact-value or inclination-value gap.

The matter is most intricate. Although logic (in the shape of universalizability and prescriptivity) is required to lead to a fact-value connection (and thus the connection has its logical aspect), at the same time this logical element cannot be so strong (read: analytic) that in the naturalistic spirit moral decisions flow immediately out of subjective inclinations (and thus the connection clearly has non-logical facets). In order to maintain his anti-naturalist stance in which values are not blown-up facts, Hare must at the crucial moment, be it only a moment, have resource to a non-logical "jump" which "connects" facts and values. Although the jump, he calls it "sincere assent," commitment or choice only occurs in connection with and according to the rules of a sophisticated logical apparatus, it is at heart non-logical and thus beyond logical grasp.

Thus at the same time, even as in his earlier work, he is insistent that a value judgment is not logically deduced from a statement of fact about a person's inclinations.

It is not a question of a factual statement about a person's inclinations being inconsistent with a moral judgement; rather, his inclinations being what they are, he cannot assent sincerely to a certain singular prescription, and if he cannot do this, he cannot assent to a certain universal prescription which entails it, when conjoined with factual statements about the circumstances whose truth he admits. Because of this entailment, if he assented to the factual statements and to the universal prescription, but refused (as he must, his inclinations being what they are) to assent to the singular prescription, he would be guilty of a logical inconsistency. (*FR*, 109)

That is to say, the all-important, all-decisive constituent of moral argument; viz. inclinations, does not have a place in the logical syllogism as such. It does its work alongside, under, prior to and concurrent with logical calculation. Inclinations dictate what one can assent to or dissent from. Then, and only then, does the logical computation begin: certain combinations of prescriptions are reckoned to be logically consistent or inconsistent with the original choice. Thus the "can's" and "cannot's" involved in any statement of the form "His inclinations being what they are, he can (cannot) assent sincerely to a certain singular prescription" are *not* logical in nature (cf. *FR*, 111, 193). Logical "cannot's" enter in when one proceeds to adopt other prescriptions inconsistent with the first one. Although logic filters out, so to speak, inclination-based prescriptions which do not measure up as moral judgments, logic does not by itself establish the connection. Apparently, if one is persistent as well as logically consistent, any inclination-statement, no matter how perverse, can be turned into a moral judgment. In the final analysis choice or commitment is the crucial factor. The act of choosing is the catalytic chamber in which the fact-value coalescence takes place. Logic is the catalyst required to ensure the success of the reaction. "Assent," to change the figure, operates as a blind behind which "is" pulls off an identity change reappearing as "ought." How any factual-statement which has undergone the universalizability treatment can suddenly take on normative character is a never explained secret. It just does!

Is it any wonder that Hare's critics have murmured that any connection which hangs by the thin thread of personal decision is not worthy of the name "logical" and is to say the least fragile, enigmatic and unreliable. Dangling everything on the peg of personal decision endangers the very "rationality" which Hare has won for ethics. He ends up ensnared in the same quicksand of irrationality as Stevenson, albeit along more "rational" roads. And is there not a notable similarity, despite the obvious disparity, between Hare's contention that logical deduction is only possible in ethics *after* a moral choice is taken and Toulmin's view that a moral principle functions simultaneously as a logical rule of inference?

The fact that Hare has seen the more-than-logical character of decision is

133

itself most praiseworthy. At this point, however, it is our concern to point out that despite his insistence on this matter, at the same time he does everything in his power to minimize the decisive importance of the non-logical. Thus, for example, he endeavours to logicize the non-logical element of "assent" by reading it into the very definition of the logical notions of analyticity and entailment. "A sentence is analytic if, and only if, either (1) the fact that a person dissents from it is a sufficient criterion for saying that he has misunderstood the speaker's meaning or (2) it is entailed by some sentence which is analytic in sense (1)" (*LM*, 41-42). "A sentence P entails a sentence Q if and only if the fact that a person assents to P but dissents from Q is a sufficient criterion for saying that he has misunderstood one or other of the sentences" (*LM*, 25).

This ambivalent, dialectic movement reappears throughout Hare's views. Although he rightly aspires to hold fast the more-than-logical character of ethics, having absolutized logic, he is constantly induced to yield that claim. The result is that one never quite knows where he is. One is tossed back and forth, so to speak, between the Scylla of reason and the Charybdis of freedom. Rather than deflating or defusing the antinomy between freedom (value judgments, decision, prescriptivity) and reason (facts, inclination, logic, universalizability) he only succeeds in exposing the deep-rooted, recurrent dialectic of the *antinomy*.

Ethics as Morally Neutral

According to Hare ethics is both morally neutral and a powerful tool in healing moral disputes. This remarkable double-edged claim deserves our close attention. The first feature which calls for discussion is the fact that, despite subtle pretensions to the contrary, the thesis of universalizability is impotent *by itself* in producing moral agreement. Hare must admit this. Without "another factor . . . the logical requirement of universalizability cannot, as we might say, get a hold on the questions. . . . This other factor is the bearing of a question on another person's interests. If this is lacking (if, that is to say, no other person's interests are involved) universalizability cannot by itself generate golden-rule arguments" (*FR*, 138-39). When this interest-factor is ignored, as for example, by non-utilitarian idealists, moral reasoning is not only ineffectual, it is impossible.

Why is Hare nevertheless able to claim that his logical thesis is an "immensely powerful engine for producing moral agreement"? He can say this with apparent impunity because "people's inclinations about most of the important matters in life tend to be the same (very few people, for example, like being starved or run over by motor-cars)" (*FR*, 97). Even when differences turn up, they can be smoothed over if the contesting parties agree — and only fanatics refuse — to consider the interests of others. All clear-headed, clear-thinking individuals will always push aside any urge "to prescribe universally that people's likes and dislikes should be disregarded by other people, because this would entail prescribing that other people should disregard his own likes and dislikes" (FR, 113). It is this (almost) universal unanimity which enables Hare to keep the spotlight on the logical thesis.

The consensus is so self-evident that one tends to overlook its crucial role. Not Hare: he is most conscious of the impotence of the logical thesis apart from the interest-consensus. In fact, he tends to telescope the logical argument and the interest-consensus into one factor. It is, he claims, a "logical consequence of universalizability when coupled with prescriptivity . . . [that] we have to allow our choices to be circumscribed by the desires of other people" (FR, 195). Or again, the principle that "everyone is entitled to equal consideration . . . is a corollary of the requirement of universalizability. It must be emphasized that it, like the principle of universalizability itself, is a purely formal principle" (FR, 118).

On this basis Hare's conclusion follows: having certain inclinations and interests, one cannot accept certain singular prescriptions which will logically force him to endanger or even sacrifice these interests. As we have already seen, "cannot's" as used in sentences of this form are not logical in nature; it is only subsequent to such a non-logical "cannot" that the vice of logic can begin to squeeze.[42] And since the interests giving rise to the "cannot's" are generally the same, logic can then, but only then, force us to act consistently and thus promote moral agreement. By itself logic is sterile when it comes to producing moral concord; when combined with the interest-consensus it is a powerful tool in generating moral accord. On the one hand, since logically any and every choice is open,[43] Hare is able to boast, "my own theory does not get the content into our moral judgements by verbal legislation; we have to put it in by exploring the logical possibilities" (FR, 195). Ethical science is morally neutral. A moment later, trading on the "fortunate, contingent fact" (FR, 172) of the interest-consensus, he is able, on the other hand, to acclaim ethics as an indispensable panacea in healing the besetting ills of humanity. Ethics is thus, in spite of its neutrality, morally relevant.

The surprising role once again played by inclinations in Hare's view induces us to fix our attention somewhat longer on this matter. The first facet which strikes one is the sharp contrast maintained by Hare between "interests" and "ideals." Since, in contrast to interests and inclinations, ideals are not open to the universalizability argument (they are already by definition universalized),

---

[42] "Universalized self-interest . . . is the foundation of the argument that we have been considering" (FR, 105).
[43] "It is, indeed, in the logical possibility of wanting anything (neutrally described) that the 'freedom' which is alluded to in my title essentially consists" (FR, 110).

they cannot be argued (*FR*, 155-56). This conclusion, in view of the diversity and importance of ideals or pre-eminent goods, as Hare defines them (*FR*, 159), is most revealing, and that in at least two respects. First of all, one now begins to understand how Hare can talk about an almost universal consensus of interests. He simply (?) calls the "higher interests" about which there is obviously a much greater diversity, "ideals." At this point, he insufficiently takes into consideration that ideals *dictate* interests and set up a hierarchy of preferences. And is not the pursuit of ideals one of our most important interests. Secondly, this discovery casts a shadow over the entire moral enterprise as conceived by Hare. We are left with a strange situation. Moral argument is possible and meaningful as long as there is a sharing of interests (or a common desire to consider the interests of others): both parties are open to logical raps on the knuckles for their inconsistencies. But, if this shared stance is non-existent, if an ideal is pursued to the uttermost, no argument is possible.

However for Hare the express purpose of moral argument is the reconciliation of dissenting parties. Clarification, airing-out, perhaps arbitration is the required remedy for those muddle-headed enough to be at odds when they basically agree. Here Hare's method is relevant. But is not "misunderstanding" rather than "argument" the more appropriate word in such circumstances? He is left with the following paradox: When argument is possible, it is more or less superfluous, the dissenting parties are discovered to have always been in basic agreement. When argument is necessary, it is impossible, logically no reproof is possible to either of two individuals who pursue antithetical ideals.

There is likewise a deep note of irony in the fact that moral argument has essentially to do with such non-evaluative matters as interests, universalizability, reasons; all topics which as such have little to do with what is considered morality in the proper sense of the word. Ideals, prescriptivity, freedom make up the essence of morality; but they are beyond the pull of reason (except for their tenuous, unexplainable contiguity with factual concerns).

It is time to conclude the discussion. In the first place it has become increasingly clear that adopting Hare's ethical stance involves choosing with him for a definite ethical bias. Universalizability functions not only as a logical thesis morally antiseptic, but when linked up with the interest-consensus it is the epitomy of a definite moral stance[44]. Only a person of a "utilitarian"-stripe or, shunning labels, one who affirms the principle of equal consideration as the

---

[44] Alan Montefiore in his perceptive essay "Fact, Value and Ideology" (in *British Analytic Philosophy*, ed. Williams and Montefiore, 1966) makes a similar observation. The enigma emerging from *The Language of Morals* is for Montefiore "the problem of an 'evaluative' or 'ideological' position so embedded within the framework of a language that it may perhaps resist even the most emphatic and explicit of disavowals," (p. 190; also 186). The whole essay is, in fact, a good example of the increased concern in analytic circles for what can be called the more basic issues.

highest ideal is *in principle* able to accept Hare's position. And even such enthusiasts, as our discussion has intimated, have their scruples.

Are all interests of equal weight, and thus worthy of equal consideration? Obviously not; but whose "scale of values" is to be employed as *normative* in settling disputes? And on whose authority normative? For Hare principles which "cannot be overridden" are worthy of the name "moral" (*FR*, 169). But this approach is of little help as long as further "material" specification of "moral" goes abegging; depending on the ideals adhered to, various principles are wielded as "overriding." Why should one, for example, be tolerant of another's interests if it is in the best interest of that person himself to be in-tolerant? Hare himself sees this as a real possibility, as for example in the case of drug addicts. Disregarding their loud protestations, we restrain them for their own good (*FR*, 174). But when and on whose authorization are such "exceptions" justified? Whose wishes, or which law serves as the final court of appeal? If, as in Hare's view, every man is a "universalizer," that is to say, law-giver, whose prescriptions are to be elevated to the status of the ultimate Answer, the Last Word, the Law?

Although utilitarianism has always been plagued with this question, it pesters Hare with merciless intensity. Due to his boast of neutrality he is prevented from making appeal to the utilitarian principle anything more than "formal" (cf. *FR*, 118ff.).[45] Coupling this with the consideration that each man is his own law-giver or universalizer, he had no choice but, despite his passionate desire to condemn fanatics, to acquit anyone regardless of his activities — with the lone proviso that he must act consistently.[46] He lacks any final ground for condemnation. Insofar as he does issue moral verdicts, he is going beyond his competence as ethicist. In the last analysis, his edifice stands or sinks in the notorious quicksand of "human goodness." Its hope of survival hangs by, certainly for him a frighteningly slender thread, the "fortunate, contingent fact" that the number of hidebound fanatics is minimal. "Men and the world being what they are, we can be very sure that hardly anybody" will choose to follow his own interests at the cost of the interests of others (*FR*, 111).

One last comment — an appreciative tribute: in his stress on and sensitivity for the more-than-factual, more-than-logical character of reality, Hare deserves

[45] As we have already noted, Hare maintains that for the utilitarian both the universalizability theory and the principle of equal consideration are "purely formal" (*FR*, 118). At the same time, the (material) cutting teeth of these principles show themselves when we recall his claim that prescriptions promoted by "substantial inclinations and interests" are only considered *moral* if they are *universalizable*. Judgments which fail to equally consider the interests of others can never enjoy the status of *moral* judgments.

[46] Thus, his decision to call non-utilitarian idealists "fanatics" is within his own viewpoint out of place. At the same time, it clearly illustrates that his position is not as "morally neutral" as he claims.

his leading position in contemporary ethics. In this light one must read our relatively lengthy treatment of his position as an acknowledgement of its importance.

"Contextual Implication": P. H. Nowell-Smith

The novel type of ethicizing exemplified by Urmson, Toulmin and Hare is still in full swing. It has in fact become what could be called "the new orthodoxy." One cannot, nor need he, discuss all the contributions. The most influential works have already been discussed. However, because it is fast becoming one of the classics in the field, more importantly because it announces a "middle way" between Toulmin and Hare, P. H. Nowell-Smith's *Ethics* may not be shunted aside without notice. Since it is, on the basic issues, in agreement with the previously discussed authors, a brief summary of his position will suffice.

In 1954 Nowell-Smith suggested that neither "evaluative inference" à la Toulmin nor strict "entailment" à la Hare characterized the logical relations of value judgments. Translated this means that Nowell-Smith softened the contrast: ethics does not need its own logic (*contra* Toulmin) but neither does it restrict itself to strict logical entailment (*contra* Hare), rather there is a weaker, informal relation which could be termed "contextual implication."[47] "Statement p contextually implies a statement q if anyone who knew the normal conventions of the language would be entitled to infer q from p *in the context in which they occur*" (80). And instead of talking of contradiction, Nowell-Smith speaks of "logical oddness" (in a particular context).

Three rules regulate contextual implication.

Rule 1. When a speaker uses a sentence "to perform any of the . . . jobs for which sentences are used, it is contextually implied that he is using it for one of the jobs that it normally does."

Rule 2. "A speaker contextually implies that he has what he himself believes to be good reasons for his statement."

Rule 3. "What a speaker says may be assumed to be relevant to the interests of the audience." (cf. 81-82)

In spite of its seeming harmlessness, the third is "the most important of the three rules." In effect, it discloses Nowell-Smith's approach to the fact-value problem. The third rule helps us "to show that there is no gap to be bridged because the reason-giving sentence must turn out to be practical from the

---

[47] In "Contextual Implication," *PASS* XXXVI (1962), pp. 1-18. Nowell-Smith has revised his position. Page numbers refer to Nowell-Smith's *Ethics*, 1954 (Paperback Edition).

start and not a statement of fact from which a practical sentence can somehow be deduced" (82-83).[48]

Lacking strict rules of entailment, one judges the validity or invalidity of such contextual implications by presumably practicing the "look and see" method and thereby classifying how people ordinarily react to various conjunctions of judgments, when they believe a certain conjunction "logically odd" and when not. If, for example, I affirm both that "X is wonderful" and "I dislike X," there is evidence of "logical oddity" (not contradiction because in some contexts this conjunction may be perfectly in order). Indeed, it is the task of the moral philosopher "to map the mutual relationships of moral words, sentences and arguments; and this is a task, not of showing how one statement entails or contradicts another, but of showing that in a certain context it would be logically odd to assert one thing and deny another or to ask a particular question" (83).

All this leads Nowell-Smith to conclude that the connection between the different uses of value words ("to express tastes and preferences, to express decisions and choices, to criticize, grade and evaluate, to advise, admonish, warn, persuade, to praise, encourage, and reprove, to promulgate and draw attention to rules; and doubtless for other purposes") is "partly logical and partly a matter of fact; and it is for this reason that, in such cases at least, the analytic-synthetic dichotomy breaks down" (98).

A RETURN TO "NATURALISM"?

The general direction of Anglo-American moral philosophy is clear: away from the so-called "non-cognitivist" denial of truth-claims for ethical utterances towards a recognition of the logical foundations for any and all ethical utterances. But there is no consensus as to how this is to be accomplished and explained. Hare's work is generally and justifiably accorded the deep respect which is its due. Nevertheless, there is at the same time a smouldering layer of discontent at the current state of affairs in ethics. There is a general, inexpressible suspicion that everything is not well. Hare's position, it is granted, may be invincible under attack, but the victories often have a thin, logical ring.

---

[48] Thus, Nowell-Smith emphatically rejects the idea that value judgments follow logically from descriptive statements (cf. 37, 181). Nevertheless, a quasi-logical link, due to contextual implication, remains. Nowell-Smith is hard put, just as his fellows, to say more than that. But he, even more than Hare and Toulmin for example, has a problem: if contextual implications hold because of certain "empirical facts," e.g. when people hear this or that, they react in certain ways, how can he avoid raising "facts" to the level of "values" (read: norms). Does not, in other words, the doctrine of contextual implication challenge, rather than presuppose the fact-value dichotomy?

139

In this rapidly evolving situation drawing conclusions or issuing predictions is a hazardous venture. Nevertheless, we may take note of a number of features which come to the fore with greater or lesser intensity.

(1) The more or less conscious restriction of ethics to an analysis of ethical words is fast terminating in a blind alley of endlessly multiplying sub-distinctions and "senses."

(2) In the process of retreating into such linguistic vacuums, ethics has systematically severed its connection with the concrete moral realities of the world at large. In reaction the present tendency, fast becoming fashion, is to demonstrate the practical implications of ethical theory.

(3) The growing concern for the logical foundations of ethical judgments is now being accompanied with the suggestion that it may be proper and even necessary to begin speaking (again) of ethical statements as valid, true, and correct. But this stress on the logic of moral reasoning threatens to endanger the major thesis that ethical statements are not primarily cognitive.

(4) How must one relate and integrate the factual and the valuational? If the factual begins to devour the valuational, "scientific objectivity" is (re)gained at the cost of a fall into Naturalism. If the valuational goes its own way, the "autonomy" of ethics is saved at the cost of "objectivity." But how to strike the proper balance?

(5) Not every reason which is *logically* "good" is *morally* "good." Meta-ethics requires rules to determine such matters. But where must they come from? Will their presence not pollute the morally antisceptic categories of meta-ethics? Are such rules objectively, that is factually ascertainable, or are they the results of personal, subjective decisions? And, just what is a *moral* rule?

It is especially around this last complex, in which all the problems come to a head, that the current controversy whirls. A burgeoning group of philosophers cannot reconcile themselves to Hare's judgment that "a permanent radical moral disagreement" is a possibility with which we have to live. Despite the worth of Hare's service in clearing a place for reason in ethics, he turns around, they argue, and sells out to irrationalism by declaring that the rightness of a judgment depends ultimately on what principles *one chooses* to accept. This amounts to suicide — against the onslaught of fanatics we are left without a weapon in our ethical arsenal. *My* reasons are not *per se* reasons *for him*. If he chooses to ignore them, they are in fact *not* reasons for him. But, fulminates this group, is that the end of the matter? There must be more "certainty," more "objectivity." One reason is morally wrong *simpliciter*, the other is morally right *simpliciter*.

Thus, for example, "spectator" theories have developed (and are developing) which, lacking any reference to a particular person and place as well as to the existence of actual persons, attempt to regain "objectivity" for ethical judgments.[49] "X is right" means that an *ideal* spectator would approve X.[50]

"X is better than Y" means "If anyone were, in respect of X and Y, fully informed and vividly imaginative, impartial, in a calm frame of mind and otherwise normal, he would *prefer* X to Y."[51] R. B. Brandt has further devised a "general rule or directive that has the same status in ethics, as a rule of induction has for empirical science." According to this view, ethical thinking is a complex interplay in which 1) appeal is made to principles and attitudes, 2) principles are corrected and filled in on the basis of "criticized" attitudes, 3) judgments are tested by the demands of consistency and generalizability, 4) attitudes are criticized and discounted if not impartial, informed, the product of a normal state of mind, or compatible with having a consistent set of general principles not excessively complex. From this testing procedure — the Qualified Attitude Method which is a "definite account of how exactly we do or should go about answering ethical questions" — emerges the principle "Assert an ethical proposition if and only if it satisfies the conditions of the Qualified Attitude Method."[52]

A New Naturalism: Philippa Foot

In addition to the lively on-going efforts to reinforce or modify current meta-ethical theories, there are rapidly gathering signs that moral philosophy is once again to be shaken by a new tidal wave which could be described as a "new naturalism." In retrospect the initial indications that such a storm was in the offing appeared in 1958. In that year with a frankness all her own, the Oxford

[49] Hare has recently pointed to the affinity of these theories (as well as the differences) with his own theory (cf. *FR*. 94-95). He appends the note that "since for many Christians God occupies the role of 'ideal observer', the moral judgements which they make may be expected to coincide with those arrived at by the method of reasoning which I am advocating."

[50] For example, R. Firth, "Ethical Absolutism, and the Ideal Observer," *Philosophy and Phenomenological Research* XII (1952); F. C. Sharp, "Voluntarism and Objectivity in Ethics," *PR* L (1941); W. Kneale, "Objectivity in Ethics," *P* XXV (1950), reprinted in W. Sellars and J. Hospers, *Readings in Ethical Theory* (1952); J. Harrison, "When is a Principle a Moral Principle?" *PASS* XXVIII (1954); R. B. Brandt, *Ethical Theory* (1959), pp. 173-76; 264-65.

[51] R. B. Brandt, due to the absolutist tinge (if *anyone* were . . .), has projected a relativistic version which he calls "quasi-naturalist" (cf. Brandt, *op. cit.*). W. K. Frankena inclines towards a "noncognitivist" version (cf. "Ethical Theory," *Philosophy* 1964, and Brandt, *op. cit.*, p. 229).

[52] Brandt, *op. cit.*, pp. 250-52; 267. An influential American theologian-ethicist, Paul Lehmann has enthusiastically acclaimed Brandt's method "an achievement of no small gain to ethical theory." It "does in fact bridge the gap between fact and value, between empiricism (naturalism) and formalism (rationalism) in ethical theory" (cf. *Ethics in A Christian Context* 1963, pp. 234-35).

philosopher G. E. Anscombe judged that modern moral philosophy was, to put it mildly, a profitless venture. She consequently advised an enforced layoff for all ethicists until an adeqate philosophy of psychology (furnishing "an account of human nature, human action, the type of characteristic a virtue is, and above all of human 'flourishing'") was developed. Further, she recommended jettisoning the concept of a special *moral* sense of "ought." All that is mandatory is an ordinary sense of ought: just as a machine "needs" oil or "ought to be" oiled, a man "needs" or "ought to be" honest.[53]

In the same year another Oxford philosopher, also a member of the fairer sex, Philippa Foot published the first of a series of influential articles which sparked off a new round of debate on the is-ought, fact-value dichotomy.[54] Up to that time, following the lead of Moore, the great majority of ethical philosopher's had assumed the logical impossibility of deducing "ought" from "is."[55] Suddenly it is once more the center of debate.

Foot's attack on the is-ought distinction is (at least began) indirect(ly). It springs from her concern with a matter to which we have already called attention: the "breakdown" of moral arguments into a confrontation between two mutually-opposed *decisions* in which further discussion is excluded. This, so she reasons, simply cannot be, it is not the state of affairs in reality. "A man can no more decide for himself what is evidence for rightness and wrongness than he can decide what is evidence for monetary inflation or a tumor on the brain."[56]

Since a man cannot pick and choose which facts are relevant to a moral conclusion, there must be a logical connection between factual and evaluative judgments. Such a clear-cut hook-up has, Mrs. Foot is aware, been declared illicit. But "it has not even been proved that moral conclusions cannot be

---

[53] G. E. M. Anscombe, "Modern Moral Philosophy," *Philosophy* XXXIII (1958), pp. 1-19. Cf. also, Peter Geach, "Good and Evil," *Analysis* VII (1956-57), pp. 33-42.
[54] "Moral Arguments," *Mind* LXVII (1958), pp. 502-13; "Moral Beliefs," *PAS* LIX (1959), pp. 83-104; "Goodness and Choice," *PASS* XXXV (1961), pp. 45-61.
[55] This is not in the least to deny that individual modern philosophers have propounded a naturalistic theory of value. To cite a number of the more important volumes: Edward Westermarck, *The Origin and Development of the Moral Ideas* Vols. I-II (1906); *Ethical Relativity* (1932) (cf. Moore, *PS*, 332ff.); Ralph Barton Perry, *General Theory of Value* (1926), *Realms of Value* (1954); W. T. Stace, *The Concept of Morals* (1937); John Dewey, *Theory of Valuation* (1939); C. I. Lewis, *An Analysis of Knowledge and Valuation* (1946); A. G. Garnett, *The Moral Nature of Man* (1952); Bertrand Russell, *Human Society in Ethics and Politics* (1955); P. B. Rice, *On the Knowledge of Good and Evil* (1955); D. H. Parker, *Philosophy of Value* (1957); S. C. Pepper, *Sources of Value* (1958); P. Ziff, *Semantic Analysis* (1960); S. Zink, *The Concepts of Ethics* (1962).
[56] Foot, "Moral Arguments," *Mind* LXVII (1958), p. 505. Here it is clear that Mrs. Foot has hit upon a sore point in the "subjectivist" position. The question is, however, if it is anymore feasible to go the opposite extreme of viewing reasons as objective, universally-valid, same-for-everyone facts.

entailed by factual or descriptive premises." To cite an example, if a man is prepared to discuss questions of "rudeness," then he must accept the evaluative conclusion that "X is rude" if the factual premise "X fulfills the criteria for rudeness" is proven. So doing we have moved from a factual to an evaluative statement.

Analogously, once the criteria of morality are accepted, all moral disputes can be objectively settled. One can, of course, refuse to accept such criteria, but only at the cost of placing himself "outside the pale of moral discussion." Such a person must "abjure altogether the use of moral terms."[57]

In all her writings Foot struggles to enmesh the "content" of morality. Although her (fishing) expeditions have only really begun, at this stage she suggests that there is an intimate connection between the content of morality and factually verifiable "human good or harm."

The Content of Morals: G. Warnock

The most recent and perhaps the most striking evidence that a new wave is about to break (or is breaking) is G. Warnock's *Contemporary Moral Philosophy*.[58] Convinced that modern moral philosophy is derailed, his monograph contains the first rough instructions about how to get it on the right track. "Intuitionism, to begin with, emptied moral theory of all content by making the whole topic undiscussably *sui generis*." The emotivist "had nothing to say on what moral judgments are, or say, or mean: he was interested only and somewhat crudely, in what they are *for*." And even prescriptivism "stopped short of considering what such utterances actually say, what they mean, what sorts of grounds can be urged for or against them." He concludes that "all that is of distinctively moral interest" has been out of view, "or at least at the margin of attention" (2, 3).

As a cure-all for this grave short-coming, Warnock sees only one possibility: *back to the content of morals* (48 ff.; 75 ff.). Morality ought to be characterized "by its subject-matter — the idea that what makes a view a *moral* view is, ... primarily its content, what it is about, the range or type of considerations on which it is founded" (54). In the same way the complex of questions revolving around the matter of moral argument "needs to be discussed in substance, not in form; for there is nothing formally peculiar in, or distinctive of, argument in morals; if there are special features here, as quite probably there are, I would suppose them to be founded in what argument in morals is *about*" (76).

[57] *Ibid.*, pp. 510-11.
[58] G. Warnock, *Contemporary Moral Philosophy* (1967) (page numbers refer to this work). For Hare's critical reaction, cf. his review, *Mind* LXXVII (1968), p. 436ff. The thrust of Mary Warnock's concluding chapter of *Ethics Since* 1900 (1960) adumbrates her husband's position. She judges that an "obsessive fear of naturalism" has led to the "trivializing of the subject." Ethics "as a serious subject has been left further and further behind" (p. 203-04).

The quandary in which ethics presently finds itself is directly traceable to the fact "when we talk about 'morals' we do *not* all know what we mean" (75). With the hope of offering a way out, Warnock suggests that moral "judgment is concerned by definition or *ex officio*, in one way or another, with human good or harm, needs, wants, interests, or happiness" (61). It is just at this point that he reveals himself as the champion of what I have termed "New Naturalism."

It is true, and ought to be mentioned, that Warnock does not in one respect question the logical independence of evaluation and description. He grants that there are no moral standards which must logically be accepted by anyone who describes the world in a certain way. But, and this is the heart of the question for Warnock, *if* one claims to be judging "from the moral point of view," he is duty-bound to accept certain necessary standards of *moral* evaluation. Thus, "certain kinds of facts or features are necessarily relevant criteria of moral evaluation"; from these facts, in Warnock's case facts about people's needs and interests, happiness and wants, one can deduce a particular moral judgment (cf. 66-68).

The Practical Syllogism: G. H. von Wright

In view of our special interest in the fact-value relation, it is well that we take note of the work of George Henrik von Wright. A logician of renown, von Wright has provided in his 1960 Gifford Lectures a book-length embodiment of an ethical position which serves as a foretaste of what can be expected to appear under the influence of the revived naturalistic spirit.[59] There are, von Wright is confident, many *Varieties of Goodness*, instrumental, technical, utilitarian, medical, hedonic etc. The so-called *moral* sense of "good" is, however, at best a derivative and secondary sense explainable in the "terms of non-moral uses of the word" (1). (The same holds true for the *moral* sense of "ought" and "duty".) Moral goodness is

the sub-form of utilitarian goodness which we have called the beneficial. To put my main idea very crudely: Whether an act is morally good or bad depends upon its character of being beneficial or harmful, i.e. depends upon the way in which it affects the good of various beings. (119)

In effect, and this is more explicit as the exposition unfolds, von Wright denies that value concepts are intrinsically normative (cf. ch. 8).[60] Only norms (in distinction from values), be it as commands, as "deontic" rules ("ought to,"

[59] George Henrik von Wright, *The Varieties of Goodness* (1963) (page numbers refer to this work). Cf. also Anscombe on the Aristotelian doctrine of the "practical syllogism" (*Intention*, 1957).
[60] The contrast with Hare is obvious. Value-statements are no longer normative, but are in a class with statements expressing wants and inclinations.

"may," "must not"), or as "anakastic" practical necessities ("must," "need not," "has to," "cannot"), are prescriptive for human actions.

From a *want-statement* (equivalent for von Wright with a "good" or "value"-statement) combined with a statement of *natural necessity*, von Wright arrives at a normative statement of *practical necessity*. "In this way norms may be said to 'hook on' to values" (176).

You want q.
Unless you do p, you will not get q.
∴ you must do p. (161)

Such practical syllogisms, as von Wright calls them, are logically conclusive in spite of their failure to conform to the patterns sanctioned by the rules of "ordinary logic." Indeed, they require a logical theory all their own (cf. 161-62; 167-71).[61]

The Swing to Content and Institutional Facts

Three comments are in order in regard to this latest shift. Leaving aside for the present the inadequate as well as misleading character of the terminology, the general swing from the "form" to the "content" of morality is both understandable and laudable. However, the effort to designate the content in terms such as "human happiness, interests, needs, wants or desires" or the like is less promising. Does not everything in creation have something, be it more or less, to do with human interests, wants or happiness? A more precise marking-out is certainly required. Neither does it help, in the fashion of philosophers as Baier,[62] to delimit the range by reserving the accolade of morality for altruistic measures (as over against egotistical ones) or for beneficial (and not harmful) interests. In such a setup, it is no longer possible to talk of an *im*moral act. That which is moral is by that token alone good. By the same token the suggestion is unavoidable that the non-moral or *a*moral is evil. But is this the state of affairs one meets in reality?[63] Moreover, by what criteria shall such awards be made? Each man, consonant with *his* own stance, will judge this or that to be in *fact* a good interest. The verdicts

---

[61] Von Wright has indeed projected a special "logic of norms" dealing with patterns of reasoning in which *both* premises and conclusions are norms called Deontic Logic (cf. "Deontic Logic," *Mind* LXII 1953 and especially his 1959 Gifford Lectures *Norm and Action: A Logical Enquiry* 1963). He has not, to my knowledge, worked out a theory treating patterns of the kind we are primarily interested in, patterns in which "one normative and one factual premise yield a normative conclusion" (162). Cf. also Alf Ross, *Directives and Norms* (1968).

[62] K. Baier, *The Moral Point of View* (1958), chs. 7 & 8.

[63] Cf. further discussion, pp. 201-04.

will not always, to say it mildly, coincide. Warnock, Foot *et al.* must stipulate in detail the content of "human good and harm." Is it possible, as they suggest, that this is a matter about which everyone will (in principle) agree — and thus considered, be a matter of fact.

Our second comment simply calls attention to the fact that these views resemble in basic respects those castigated by Moore as fallacious and untenable. Once again philosophers are boldly claiming to move logically from factual premises to evaluative conclusions. In the current discussion on this matter,[64] there is especially one novel twist which deserves attention. One distinguishes "brute" and "institutional facts."

A man hits a home run only given the institution of baseball; without the institution he only hits a sphere with a stick. Similarly, a man gets married or makes a promise only within the institutions of marriage and promising. Without them, all he does is utter words or makes gestures. . . . that a man has a bit of paper with green ink on it is a brute fact, that he has five dollars is an institutional fact.[65]

Institutions are systems of constitutive rules, rules which "constitute (and also regulate) forms of activity whose existence is logically dependent on the rules." Within systems of constitutive rules involving obligations, commitments, rights and responsibilities, one can derive "ought's" from "is's." By invoking the institution of promising, I can, for example, move from the factual statement that "Jones uttered the words, 'I hereby promise to pay you, Smith, five dollars'" to the evaluative judgment that "Jones ought to pay Smith five dollars."[66]

[64] R. F. Atkinson, and A. C. Montefiore, "'Ought' and 'Is'," *P* XXXIII (1958); J. R. Searle, "How to Derive 'Ought' from 'Is', *PR* LXXIII (1964); A. Flew, "On not Deriving 'Ought' from 'Is'," *Analysis* XXIV (1963-4); Max Black, "The Gap between 'Is' and 'Should'," *PR* (1964); W. D. Hudson, "The 'Is-Ought' Controversy," *Analysis* XXV (1964-5); James & Judith Thomson, "How Not to Derive 'Ought' from 'Is'," *PR* LXXIII (1964); A. C. MacIntyre, "Hume on 'Is' and 'Ought'," *PR* LXVIII (1959). Mendel F. Cohen, "'Is' and 'Should': An unbridged Gap," *PR* LXXIV (1965); R. Montague, "'Is' to 'Ought'", *Analysis* XXXI (1965-66).
[65] J. R. Searle, "How to Derive 'Ought' from 'Is'," *PR* LXXIII (1964), pp. 54, 55. Prof. Hare devoted his 1963 British Academy Lecture to a refutation of this revived Naturalism, or "Descriptivism" as he prefers to dub it. Cf. "Descriptivism," *The Proceedings of the British Academy* XLIX (1963), pp. 115-34.
[66] J. L. Austin was perhaps the first to call attention to the state of affairs now covered by the term "institution." He stressed that in the case of performatives "the *circumstances* in which the words are uttered should be in some way, or ways, *appropriate*." If the circumstances are not in order, the uttering of a performative is a "misinvocation" and the act is disallowed. Cf. *How To Do Things With Words*, p. 8, 15 ff. On "brute facts," cf. G. E. M. Anscombe, "Brute Facts," *Analysis* XVIII (1958). Mrs. Foot has also called attention to the supreme significance of the "background" in ethical theory. According to her, the characteristic mark of morality cannot be located in the subject, whether in a pro-attitude or a prescriptive act, rather a certain conceptual background is necessary in order to know the meaning of calling something a moral principle. Cf. "When is a Principle a Moral Principle," *PASS* XXVIII (1954).

146

Other philosophers have been quick to retort that since such institutional facts are parasitic on the notion of standards or norms, there is no simple passage from facts to moral conclusions.[67] Searle, himself, recognizes the problems involved: the word "promise" is at the same time evaluative and purely descriptive. He concludes that the whole distinction between description and evaluation needs to be "re-examined."

At the same time, and this is our third comment, it is necessary to notice that this renascent Naturalism differs in important respects from its earlier form. It clearly bears typical mid-twentieth century traits. The emphasis is no longer, as it was with pre-Moorean Naturalism, to capture or map out reality *logically*. In the earlier period the world was "out there," in front, as something to dominate and exploit, as yet another challenge by which man could exercise and prove his mastery. In this situation Moore protested that a certain area (values) was logically inaccessible. At present the burgeoning Naturalism is of a different spirit, less concerned to put it crudely with the logic of the matter. Chastened by the turns of world history, faced with rapid social change and the irrationality characteristic of our times, it throws itself on primordial facticity as a universally-given foundation and resting-place. In contrast to existentialism which considers facticity, as a component of human existence, a threat to that very existence which must be put down, this new Naturalism accepts the givenness of facticity as something on which it can count, as something about which it need not worry. It aspires to employ this rudimentary layer as a platform from off which imaginative projects can be launched and to which one can always return in adversity. Whereas the "old" Naturalism was a

[67] For example, D. Phillips and H. O. Mounce, "On Morality's Having a Point," *P* XL (1965), p. 311. Also, D. Phillips, "Does it Pay to Be Good," *PAS* LXV (1964-65). Morton White, the noted exponent of "reunion" between neo-positivism and pragmatism, agrees that the deduction of "ought" from "is" can only be accomplished *via* reference to moral principles. The question for him, however, is whether it is possible to exclude moral principles from the category termed *factual* statements. Can one, he asks, even distinguish a so-called factual principle and a moral principle? White ends by affirming a one-hopper beyond-all-isms theory which involves "a breakdown of the epistemological differences between the logical, the physical, and the ethical ... a breakdown of the semantic walls between the analytic, the synthetic and the emotive" (*Toward Reunion in Philosophy* 1956, ch. 14, especially pp. 251, 257, 263). Dorothy Emmet, a noted devotee of Whitehead, is also convinced that "we must accept the logical rule that no obligation is deducible from mere facts." At the same time, she adds "but facts are seldom 'mere' when they are facts of social situations." She suggests that in the notion of role – "a role is a relationship of a recognized kind within a given society, with some notion of the kind of conduct appropriate to it built into its description" – provides a "link between the factual descriptions of social situations, and the moral decisions about what ought to be done in them. It has, so to speak, a foot in both camps." The facts of social situations are "already charged with the norms of roles as established within a social tradition" (*Facts and Obligations* 1958, pp. 20, 8, 10, 11).

147

rationalistic positivism, the "new" Naturalism is irrationalistic neo-positivism with pragmatistic overtones.

Moore and Deontologism

A. To deliver ethics from the bondage of "Naturalism" and other "metaphysical" systems, Moore posits the independent, absolute and objective occurrence or subsistence of values in respect to both (subjective) Mind and (factual) Matter. Ethics is an autonomous and objective science.

B. Threatened by the clear and present danger that absolute (*absolvere*) values, cut-off from the natural world of things, not only appear anarchistic, licentious, and capricious, but are also sterile, emasculated and impotent, Moore hedges on their autonomous nature by promulgating a *necessary, unconditional* conjunction between objective values and objective natural facts.

Emotivism

A. Under the sway of Moore, Ayer agrees that values are not facts. At the same time brandishing the verification theory of meaning, he robs them of all pretensions to objective existence, exposing values as psychosomatic ejaculations deprived of all factual content and thus meaningless for scientific knowledge. Devoured by psychology and sociology, ethics is banished from the ranks of the sciences.

B. Circumspectly avoiding the pitfalls of Naturalism as well as non-naturalism, Stevenson suggests that value judgments, although primarily emotive in character, also *describe* the attitudes of the speaker and to that extent are "verifiable." This implies that facts can once again function as reasons in support of value preferences (ethical science is once again possible!). However, since such facts serve as valid reasons if and only if they are *psychologically effective*, ethics returns bereft of its (logical) objectivity.

Oxford Meta-Ethics

Armed with the revolutionary insight that value judgments need *not*, at least in the first place, *refer to* anything in order to be scientifically respectable (previous ethicists were bewitched by the descriptive language-model), refreshed with the discovery that words are multi-functional (they are "tools" to be used, rather than "pictures" depicting hidden meanings), largely ignoring the ontological issues involved (one simply has to do with the practical uses of language), the Oxford meta-ethicists set out to rehabilitate ethics as a reputable, autonomous science by making room for factual concerns within the ethical perimeter.

A. Toulmin and Hampshire insist that ethics, in keeping with its *sui generis* character, enjoys a unique, evaluative kind of logical inference from statements of fact to judgments of value. Value judgments can thus be supported by "good" reasons; nevertheless, ethics is clearly autonomous.

B. Taken back by the contention that logical validity is in any way a moral matter, Hare champions a morally-antisceptic ethics subject to the "ordinary" rules of deductive inference. The connection between factual and valuational statements must be made *via* moral "decisions of principle." But having restricted ethics to the logical investigation and control of ethical language, Hare is in the final analysis impotent to judge any decision morally wrong – "fanatics," if they are *logically* consistent, roam the land at will. Ethical science remains, it is true, autonomous over against "Naturalism," but it is exhausted in logico-lingual concerns.

New Naturalism

Stung by the moral emptiness and fleeting objectivity of such formal approaches, Foot and Warnock, among others, desire to restore "content" to ethics and in the process regain "objectivity." To this end they have gone "naturalistic" – value judgments do in fact follow from factual statements concerning human wants and interests. Ethics as a "natural" outgrowth of empirical, factual science forfeits its *sui generis* nature. Values are *in concreto* euphemisms for or extrapolations from factual human needs and wants.

In critique: G. E. Moore

5

In the previous chapter our appraisal of Moore was launched in a rather unusual fashion. Instead of focusing narrowly on Moore's structures, we examined more recent ethical mansions erected, at least in part, to remove the faults and flaws detected in Moore's. This being the case; namely, that the areas of weakness in his ethics have already been duly located and corrective measures instigated, one may be inclined, upon taking in the title of this chapter, to question the necessity as well as the utility of further critique. Nevertheless there would appear to be weighty reasons for taking a long look at Moore. First of all, there is the simple fact that one cannot understand present developments without "knowing" Moore. He is, after all, the "father" of the modern approach. Secondly ethics, to put it bluntly, is caught in an impasse at present. And, as previous discussion made clear, in spite of advance and refinement, the same basic problems that beset him harass his successors. In general they have only been able to avoid his specific errors by leaving themselves embarrassingly exposed on other flanks. In fact, we noted that current ethicists in their search for "rationality" and "objectivity" are unmistakably shifting away from the extremism of Ayer in the direction of Moore. Certain trends have even been signalized warning that re-adjustment may not cease until ethics once again founders in the primordial waters of facticity — a morass reminiscent of the one from which Moore extracted ethics a short sixty years ago.

ETHICS AND ONTOLOGY

The "Is" — "Exists" Tension

On account of the fact that, as we have noted on more than one occasion, Moore's central contention that goodness is non-natural rather than natural is the ethical reflection of a basic ontological pattern in which particulars "exist" and concepts only "are," our critique will win a new depth perspective by beginning with an investigation of the ontological foundations. He adopted

150

this schema in order to be able to avoid both the nearsightedness of Positivism and the speculation native to Metaphysics. For Moore, Positivism, Empiricism and Naturalism are doctrines which, regardless of possible differences among them, are one in their preoccupation with the natural, the empirical, the sense-perceivable. Metaphysics is a pejorative cover-term employed by Moore to express in the first place his rejection of Idealism or any "subjectivistic" theory, but also of a Platonic-type theory with its value-realms or supersensible existents.

Moore endeavours to avert both intoxication with the "subject" as well as submersion in or flight from the natural world. Faced with this praise-worthy but hazardous assignment, he chooses on the one hand for a theory which stresses the mind-independent or extramental character of reality. "It is the very reverse of obvious that there could be no facts in the Universe, if there were no minds in it. And as soon as we realize that 'a truth' is merely another name for a fact, and is something utterly different from a true act of belief, it becomes quite plainly possible that there *could* be truths in the Universe, even if there were no minds in it" (*SMPP*, 298, also 302-03, 370-71). On the other hand — and here because the threat is two-edged, the strategem is complex — he points to the importance of non-natural concepts which enjoy "being" (thus there *is* more than the natural) but not "existence" (thus there is *no* supersensible, extra-cosmic realm).

As can readily be imagined and as we have seen, this ontological schema is not without its tensions. Moore is well aware of the difficulties. In regard to his theory of intrinsic value, he realizes that in distantiating himself from a "*naturalistic* or *positivistic*" theory he will be accused of "erecting into a 'metaphysical' entity of what is really susceptible of a simple naturalistic explanation" (*PS*, 258). This critique is not difficult to understand: how is one to conceive of concepts which "are" but do not "exist." Such concepts cannot for Moore be the fabrications of the subject, but neither can they be the inhabitants of some realm behind, beyond or above reality.

A more general way of expressing the tension in Moore's ontology is to say that he essays to effect a synthesis of what is traditionally known as nominalism and realism. In the "realistic" spirit he makes particular objects dependent on universal concepts in the sense that things are composite-concepts. In the "nominalistic" spirit only existents enjoy real and substantial existence. Although he clearly emphasizes the importance of *universals* and defends their "being" over against all attack, he is adamant in his refusal to grant them any kind of "existence" — not even in a super-sensible realm. It is just *the* mistake of metaphysicians that they "supposed that whatever does not exist in time, must at least *exist* elsewhere, if it is to *be* at all — that whatever does not exist in Nature, must exist in some supersensible reality, whether timeless or not" (*PE*, 111). Concepts have *being* but they lack *existence* of any kind. But if "being" is not just another word denoting existence — and Moore's denial is incapable of misunderstanding at this point — the only alternative would seem to be that concepts must be thought-constructions lacking all ontic pretensions. But if one thing is clear in Moore, it is his concern to point out that concepts are mind-independent. "Being" is obviously an ontic category: But how to conceive of "being" without "existence?" The complication mounts when we recall that all existent objects, particulars and things are composed of non-existent concepts. Whereas in the realm of experience time and existence are primary, the inhabitants of this realm depend on "entities" which enjoy at best a precarious kind of onticity called "being."

In this situation it is not easy to grasp Moore's meaning. It would seem clear, especially when placed against the background of his concern to prevent any enthronement of Pure Will, of God, or of any "subject" (E, 93-94), that he does not conceive of a Platonic Demiurge who "fabricates" objects out of concepts. Nor is there any suggestion that the concepts possess power in themselves to combine into objects. He rejects the evolutionary theory (PS, 256). This being the case, despite the misleading word "composed of," it seems likely that he has in mind (or at least something like) the normative, universally valid, law-character of universals in relation to particulars. Thus, every particular has its universal, i.e. the law which holds for and determines it. And although a particular requires a universal in order to exist, the universal itself cannot exist (it is just existence-determining). But this genuine insight of Moore into what we prefer to call the relation of law-order and the facticity subject to that law is immediately obscured and distorted when these universals are *substantialized* and made to function as the component parts of existents. He dialectically asserts that existent objects are in fact *made up of* non-existent concepts. And this is impossible. Existent objects cannot -- at least without antinomy — have non-existent concepts as their constitutive parts.

Once this road is entered upon; namely, once radical differences in nature are overlooked and that which is law (concept) is treated as if it can also be subject to the law (objects or things), problems multiply. The *correlation* of law and subject[1] devolves antinomiously into identity on the one hand and contra-position on the other. In spite of the fact that things are composites of concepts, concepts become the pendants of things so far above them that there is no contact possible. Meaning-determinig law can no longer order existence. However, contact is required and to mediate the gulf propositions and later facts are introduced by which the *meaning* of things can be known. Propositions are not so much above reality as law, but the screens in front of the viewer from

---

[1] When so employed, "subject" has the meaning of "subject to the law." As such it includes both subjects and objects. Cf. *infra* and Ch. 7, pp. 182-83.

The cogency as well as feasibility of a position holding to a distinction-in-correlation of a law-side and subject- or factual-side is outlined in chapter seven.

off which he can come to know the landscape (things). On the one hand, as a complex of concepts a proposition "is," on the other it mirrors a reality which "exists."

This crucial but ambivalent role is later ascribed to facts. But the basic situation has not changed. Facts have a certain universal validity or law-character (along with universals, facts "are," only things "exist") and at the same time they are inseparably and unmistakably related to "things" (and are generally treated as things, be it of a special kind). The split between being and existence is bridged for Moore in an important sense by facts and propositions. But the situation and the interrelation remains opaque and murky. It could not be otherwise when the law-subject distinction-in-correlation is broken. That which is law cannot at the same time be subject to the law, all dialectical attempts to the contrary. The persistent enigmas surrounding propositions and facts to this day (what are they? do they differ? if so, how do they relate to each other, to persons, to things?) are in a large measure the result of and explainable by their in principle compromising position.[2]

The inherent difficulty given ontological status in Moore's theory which we have just exposed also places his perplexity in relation to synthetic a priori in a wider perspective. In the realm of existent things, Moore ascertains causal necessity between objects and logical (analytic) necessity in the whole-part relation of "containment." But what kind of necessity is involved in the relation of "being" and "reality" as such — how do simple concepts combine to form existent objects?[3] What is the necessity involved in the part-whole relation (*PE*, 29)? Or, as we have discussed, what kind of necessity characterizes the relation between natural things and non-natural values known as supervenience? Moore advocated, we recall, a non-causal, non-logical yet necessary connection; in effect synthetic a priori.

However, since his contemporaries deny the possibility of synthetic a priori, and since, in view of the non-logical element involved, the apprehension of such propositions requires the introduction of the psychological intuition, Moore grows increasingly hesitant. In any case Moore's increasing anxiety throughout his life in respect to the analytic-synthetic problematics can thus be directly related and made parallel to his growing mystification in relation to ontological issues. It is interesting to note that Moore already in his neo-

---

[2] This remains true despite the general rejection of Moore's ontology. A prime example is the recent Austin-Strawson debate as to the nature of truth. Although Austin on the one hand considers facts to be universally valid (as law) in correspondence with which statements are true, he treats them more or less as things. And this ambiguity has furnished Strawson with a reason to deny the existence of facts as entities in the world to which statements correspond differing from things (cf. transcript of debate in *Truth*, ed. Pitcher).

[3] What is clear is that "to exist is merely to stand in a certain logical connexion" (NJ, 183).

153

Idealistic period was plagued with the same problem of connection. To link up the two realms, then called reality and appearance, he required an unusual tie-up neither merely logical nor merely causal; it had to be at the same time both logical *and* existent. He chose for a "synthetic" though logically necessary connection and at the same time cautioned that we cannot understand it "because we have no intelligible intuition" (F, 202; cf. 183).

The Concept "Goodness"

The basic dialectic nature of Moore's ontology receives a new complication when we consider the place of "goodness." The added complexity results, it would seem, from the fact that goodness is a "latecomer" on the ontological stage. Perhaps the best indication of this is Moore's 1899 declaration that "no one concept [is] either more or less an adjective than any other" (NJ, 193) when compared with his 1903 treatment of goodness as a "mere" predicate lacking all claims to substantiality (*PE*, 41).

At the same time this discrepancy serves to warn us that goodness may not fit as snugly into the ontological pigeon-hole as first appearances lead one to believe. Further investigation confirms this suspicion. Goodness turns out to be a maverick-like concept for Moore. In contrast to natural objects which exist, goodness along with all other concepts only "is." To be non-natural in this sense is to be a universal, a concept. The tensions involved in this set-up we have already examined. But Moore also — and this is his dominant stress — declared goodness to be non-natural over against other concepts (in particular empirical concepts). Goodness is a *non-natural universal* — and this is no pleonasm. Goodness is a predicate just as empirical concepts and not a relation. It is something which *belongs* to objects rather than relates such objects. But, in that it cannot exist in time by itself, it is a *mere* predicate and never a *necessary* constitutive property. Goodness can be withdrawn without the object losing its identity (*PE*, 41).

This non-essential character of goodness gives it a certain similarity in function to (external) relations. Just as such relational universals, goodness is not "contained" in the object as a substantial part. Neither relations nor goodness may be considered "essential" to an object.[4] Nevertheless, although resembling relational universals in this way, goodness clearly remains a non-relational property. To point out this hybrid character Moore christens it a non-natural property. This non-essential, non-temporal character of goodness is what Moore desires to defend in his ethical writings. Thus to confuse good-

---

[4] In fact to say that a thing is relative (meaning that connection is essential to it) is self-contradictory. This is to imply that one can distinguish things and the relations involved at the same time as one declares the distinction illegitimate. Cf. *Baldwin Dictionary* under "Relative."

ness with a notion which can exist in time is to commit the naturalistic fallacy (in the specific sense). "If indeed good were a feeling, as some would have us believe, then it would exist in time. But that is why to call it so is to commit the naturalistic fallacy" (*PE*, 41).

Since pleasure is a natural property and goodness a non-natural property, it is always an *open question* for Moore if pleasure is also good. Just *because* this question is *always* significant, it is impossible that pleasure and goodness are identical. On account of this basic distinction, natural terms like "pleasantness" and non-natural terms such as goodness are also of *different* logical kinds. To identify them is to take a logical mis-step.

Moore sensed the irreducible, unbridgeable difference in nature between concepts (more appropriately termed in my opinion law-order) and things. But, as we have already seen, he violated the distinction and involved himself in contradictions by asserting that existents are made up of concepts — empirical concepts. However, in the present discussion of goodness, we discovered that Moore emphatically castigates such violations in regard to other concepts such as goodness and beauty. Here he no longer faces the difficulty of distinguishing natural universals and natural particulars, but the opposite one of finding a meaningful way to relate non-natural universals (e.g. values) and natural objects.[5]

This problem of relation becomes in the last analysis insoluble for Moore because he has goodness play two radically different roles, two roles which he attempts to telescope into the one concept of value. For Moore, it could be said, intrinsic value is supposed to be both norm and at the same time value (that which answers to the norm and is valuable). On the one hand value is absolute and normative (goodness ought to be), on the other hand it is a unique quality (with which certain objects are festooned). But it is impossible for a quality, regardless of kind, to be at the same time norm; it itself answers to norms. Moore admits this and moves in the direction of considering natural good-making characteristics to be norms. However, since such criteria are natural, Moore cannot in the last analysis recognize them as full-fledged norms. For then ethical value will have been determined by natural criteria. Yet, if there is to be any subjective certainty as to the movements of goodness, natural intrinsic properties must serve as norms.

Moore's problem can be put in more general terms: he essays to employ "intrinsic" (as well as "non-natural and "objective") to mean both universally valid and mind-independent. And, although generally confused, these two matters must be distinguished. Mind-independence need not in the least imply universal validity in the sense in which a norm holds without exception for that

---

[5] Here we concretely encounter the intermediary role played by propositions. Revealing what things are necessarily good, self-evident propositions are called in to make the connection.

which is subject to it. Mind-independent entities such as objects certainly condition subjective existence in the sense that the subject must continually deal with them, but this does not mean that they norm man's existence. Objects along with subjects are subject to law; they cannot function simultaneously as laws (holding for themselves).

THE ETHICS OF G. E. MOORE

Having examined the framework of the Moorean mansion, we are now in a better position to appraise the (ethical) furniture within. For the same reasons presented at the outset of chapter two, our critique will concentrate on Moore's position as it is (largely) set forth in *Principia Ethica*. Obviously, however, we will relate Moore's subsequent efforts to our discussion.

Goodness as Intrinsic Value

According to Moore "intrinsic value" is in itself out-of-touch with everything — with the human subject as well as with the realms of nature and super-nature. Autonomy is its very quintessence, its distinguishing characteristic. It is non-relational, self-contained and self-sufficient, hermetically sealed off from all non-ethical influence. One could go on: it is simple, non-natural and unique. It is Absolute. Goodness has as many faces as vantage points from which it is viewed. But they all express one thing: isolation, logical inaccessibility, constancy.

There are, however, two distinct facets to Moore's position. On the one hand, he is concerned to defend the objectivity of the world (including goodness) over against subjective arbitrariness — Moore's anti-subjectivism. On the other hand, he is out to defend the independence of goodness over against the natural world (including the long reach of science) — Moore's anti-naturalism. Moore must rehabilitate mind-independent entities, in this case, values, *without* surrendering to the tugging harness of Naturalism. Both facets are indispensable to his position, and, since they are expressions of *one* fundamental drive, Moore's ethical philosophy has an unmistakable inner unity. Nevertheless, it is incontrovertible that there is an inherent tension between these two expressions. In fact one could say that his position is an outgrowth of his ongoing endeavours to reconcile these two concerns. "Reconcile" is the appropriate word because these two concerns as *leading ideas*, not only join forces to produce the peculiar configuration which is Moore's ethics, they also continually resist and negate each other. Thus, although Moore is a firm believer in the scientific method, at the same time he is not unaware of its Faustian passion to dominate, which, if not checked, offers universal validity at the expense of freedom, the security of prison. Moore's solution: by shortening the leash on which science runs free, he creates a "safe" place for value. Universal validity is retained in so far as possible without prostituting value on the altar — of science.

To say it in fact-value terms:[6] to fend off his archenemies, Idealism and Naturalism, Moore holds that *both* natural objects and values are irreducible entities. It is as illicit to degrade values to the status of facts ("values are *only* facts") as it is to deny the independent existence of facts ("values are *the only* facts"). Nevertheless, although the fact-value dichotomy shows its worth in fending off hostile forces, Moore is hard put to delineate the nature of the distinction itself and thus of the relation. And here we notice the tension involved. If he connects facts and values too intimately, the closing of the gap becomes teasingly real and then we are trapped in one of the snares from which ethics has just been extracted. But if the gulf is too wide, then for all intents and purposes one side is ignored. But such neglect, whether it be of facts or values, is a fall into extremism: Metaphysics or Naturalism. And both are anathema for Moore. Even though complementary, facts and values are also and at the same time antagonistic.

It is clear that the fact-value bifurcation plays the predominant role in Moore's ethical thought. This is immediately obvious when we recall that Moore considers the "is" — "exists" (or concept— thing) split an ontic given. In that it reflects an ontic given, the fact-value distinction has its ramifications in every nook and cranny. Perhaps the most obvious tension which plays itself out is that between (the insight of) intuition and (the reasoning of) logic.

Logic and Intuition

The point that 'good is indefinable,' and that to deny this involves a fallacy, is a point capable of strict proof: for to deny it involves contradictions. (*PE*, 77)

The importance of the fact that the answer to the first question (what is the meaning of good?) is capable of direct and strict logical proof comes to the fore when compared to the situation in relation to questions two and three (what things are good? and, what is right?). Question II is not open to logical (dis) proof, rather the answer is self-evidently known through introspection (intuition). Question III is open to proof but the attainment of certainty is impossible. Question I is, in contrast, both open to logical proof and certainty is possible.

[6] It must be noted that, due to Moore's ambiguous use of "fact," it is more exact in his case to speak of a thing-goodness, object-value, or natural/non-natural dualism. When this is understood, however, and when it is recalled that Moore himself treated facts as things, and that he clearly distinguished facts and universals, the fact-value terminology can be employed in line with current fashion without misunderstanding.

The question which pushes to the fore is the relation of logical reasoning and intuitive insight. It is, to begin with, clear that Moore begins by allowing each sovereign sway in a certain area: logic in Complex QI, intuition in Complex QII (Complex QIII is to serve as the land of reunion). Is logical reasoning subordinate to or superior to introspection? The very numbering of the complexes implies a certain priority. Therefore, it is to be expected that Moore argues that logic must first determine the meaning of good before intuition can introspect what is good. He provides two reasons. One must know what "good" means before he can understand what it means that this or that is good. The second "is a reason of method. It is this, that we can never know on what *evidence* an ethical proposition rests, until we know the nature of the notion which makes the proposition ethical" (*PE*, 142-43).

Thus, because the concept good has been shown to be indefinable; that is, because it cannot be conceived of as a constituent part of an object involving the *analytic* relation of containment, all propositions of the form "X is good" are *necessarily* synthetic. In turn, since logical (analytic) certainty is out of the question in relation to synthetic propositions, Moore is forced, if he would fence off arbitrariness and relativity, to invoke the *self-evidence* of such propositions. All this, argues Moore, "follows from our first investigation" (*PE*, 143). Since intuition is required to receive such self-evident propositions, Moore in effect states that the logical investigations of QI make it inescapably clear that intuition must have the say in QII.

In this situation it would appear justifiable to judge that logical reasoning has the first and thus the last word with Moore. But it is not that simple, as we have clearly seen in chapter two. At the crucial juncture, the logical proofs of QI only hold on the basis of an intuitive awareness of the unique notion "goodness." On the other hand, attention has also been paid to the usurper's role which logic plays within the confines of QII.

The relation of logic and intuition comes to a head in QII. Moore is caught between two fires. On the one hand, it is evident that for him only logical proofs are universally binding. A logical reason is a "reason why something is true . . . a reason why *the proposition itself* must be true" (*PE*, 143). Only then can one in the full and strict sense of the word talk of proof. On the other hand, it is equally certain that for Moore intrinsic value lies outside of the purview of logic. To gain access to value, psychological intuition arrives on the scene. In this way the power struggle between logic and value passes over into a competition between the universal validity of logical reasoning and the insight of psychic intuition.

But it is a contest of incomparables. "Intuition can only furnish a reason for *holding* any prposition to be true: this however it must do when any proposition is self-evident, when, in fact, there are no reasons which prove its truth" (*PE*, 144). A strange situation has developed. Only logic can prove what is true, but only intuition can know goodness and truth. And since a true and valid process of reasoning must begin with an undoubted premise, logic ultimately depends on the givens of intuition. Nevertheless, in that intuition is a subjective organ, its reception can be affected by atmospheric disturbances. It may on occasion distort and even mis-take the impulses which impinge upon it. There is no subjective certainty, there is no certain "warrant of truth."

Logical reasoning and intuitive insight need each other. Without logic there are no universally valid truths. Without intuition there is no contact with goodness or truth. Yet logic and intuition are even more basically opposed to each other. How they supplement each other even as they oppose will be more obvious in the sequel.

Indefinability

This need-each-other but oppose-each-other-even-more phenomenon of logic and intuition is exemplified in Moore's doctrine of indefinability. Everything in his ethics sooner or later, and as a rule sooner, revolves around the complex notion of indefinability. Indeed the difficulty which we encountered in tracing out its contours stems from its many-faceted character. All the various threads woven into Moore's fabric come together and are knotted in this notion. Faced with this Gordian knot, one's first impulse is no doubt to slash away. But what can one do with a handful of loose ends? One must try to unravel the tangled skein if he is to discover the precise intertwinement.

Indefinability is the pride and at the same time the embarrassment of Moore's ethics. Intrinsic goodness is indefinable (in the special sense):

(1) to distinguish it from natural or metaphysical concepts (but it retains its objectivity);
(2) to protect it from the caprice of the subject (but common sense intuitively knows it);
(3) to save it from the logical grasp of natural science (but a *scientific* ethics is the goal);
(4) to make ethics possible as a *science* (but, even then, ethics is an *autonomous* science);
(5) to insure a morally antiseptic ethics (but the chief task of ethics is the search after material or normative answers);
(6) to safeguard the objectivity of judgments concerning intrinsic value (but such judgments are essentially formal and content-less).

In a real sense it is impossible to isolate the various strains. Nevertheless for purposes of analysis it is helpful to distinguish as clearly as possible the diverse threads. As soon as we reflect on the purposes listed, it becomes manifest that

159

we have to do again with the previously mentioned polarity. In order for one feature to function properly in the system, it requires the complementation of another element. Simultaneously this other factor also limits, challenges and contradicts the first feature. The six items form three pairs, 1 and 2; 3 and 4; 5 and 6; in which the pairs are the manifestations of a single two-pronged basic drive, call it the freedom-domination drive. Items 1, 3, 5 give expression to one pole, the freedom drive, and their pendants 2, 4, 6 to its antipode, the domination drive. In each case the bracketed but-clauses give voice to the opposite drive from that expressed in the main clause.

At one moment, in the name of freedom, Moore must distinguish goodness from the natural and metaphysical (1). To maintain the integrity of goodness, it must be beyond the long arm of science (3). This in turn forces him to espouse an ethics devoid of content (5). At the same moment, in the name of science, Moore is driven to defend value from arbitrariness (2). Ethical science is now possible (4) and the objectivity of value is guaranteed (6).

Turning to the pairs themselves, one is struck by the obvious complementation — only to be astounded at the implicit contradiction. To preserve its non-natural character goodness must be guaranteed independence from objective nature. Yet goodness requires objectivity in order to eschew the arbitrariness which is native to subjectivity. The solution honoring both requests: goodness is a non-natural quality, objective but not natural.

The conception of "intrinsic value" was for Moore the prime embodiment of his ideals. In it he was enabled to present a united front against diverse enemies. At the same time, closer scrutiny reveals inner tensions of no small dimensions. Natural, it turns out, as well as non-natural concepts can be "intrinsic." What then is extra-special about being non-natural? Just how can the subject obtain certain knowledge of values? The problems at hand emerge with unusual intensity in relation to ethics as a science (3 and 4 above).

Ethics as a Science

To keep ethics ethics (and not a sub-department of psychology or one of the other natural sciences) Moore declared the heart of ethics ("goodness") to be off limits for scientific logic. To keeps ethics scientfic (and retrieve it from the regions of faith or superstition) Moore pronounced the subject-matter of ethics to be "assertions" or "judgments" (*PE*, 1, 36). Protecting goodness from the ravishment of science pays Moore a double dividend. Goodness need not endure devaluation to the status of facts. Secondly, ethics can remain a *neutral* and *autonomous* science. If goodness could be "defined," ethics would be by definition normative, that is biased. Likewise, it would be a sub-department of some other science.

One could say that in Moore's theory goodness is both inside and outside

160

ethics. It is "inside" in that ethics deals with sentences involving the predicate good. It is "outside" in that this predicate in all its allure remains scientifically inaccessible. Once this situation is fully realized the illusion that Moore's ingenious manoeuvres have delivered what he promised falls away. Ethical science is at best only incidentally, *per accidens*, ethical. The real terrain of ethics is off-limits as a matter of principle. Thus if, to cite an example, the central concepts of economics were indefinable, economics as a science would be in essence indistinguishable from ethical science. The science of ethics is in fact suspended and replaced by or reduced to logico-lingual investigations. Moore himself cannot escape the consequences: the psychological organ of intuition is called in to give ethics *real* ethical content; it must intuit what things are good.

The conclusion of the matter is somber: Moore's aim to develop an ethical science (under the drive of the domination-motive) is in principle impossible (due to the countervailing force of the freedom-motive). Insofar as it is ethics, it is not scientific; insofar as it is scientific, it is not ethics.

Although this capsule summary is basically correct, attention must be paid to Moore's unique efforts to avoid such a cul-de-sac. He essayed by means of the techniques offered by formal logic to curtail the imperialistic tendencies of science without abandoning ethics to the mercies of mercurial subjectivity. In the logical environs of Complex QI the motive-force driving him concentrates its efforts. Utilizing logic Moore seeks to prove that value is beyond the logical grasp of science. In one grand moment his anti-subjectivism (the domination-motive) and anti-naturalism (the freedom-motive) touch and join forces. Ethics has not been delivered up to superstition but neither has it been offered up to science. But the price of this reconciliation is high — too high; ethics is drained of all (non-logical) content and threatens to become meaningless. "Good is indefinable" — period.

The respective forces regroup (as comes to focus in Complex QII). On the one side, intuition is called upon to bring back the non-logical content. On the other, a logical method of isolation is called into play in order to set the stage for intuitive insight. But this supplementation soon shows itself as contraposition. After the logical preparation any appeal to intuition becomes more or less superfluous. Indeed, since the insights of intuition are always uncertain, and since logic offers universal validity, the method of isolation receives the nod. Nevertheless logical investigation always ends up with a proposition which is beyond further proof or disproof.

In that formal logic by definition is touted to be strictly logical, it can be employed to good advantage as a reconciler of interests.[7] However, as the sequel has revealed, it only succeeds in camouflaging the tensions and in

[7] See our later remarks on formal logic, Ch. 6, pp. 176-78.

161

postponing open confrontation. Moreover, in that the matter becomes too concentrated in the logical (logic is absolutized), the resultant loss of content and meaning (as far as the non-logical is concerned) deprives the victory of its sweetness. Since goodness has previously been drained of content, subsequent efforts to avoid the formalization of ethics or to mitigate its effects by appealing to intuition are futile. As science ethics remains in principle non-ethical and formal, in this case, logical.

There is another — and important — place in which Moore depends on intuition. It deserves separate mention because, although his whole position depends upon it, Moore largely ignores the matter in his ethics. Moore requires an *initial* intuition of the non-logical and of the non-natural before logical argumentation and ethics can commence. And he (rightly) acknowledges this fact — at least in the latter instance. The difficulty is that he (wrongly) conceived of intuition in psychologistic terms.[8] Consequently, in view of his high regard for the universal validity afforded by logical reasoning in comparison with psychological intuition, his recognition of the role of intuition cannot properly work itself out. Stronger, Moore felt compelled to present strictly logical proofs of the non-natural character of goodness and only allowed the intuition to play a role at a latter stage; that is, when such an appeal could no longer be postponed.

The Vacuity of Goodness

In defense of goodness Moore overplayed and overextended himself. His strength; to wit, his uncompromising defense of the uniqueness of goodness, was also his weakness; to wit, an intuitive, always uncertain, leap is required to break through the splendid isolation of goodness. Science cannot enter the impregnable fortress; by the same token goodness is a virtual prisoner in its own castle. "Saving" it from science involved "castigating" it from human life. The very absoluteness of its freedom has made the freedom meaningless.

Moore's intuitive leap is in effect a leap in the dark, and in two respects. There is no subjective certainty as to the truth of the intuitions. Secondly, even if certainty were attainable, contact with goodness avails nothing. Goodness is vacuous, empty. How could this be otherwise when goodness is severed from all that is natural and non-ethical, from all that is necessary for its proper functioning. In absolutizing goodness Moore emptied it of all content.

Moore obviously was aware of the formal nature of his inquiries into goodness. Thus he stresses the need to separate the formal question concerning the meaning of goodness from material questions concerning what things are good

[8] For Moore's views of intuition, cf. ch. 3, pp. 76-79; for the writer's, cf. 7. pp. 184-85, especially fn. 4.

and right. Further, as we recall, it is not until Complex QIII that Moore addresses himself to the practical question: what ought I to do? But even here the vacuity of goodness affects the outcome. Moore is emphatic that judgments concerning the right depend in the final analysis on intuited answers to the question re the good. The result — contrary to Moore's explicit intentions — is that one lacks any lodestar by which to guide his life. To avoid going by subjective, individual preferences, to prevent oneself from being swept along by the contingencies of history, Moore attempts to make a case for the status quo. The irony of the matter cannot be hidden. Goodness is absolute, certain, constant. However, I am never sure that I know what is good and I can have no firm confidence that I am doing what is right. And unable to have certain knowledge of values, Moore, who relativizes laws because they originate in subjective volition, ends up submitting to the rules of the status quo.

Goodness is a logical, formal concept. Thus any content that it may be discovered to have is a subjective deposit. That is to say, one initially fills the "box," later claiming to find the box with its content as a "given." Such formal concepts are employed to serve various and often cross-purposes. What one individual views as good, he exclaims to be so on the basis of revelation. It is now normative for *everyone*. What one receives as the voice of goodness is in effect a replay of his own subjective desires and prejudices. Self-evident intuitions as to what things are good are an individual's ideas raised to universal status by palming them off as indubitable pronouncements.

All this means that Moore's "objectivism" shows itself at this point as a moderate or disguised subjectivism. His attempt to usher in a second Copernican revolution in philosophy, a Kantianism-in-reverse, failed — not in the least because of the first revolution. Moore wished to return to things, to values in themselves, to that which is mind-independent. But the impossibility of apprehending objects as they are in themselves without subjective mediation is clearly evidenced in Moore's work. He is forced to limit his discussion to (subjective) *assertions about* things and values.[9] This is true in ethics as well as in his general philosophy. He demonstrates the existence of things to us, not by an examination of "things," but from an examination of knowledge contained in common sense.[10]

---

[9] R. McKeon has also been struck by this inconsistency. Cf. *PGEM*, 475 ff.

[10] Moore does employ diversionary tactics to evade this damaging conclusion. For example, as we have previously noticed, he claims that "propositions" (expressed in assertions) have an *an sich*, objective status. The impossibility of such a gambit is evidenced by the very term "proposition" itself. Propositions (*proponere*) depend for their existence upon human subjects who propound, that is, "set before."

Before concluding our examination of Moore's ethics, it is instructive to bring Moore's second thoughts into our discussion. We can be brief and for two obvious reasons. Phase two is a revision as well as a de-radicalization of phase one, and it is an unfinished revision.[11] In *Principia Ethica* goodness, so to speak, lives its own life by its own rules. No logical investigation is able to trace out with regularity the movements of goodness, when and when it will not attach itself to natural objects of its choice. Intuition must "see" what things are good. But there is no certainty about such sight, it may be myopic; in any case different people intuit different "self-evident" propositions.

Moore was not untouched by this state of affairs. In later publications (in particular, "The Conception of Intrinsic Value") he endeavoured to correct this situation. He attempts to tighten the connection between the natural world and goodness. But, and Moore is most conscious of this, a fixed connection of values with facts endangers his major thesis that values are not reducible to natural facts. On the one hand, impelled by the paradoxes of his first phase, he is convinced that some kind of *necessary* bond must be accepted between facts and values. But of what kind; and here Moore is bewildered. A causal or factual tie is too loose, but a logical (analytic) linkage is too tight. As we have investigated, Moore without ever explicitly saying it is led to think of a synthetic a priori connection. Once again we are in the middle of all the problems. If the fact-value nexus can be characterized as synthetic a priori, Moore must call upon intuition to ascertain its presence. But then the earlier uncertainty which he is now trying to escape has not decisively been overcome. Knowledge of the connection still depends on the admittedly fallible human intuition. In addition, such necessary relations (synthetic a priori) also occur between natural qualities. Moore is forced to admit that he is unable to delineate the nature of the fact-value relation other than to say that it is "unconditional."

Dialectic and Dilemmas

Throughout our analysis it has become increasingly apparent that Moore is operating on two fronts. Alarmed by the speculative excesses of Idealism as well as the leveling tendencies of Naturalism, he set out to avoid both extremes by doing justice to, i.e. harmonizing, the interests of both science and freedom. But, as we have discovered, such an operation is tenuous to say the least. Danger is acute on both fronts. One must demolish Naturalism without disposing of the weapons necessary to repel Idealism. One must destroy Idealism

---

[11] It should be recalled that the same gradual process of de-radicalization takes place in Moore's philosophy generally.

without falling prey to the forces of Naturalism. And both dangers must be averted without falling into (objectivistic) metaphysics.

Another metaphor is perhaps more helpful at this point. The various considerations which play their role in Moore's ethics form, as it were, two "poles" with their attendant magnetic fields; the so-called domination (or science) pole and the so-called freedom (or value) pole. In line with the nature of polarization, the poles reciprocally presume even as they mutually exclude each other.

Feeling the magnetic pull of both poles, Moore is induced (by the domination-pole) to consider goodness a quality, and at the same time (under the attraction of the freedom-pole) a non-natural, indefinable quality. Both poles or motive-forces — for that is what they are, the poles are "charged" — have their say, but neither has its way. And now the dialectic involved reveals itself in antinomies. Goodness in that it is completely free and yet completely objective — absolute in both senses — disintegrates into nothingness. In relation to science and logic, goodness remains at large; in its freedom it is no longer "objective." Viewed by the insight of intuition, goodness is bereft of all content: in its very "objectivity" it is "freed" of all content.

As we have noticed, this pattern of reciprocity, both in complementation and in contraposition, returns at every point. That one can speak, despite the presence of two competing ideals, of a certain oneness in Moore's theory is to be attributed to the fact that the two ideals find a common rootage in a single pre-theoretical motive-force, and that this motive works out its dialectic largely in the arena of logic. The two-faced character is possible in that the motive-force taking on expression in the ideals is itself dialectic. Moore's theorizing is ruled by this single, yet ambivalent freedom-domination motive. Whereas Moore attempts to do justice to the demands of both ideals by means of his concept of intrinsic value, our investigation reveals a certain primacy for the science-ideal. In *Principia* Moore indeed took it up for values, but only to clear a legitimate place for them alongside of nature. Further, the goal of his investigations was the establishment of a scientific ethics with the result that ethics threatens to become merely a logico-lingual exercise. Still Moore must receive credit for realizing the dangers of complete domination by the science-ideal. Moore's later amplifications strengthen our case. For in this period, concerned that he had given values too much freedom and leeway, he tightens or tries to tighten the connection with the natural. But now he has swung even closer to the nature-pole. He cannot allow values to be free and yet, since he still has an eye for value, he cannot allow them not to be free (autonomous).

In conclusion, Moore's rejection of metaphysical realms, subjective arbitrariness as well as of naturalistic, positivistic theories deserves wide acclaim. The significance of his efforts in this direction cannot be emphasized enough — especially when seen in their historical setting. That Moore's positive contributions were not of like merit results from his failure to carry the reforms radically through. He sensed that there was "more" to the universe than the natural. But his ontological schema being what it was, his insight was sapped of meaning and strength. Conceived to be non-natural, normative and thus universally valid, at the same time identified as a quality (which itself obeys norms), intrinsic value lapsed into a "nothingness" value-less for life on earth.

In survey: Basic problems

6

As we have discovered in chapter four, not only Moore but twentieth-century Anglo-American moral philosophy on the whole has struggled and is struggling with the problem of values and valuation. This being the case, prior to outlining a position designed to avoid the present impasse, it should be helpful to focus attention in more general fashion on a number of basic problems.

FACTS AND VALUES: AN UNTENABLE DUALISM

Variations on the Fact-Value Theme

A fact-value dualism can take on many forms. "Facts," it is often asserted, stand in one way or another over against "values." First one comes to know the facts; then, if need be, he ascertains *The Place of Value in a World of Facts*.[1] Knowing is regarded as the portion of theoretical reason, valuing the forte of practical reason. Whereas factual judgments can be true, value judgments are at best partially susceptible to such true-false designations.

Philosophically, fact-value dualisms in which objective brute facts stand over against and independent of objective absolute values are no longer in fashion. In the first place, due to increased recognition of the role of the human subject as well as a growing awareness of the worthlessness of cut-off (absolute) values, values have been more and more identified as *subjective* embodiments of human preferences, desires and idiosyncrasies. Concomitantly, but in much slower tempo, only in the last years approaching crescendo in the English-speaking world, there arose the disturbing suspicion that *an sich*, "brute" facts are simply impossibilities. Facts only speak in context. Facts are relative to situations and viewers.[2] And since they are not sacred, it is as foolish as unnecessary to worship them.[3]

---

[1] Wolfgang Köhler (1939).

For note 2 and 3 see page 168.

All this means that more recent theories, while maintaining the dichotomy, have stressed the connection and the demand to tighten it. This is not surprising in that social, ethical, political, economic, etc. facts cannot be described apart from "values" (or, as we prefer, norms) and likewise "values" lose all meaning apart from their connection with and realization in facts.

In comparison, the latest fashion as evidenced in so-called meta-ethical theories is somewhat disconcerting. The remarkable feature is a strong emphasis on the descriptive-evaluative contrast coupled with an explicit denial of the *existence* of values, whether they be objective or subjective. Value terms and judgments of value are irreducible to matters of facts or judgments of fact, presumably because of their different logical behavior.[4] In contrast to the descriptive theoretical nature of factual judgments, value judgments fulfill certain practical, i.e. non-theoretical, purposes: they are action-guiding and choice-commending. The advance in respect to previous theories is obvious and immediate. Value judgments need no longer squirm under the harrassment of the descriptive-model of language under which they could never be anything but second-rate judgments and ethics a second-rate science. With the declaration that value judgments are essentially non-descriptive, the way is open, it is said, for ethics to be a science, a *sui generis* science in the full sense of the word.

But, as we have already seen in some detail in chapter four, this novel approach to ethics is not without its own problems. Do value judgments

[2] Generally speaking, in an attempt to retain or safeguard their universal validity, facts are drained of their non-logical content and considered strictly logical. It is the *logical* object-function of facts (cf. ch. 7) which is relevant. Concrete facts are reduced to logical abstractions. Wittgenstein in the *Tractatus*, to present a telling example, is not so much interested in facts as in their logical form. Others, regarding facts as "pseudoentities," seek their point of reference in particulars or things. Thus, reversing Wittgenstein's aphorism (*Tractatus* 1.1), Strawson declares that "the world is the totality of things, not of facts" (in *Truth*, ed. Pitcher, p. 40). However, things are also largely exhausted in their logical aspect.

[3] Thus exhorted J. R. Lucas, "On Not Worshipping Facts," *Phil. Quarterly* VII (1958), pp. 144-56. Cf. also C. Van Peursen, *Feiten, waarden, gebeurtenissen* (1965). Van Peursen rightly and clearly rejects any idea of "brute facts" as well as of any jump from facts to values. However, in that he neither defines "value" nor explains his use of "logical order," the value of his positive suggestion (reversing the logical order, first values and then facts as restricted, trimmed values) remains problematic.

[4] This emphasis on the logical behavior of concepts is one of the most remarkable features of this new viewpoint. In as far as possible cut off from the subject who conceives them, such concepts, the "metaphysical entities" of neo-positivism, are treated as if they have "lives" of their own. Language is regarded more or less as a natural process functioning according to rules. Cf. P. A. Verburg, "Het optimum der taal bij Wittgenstein," *Philosophia Reformata* XXVI (1961), pp. 169-70 and J. van der Hoeven, "Filosofie op het spel," *Philosophia Reformata* XXX (1965), pp. 152, 155-56.

possess meaning if they do not refer outside themselves? The ready retort that "use" is equivalent with "meaning" is of little help. For certainly meaning is not exhausted in linguistic use — as if meaning is merely to employ words in certain ways. Can such a claim even be made in regard to linguistic meaning? Is it not rather the case that one speaks of linguistic meaning only when words are used to signify something beyond themselves?

This being the real state of affairs, the "reference" character could not be eliminated. Toulmin has his "good reasons," Hare talks of "descriptive meaning." Suddenly all the problems involved in the more traditional value theories make their appearance. Toulmin, for example, cannot permit his factual "good reasons" and moral conclusions to coincide if he wishes to save the integrity of the ethical language-game. Yet he cannot fulfill his purpose of enlightening mankind without fostering the impression that the reasons are the equivalents of moral judgments. In any case, as we have seen, his solution trades on the built-in ambiguity of "good" in "good reasons." Since Hare considers that value terms themselves possess descriptive meaning, the matter of relation is even more crucial for him. Just what is the connection of evaluative and descriptive meaning in value terms? Since the descriptive meaning involved in value terms is determined by moral substantive principles acting as criteria of application (and not by factual characteristics), the fact-value hook-up occurs in some never explained way by means of individual decisions taken in the process of formulating moral principles.

At the present time ethical theory is especially concerned to repair the break between valuational and factual judgments. Nevertheless, it remains an un-questioned assumption that a contrast of sorts is real. Even those who deny the existence of values have an undulled sense of the more-than-factual charac-ter of reality. (How else can one finally explain the retention of the descriptive-valuational dichotomy?) The attempts at reconstruction aim at narrowing the gap or throwing over a bridge. The gap remains — as deep, although not as wide, as ever. In the proportion that the width of the chasm is narrowed, its depth is accentuated. These on-going, in the heart of the matter dialectic efforts pressing for reconciliation are, however, shrouded in mist. For if they were to succeed, if the logical connection were firmly laid out, the dualism itself would collapse. Either "values" are merely blown-up facts or "facts" are merely emasculated, impoverished values. The very nature of the dualism de-mands the reality of an unbridgeable fact-value gulf.

But, and this is the thorn which rankled Moore and which chafes his epigoni: without a firm logical connection between facts and values, ethical science proper is suspended and one has to do with a disguised psychology or logic etc. It is this enigmatic character (mandatory but impossible connection) which gives the extreme positions an undeniable attraction. Here we need only remind ourselves of those who at the present feel the urge to take the plunge into the cold but bracing waters of facticity.

Perhaps the most exasperating problem for theorists concerns the very possibility of a theory of values. Within the fact-value framework there are basically and certainly ultimately only two alternatives in relation to a science of values. *Either reason (as logical subject with its logical apparatus) must be allowed complete access or it must be allowed no access to values.* If à la Moore values are declared indefinable, or à la Hare one cannot move from a factual to an evaluative judgment, a *science* of ethics is per se impossible. If à la Naturalism science is permitted free entrée, a science of *ethics* is per se impossible. In the former case, the terrain of ethics proper remains outside the pale of scientific thought. If a science of ethics is nevertheless formulated, it is without fail some other discipline masquerading under the ethical banner. In the latter instance, since ethical questions are "handled" in the same way as questions of the natural sciences, ethical science is transformed into a natural science. In neither case can one speak of a real science of ethics.

At this point there must be no misunderstanding. It is not that we are forcing ethicists into a schema of *our* making and thereafter faulting them for failing to choose either alternative. Nor are we claiming that they wish or intend to choose between these alternatives. Indeed, it is obvious that third or in-between stances are often adopted. Rather the matter at hand is that the philosophers concerned, through their absolutization of logic, make it impossible for themselves to establish a third position without falling into antinomies. Once logic is conceived to be abstract, formal and pure, cut off from all that is non-logical, the said thinkers, their desires notwithstanding, have laid upon themselves the dilemma: Either logic is taken to be everything (cosmic diversity is reduced to logical diversity) or logic remains isolated in itself (and there is no scientific contact with reality). A third position endeavouring to avoid either horn is necessarily involved in inconsistency.

The situation becomes even more complex when one considers that the alternatives are in themselves impossibilities. If it were feasible to give theoretic thought complete access to values, theoretical knowledge as such would be unobtainable. Any attempt to logicize reality is faced with the fact that if it were successful, it has eliminated its very possibility. Only *in* a previously given diversity is one able to distinguish logically.[5] At the same time, it is

---

[5] Without its coherence with the other aspects of reality, the logical aspect cannot reveal its logical sense. Logical diversity is only possible because of a prior *cosmic* diversity.

At the same time this implies that the analytic-synthetic distinction in the sense of (formal) logical and empirical (material) propositions is illegitimate. All scientific judgments are, one could say, both analytic and synthetic in character. Logical distinguishing always takes place in acts structurally made up of non-logical aspects in addition to the logical aspect. Even a tautology is logically meaningless if the non-logical is banished.

self-evident that if reason is permitted no entrance, there is no science of values. This being the state of affairs, it is clear that in-between positions are advocated. Since, however, a middle stance is thoroughly defined by its extremes, the besetting problem is to avoid and equally to justify the rejection of the extremes. And it is just here that the value theories have not been able to prove themselves. Although in themselves generally most instructive, these positions are unable to break through the basic problematics with its adherent dilemmas.

Although Ayer is often berated for his crudeness, it is to his credit that he realized the last consequences of considering values irreducible and unrelated to facts: ethical science is as such eliminated. Since then ethicists have labored unceasingly, as we have seen, to rehabilitate ethics as a science. One of the most attractive variations on Moore's theme is that of Hare. What has been exposed as a dire shortcoming (no science of *ethics*) Hare parades as a virtue. Ethics is simply logic, the logical study of the language of morals. However, since Hare is still concerned to be an ethicist, he must demonstrate that ethics does not lose out by being defined as logic. And this proved to be an impossible task. In this context it is no surprise that Naturalism, be it in new irrationalistic forms, is once again showing itself. For then an ethics with content is once again possible. But can this renascent Naturalism avoid reducing ethics once again to another natural science. It would seem, if our analysis is correct, that sooner or later another "Moore" will arrive on the scene bent on exposing the "naturalistic fallacy."

The Form-Matter Bifurcation

The same problem comes into somewhat different focus when considered, as it customarily is, from out of form-matter bifurcation (of one type or another) in which form is considered logical and matter non-logical. If one chooses for no logical access, or if values have no opening to the logical, a formal-logicistic or content-less ethics will emerge. If one chooses for logical access, or if values have an opening for the logical, a material science of sorts will develop. Since the latter choice is excluded for one who adheres to a fact-value dualism, it is not surprising that the formal note predominates in the theories we have discussed. It is also predictable that a cry will soon be raised for a material ethics with an accompanying minimizing of the fact-value dualism. As we have noticed, the chant has already begun.

Moore attempted, we recall, to reconcile both traditions in ethics. By separating the formal and material questions, respectively, what is the meaning of good? and, what things are good and right?, he sought to give both elements a respectable place in ethics. He was thus consistent in denying logical thought access to the (formal) good (QI) and in granting it access to (material) right. Nevertheless, in line with his choice for the integrity of values, the formal

171

question is the primary query and intuited answers to it (in QII) are necessary before one can answer the secondary question as to the right (QIII). The paradoxical and sterile character of this schema has already been demonstrated. In Moore's second phase the form-matter schema rears its head in the starkest possible manner. How can one relate (formal) values to their (material, natural) content?

Post-Moorean ethicists have taken the logical inaccessibility of values as something over which to cheer rather than lament. Ethics is simply the logico-lingual investigation of ethical judgments. That is to say; having witnessed Moore's discomfort in trying to bring form and matter together under one roof, later analysts restricted ethics to formal, logical investigations similar to the ones carried on by Moore in complex QI. Material, normative answers to the "big" questions are outside the purview of ethical science. Such matters are answered by the natural sciences, in some instances by "ordinary" ethics employing the tools sharpened by the meta-ethical craftsman, and often such issues are simply left to the individual conscience of the man on the street. Meta-ethics is responsible only for the "form," other authorities are responsible for the "content." Ethics has retreated into a morally-antisceptic logico-lingual vacuum.

The full implications of this formalization of ethics can only be properly seen when our horizon is lifted and we discover that other socio-cultural sciences are also in many instances claiming to be only responsible for the "form." Although this topic deserves intensive and extensive investigation, it is beyond the scope of the present work. Still, with an eye to its importance, a word or two must be said. The situation is such that all these sciences tend to relegate the question of content and normativity to the science of ethics. But ethics itself is busy absolving itself from any obligation in regard to content. The result is as clear as it is tragic. Each of the sciences claims to be formal (and thus empirical and descriptive) and regards the other as material (and thus normative). While mankind craves answers, scientists play musical chairs.[6]

Legal theory, economics, sociology, etc., it is said, need deal only with "forms." Any discussion of norms, goals and preferences ("content") apart from their logical clarification is the responsibility of ethics. But now ethics too has gone "logical" and refuses to accept the onus of "telling" mankind what it ought to do. But — and this fact deserves underlining — just because *both* the legal theorist and the ethicist can construct plausible cases supporting their positions, the unsatisfactory and eventually contradictory character of the formal-material

---

[6] The underlying cause of this distressing state of affairs must, it seems clear, be sought in the driving concern to keep science "neutral." The matter has come to a head in the present time partly because new developments in logic have anew nourished the false hope that neutrality can be achieved in the humanities, the social sciences and ethics.

distinction is revealed. The "content" of, say, economic activity cannot be so *a*-economic as is supposed in "pure economics" for the simple reason that it would then be impossible for "pure ethics" (meta-ethics) to claim that it only is responsible for the form and economics for the content. To dissect an economic act into an economically-neutral material segment and an ethically-neutral formal segment is as infeasible as the reverse, dividing it into ethically-neutral content and economically-neutral form.[7] As form and content do not exist in themselves, there is never form without content or vice versa. A denotation (form) always presupposes a connotation (content). It is always the form *of* a content. If form is separated from content, with form considered the monopoly of one science and content of another, the result is an "internally antinomic exclusivism"[8] involving the disintegration of the respective sciences.

The antinomic results of a theory built on a form-matter distinction also imply that no theory can hold to this viewpoint. The impossibility of remaining pure and formal is intimated in the very name meta-ethics. For to move beyond (meta), one must move from somewhere. "Ordinary ethics," whether officially recognized or not, is necessary as a foundation, or at least, as a jumping off place. But how can one draw a line between ethics and meta-ethics which will stand up? In the degree that meta-ethics maintains its ethical neutrality, it is simply a logico-lingual exercise. Only when the form-matter division is violated do the first beginnings of ethics enter the picture.

Thus it is to be expected that insofar as the theorists discussed wish to be ethicists they will, their theory to the contrary, be forced to deal with normative matters. Indeed this is the case. Despite his claims to operate in a neutral descriptive way, Toulmin in fact has read a normative principle (harmony) into the facts. At the same time, his good reasons turn out not only to be logically valid but also ethically normative. Insofar as Hare is able to mitigate substantial ethical disputes, he is forced to smuggle in material considerations under the cover of logical formality. In each case the re-appearance of the material insures that the science in question will indeed have an ethical bite. At the same time, its presence makes any claim to neutrality impossible.

A FUNDAMENTAL DIFFICULTY

A fact-value dualism entangles all who accept it in perplexing, not to say, intractable and insuperable situations. Must one then take flight and land up with an extreme position? From the argument presented thus far, the answer is short and discouraging: one can only avoid an extreme position by adopting some form of the fact-value dualism. Nevertheless there is another possibility.

[7] Cf. B. Goudzwaard, "De economische theorie en de normatieve aspecten der werkelijkheid," *Perspectief* Eds, van Dijk, Stellingwerff *et al.* (1961).
[8] Cf. Dooyeweerd, *A New Critique of Theoretical Thought* II (1955), p. 209f.

The strangeness of this situation lifts when one understands that a fact-value dualism in some form is unavoidable for those inclined to moderation *as long as* they operate within the confines of a certain ontological framework. And since all the ethicists considered thus far have this framework in common, they have no choice but to adopt a version of the fact-value dualism. It is this framework, consciously or unconsciously presupposed, but seldom critically examined, which demands attention and which is in fact the fundamental difficulty.

The Subject-Object (or Noetic-Ontic) Schema

The philosophers concerned accept unquestioningly, often naively, a certain assumption: reality consists *ontically* of the human subject (more or less identified with the logical function) over against the world (more or less identified with the pre-logical aspects). The "subjective" *cogito* and "objective" *cogitata*, the knower and the known, knowledge and reality — the dualism constantly returns in different dress. On the one hand, the subject, free and autonomous, stands over against law-bound Nature (the object). On the other hand, the subject is inexorably bound to Nature. In the last analysis everything must find its origin and explanation in relation to the "subject" or the "object."

This schema, the absolutization of the theoretical subject-object relation,[9] has traditionally served as the framework in which, and the vehicle by which, the freedom-nature or autonomy-domination motive has worked itself out.[10] The ethicists we have considered, driven by this motive, have *bound* their thought to the subject-object schema in a logicistic manner *as if* it squared with the states of affairs. While the autonomy drive lodges itself more or less securely in the subjective logical function (with or without another subjective function), the impulse to domination, itself especially since Kant installed in

[9] The epistemological relation characteristic of theoretical thought in which the logical subjective function stands logically over against the non-logical aspects is taken out of its place and absolutized. Three comments are in order. In the first place, the human subject operating in theoretical thought is in the schema exhausted more or less in his subjective logical function. However, man has many more functions, and as a whole he is much "more" than the sum of his functions. Secondly, the separation character- istic of theoretic thought is typically logical; that is, abstract and intentional. Although this abstraction has ontic or real status *within* the act of thought, it cannot be absolutiz- ed as if this "split" were not merely logical but an original given which squares with the fullness of reality. In the third place, even if the subject = logical subject, even if the separation were more than logical, the subject could still not exist by itself autono- mously. For to speak of the subjective logical function only has meaning in relation to the theoretical object. Cf. Dooyeweerd, *op. cit.* I, p. 39ff.
[10] In masterful fashion Dooyeweerd has traced the influence of ground-motives in the history of western philosophy. Cf. especially the first volume of *The New Critique*.

the subjective logical function, fixes its glance on the to-be-mastered objective pole.

The free subject is driven to master "nature" by means of theoretical thought. But the eventual result is the very intimidation of the subject itself. Under pressure, its very autonomy threatened, the subject reacts. Without the "object" the autonomy of the subject proves empty, but bound to the "object" autonomy is thwarted in its unfolding. The autonomy-drive which as a matter of course gave rise to the domination-drive must now in turn fight off domination itself. This in a nutshell characterizes the dialectic which is as native as it is problematic to the subject-object schema (in any of its forms). Just as an extreme is about to be reached, just as the science-ideal with its autonomous *rationality* is about to eliminate human freedom, or the freedom-ideal with its rational *autonomy* considers itself absolutely unfettered, a reaction sets in causing the pendulum to swing in the opposite direction. Consequently, under the pull of both poles and the concomitant ideals, there are frequent efforts to avoid one-sided theories. Even when extreme theories are projected, they are unable to do away with the opposite pole. Stronger, despite their intentions to ignore or push away the opposite pole, such constructions are only possible because they are not successful in their attempts.[11]

The "External Ought"

One of the persistent enigmas facing a thinker within this complex is caused by the fact that he must reckon with some kind of "external ought" in relation to the free subject. Certain heteronomous factors affect, determine and restrain human activity — and every theory must account for them. The givenness of this situation has always been the fatal blow to any theory, for example, an existentialistic theory of freedom, which desired to make good the absolute freedom of man. Correspondingly, the reality of the freedom which man enjoys (relative freedom under the law) has always been the nemesis of any naturalistic theory (of whatever vintage) which in effect ignored or vitiated the uniqueness of human responsibility and freedom.

One way, popular today especially in the English-speaking world, of trying to account for the external ought without falling into such contradictory extremes is to talk of "values." The difficulties arise when one sets out to explain and justify the place of value. For within the subject-object schema only two possibilities are in the last analysis available; either value must be explained in reference to the creative free *subject* or in relation to the static universally valid *object*. But it is just such one-sided solutions which value theories are

---

[11] These basic tensions are clearly reflected in the titles of recent works in analytic circles, e.g. *Freedom and Reason* (Hare), *Thought and Action* (Hampshire).

intent on averting. Although a choice must ultimately be made, in general a concept of value is employed as a bridge, a point of synthesis — with or without dialectics – between subject and object. Value has the ring of normativity and at the same time it echoes all sorts of subjective associations. But must one stress the objective or subjective face of value? See here the underlying cause of the pendulum-like oscillation between "objectivism" and "subjectivism" in contemporary value-philosophy.

Impressed by their normative character, one individual is induced to assign values some kind of objective existence. The question is: what kind of objective existence? For if values enjoy a non-factual objectivity, not only is the fact-value relation a delicate matter, but the human subject himself must be called in to play a special role as the re- or per-ceiver of that which is beyond the pale of ordinary sense-perception. Thus, notwithstanding the intentions of the value "objectivist," the existence of such values depends on the testimony of the human subject. All this we have seen in relation to Moore.

Denying the existence of values or at best considering them euphemisms denoting personal preferences, post-Moorean theorists have given more attention to the subject. But to the present the crucial complex of questions which surfaces around the subject has not received the critical attention it deserves. Granted, an "ought" cannot be reduced to an "is," but, short of an appeal to values, how can one even talk of universally valid "oughts"? Concretely, how can Hare finally justify his separation of value judgments and personal inclinations? Why do the former and not the latter possess normative teeth? Perhaps it will be said that judgments which are *so* defined or which are *so* employed, i.e. to guide actions, are normative. But what situation made such definition possible? Why is there such a normative use in the first place? "Subjectivists" in value theory appear to have no alternative but to find the source and seat of normativity in the subject. However, can a subject, alone or in consort, justify raising his wishes to the level of norms for all? Can one even talk of an external ought in such cases? Yet, if it is not external (at least in theory), have we not ended up with an absolutization of human subjectivity which a fact-value dualism sets out to evade?

A Note on the Use of Formal Logic

The present trend to formalization in ethics has been stimulated as well as made possible by modern formal logic. Although clearly beyond the scope of the present study, the role which formal logic plays in the ethical theories discussed, as well as in analysis as a whole, makes a brief comment desirable.

Modern symbolic or formal logic, it must be noted at the outset, can play its role of "intermediary" because logic and its laws are no longer considered the attributes of being (Aristotle) or (in the post-Kantian trend) the "laws of

176

thought."[12] Logic has an exceptional position. But whether the laws of logic are the "laws of the laws of nature"[13] or whether necessary truths are established by linguistic convention[14] is still a matter of heated debate.

This ambiguous place of logical thought and its technical apparatus is clearly connected with the subject-object schema. The logical subject must maintain its autonomy even as it penetrates to the object. This dual, in the heart of the matter contradictory, desire has led to two uses of logic. On the one hand, the logical is taken in its formal-ness as the very creator of the possibilities of experience. By means of a so-called transcendental logic, the possibility of man's freedom is created and guaranteed. On the other hand, logic is taken in its formal-ness as encompassing all material possibilities. Here by means of a so-called formal logic the significance of free decisions and new experiences is voided or at least largely obscured. Whereas in the former instance "content" is attained in arbitrary individual decisions, in the latter instance "content" is logically excluded and the peculiarly human responsibility to act and choose, formally present, threatens to dissolve into meaninglessness. It is not that the thinkers concerned fail to recognize that there is "more" to reality than the logical, but that the logical is their final criterion for determining the meaningful. Thus, even though formal logic is able to shield human subjectivity from ravishment by the natural sciences, in the final analysis this formalization squeezes the meaning, content and life out of human freedom.

As will be obvious, today the existentialist unfolds a transcendental logic designed to secure human freedom and the neo-positivist employs logic as a tool to circumscribe reality. Wittgenstein is a classic example of one who attempted to carry out the neo-positivist line to the bitter end. In the *Tractatus* he is left only with contradictions and tautologies — all the important things are "beyond," only to be mystically pointed at.

The same problem, the relation of subject and object, is at the bottom of the continued unrest in regard to the analytic-synthetic distinction.[15] The analytic

[12] Cf. Stebbing, *A Modern Introduction to Logic* (1930), p. 471.
[13] Cf. Frege, *Grundlagen der Arithmetik* (1884), pars. 87 and 93 (Eng. trans., *Foundations of Arithmetic* 1950) and also W. & M. Kneale, *The Development of Logic* (1962), pp. 739-42.
[14] Thus Strawson claims that "it is, then, our own activity of making language through using it, our determination of the limits of the application of words, that makes inconsistency possible" (*Introduction to Logical Theory* 1952, pp. 9, 11-12).
The conventionalist position has been facilitated by an identification or at least a close *rapprochement* of logic and language. This identification has also been affirmed by certain ethicists whom we have studied. Whereas on the one hand language is reduced to logical propositions and identified with thought, on the other hand a logical thesis is widely regarded as a "thesis about the meanings of words, or dependent solely upon them" (*FR*, 30). Cf. also Montefiore, "'Ought' and 'Can'," *Phil. Quarterly* VIII (1958), p. 24. Cf. also Kneale, *op cit.*, pp. 628-51 for a general discussion.
[15] Cf. fn 5, p. 170.

judgment is conceived of as "pure" and "formal." The synthetic judgment comes into the picture when content is added and contact is made with the factual world of sense-experience. Although necessary, analytic judgments can by definition say nothing (new). But can synthetic judgments be anything but contingent? If not — as current orthodoxy legislates — mankind is left without substantial necessary principles by which to guide his life. All that is certain is analytic a priori. However, aside from the hollowness of this certainty, the present Quine-White inspired attack on the sacredness of the analytic-synthetic distinction itself is a most consistent irrationalistic foray designed to deprive the philosophically engaged man of certainty even there, i.e. in his last supposed stronghold of formal logic.

Summing Up and Looking Ahead

Our investigations, brief and general as they are, are at an end. It remains only to reformulate our conclusions. Although we stand shoulder to shoulder with Moore and Hare in their repulsion of the forces of extremism, and in their awareness that there is "more" to reality than the factual and logical, we cannot (and could not) hide our fears, hardened into conviction during the course of our explorations, that fact-value dualisms of whatever calibre are finally unable to beat off the irreconcilable adversaries. Mediation cannot furnish once-and-for-all immunity. The malaise is much deeper: the autonomy motive with its fixation for the subject-object schema. No remedy less radical than a complete rejection of the motive and framework itself can offer any hope of an eventual solution to the problems at hand. And just here arise tremendous difficulties. For, although by no means impervious to the dilemmas we have sketched, value theorists continue to presume that reality in its fullness is "subject" over against and tied to "object." This failure to locate the main source of difficulty in the constrictive nature of this ontological schema forms, it would appear, the major obstacle to genuine advance.[16] If the analysis here offered is in any way valid, the fundamental problems facing value theory will

---

[16] This failure is not simply to be written off as oversight — be it a serious case. Much rather, when one is driven by the freedom-domination motive and accepts the noetic-ontic schema, he cannot be moved to give up such a prioris by argumentation alone.

Although we cannot present a positive proof of the influence of pre-theoretical motives on one's philosophizing, we can show negatively that without reference to something "beyond"or"before" scientific thought, the master-key to a basic explanation of the states of affairs (continually returning dilemmas; opposing theories built on similar evidence; tenacity with which position is maintained regardless of antinomies; impossibility of communication between various schools; etc.) is never found. This state of affairs remains closed as long as philosophers continue to claim that theoretical thought is neutral. This is itself a stance with deep pre-theoretical roots.

remain unsolved in spite of the real advances made until ethicists and philosophers alike begin to engage in a far-reaching and deep-penetrating critique of starting-points and the framework involved.

One cannot advocate a "revolution" of these proportions without suggesting a positive alternative. In a last chapter we intend to lay the main lines for a "new" perspective with the hope that it will provide a "way out." Looking ahead to the last chapter, it is our conviction that a way out of the present predicament in ethics as well as in philosophy is in principle only possible if one considers (to attach to our previous discussion) the "external ought" as an irreducible "third factor." However in the present situation, intentions notwithstanding, the "third factor" or normativity is finally accounted for in terms of subjects or objects. To put it crudely (and certainly too simply): one is forced to squeeze "three pegs" (subject, object, normativity) into "two holes" (subject, object). It just never works.

The third irreducible factor can only retain its uniqueness when recognized as a law-order which holds for subjects as well as objects. There are, so to speak, two "sides" to reality: a *law-side* and a factual or *subject-side* (including both subjects and objects). These two sides are in correlation. Without law (to condition, to determine etc.), existence is impossible. Without that which is subject to the law (*sub-jacere*), law is without meaning. The law-order is the necessary condition for creaturely existence, and, on the other hand, limits and defines that existence. Bound by the law; that is, placed in the "room" where possibilities open up, man is free to act.

Prior to developing this view in its significance for value theory and ethics in a concluding chapter, it is instructive to examine the value theories which we have considered from the vantage point offered by the "new" position.

All of the theorists concerned have felt the impinging force of the law-order. Their fall into antinomies whenever they endeavoured to ascribe this "external ought" to subject or object is explained by the basic consideration that it has its own irreducibility, in fact, it makes the existence of subjects and objects possible. In Moore's case the "pull" of the norm-laws[17] is particularly intense. Thus, he refuses to allow these norm-laws either to be presented as subjective creations or to be reduced to the "natural" aspects. Further, he sensed that the norm-laws did not "exist" in a supra-sensual realm in the same way as perceivable objects existed "below." Goodness has its own kind of existence. But Moore is caught in a bind because despite his "intuition" of goodness, his ontological schema does not allow him the room to account rightly for this third factor called normativity. Universal validity is confused and identified with that which is objective. This equivocation alone caused him to relate goodness — despite all the problems it caused him — to the "object." As a

[17] In regard to norm-laws, cf. ch. 7.

result, not only is the function and place of the subject in regard to normativity ignored and distorted, but "goodness" cannot function properly as norm obtaining for both subjects and objects.

Having chosen to deny the existence of values, Moore's critics are unable, beset as they are with the same confusion, to account for the element of universal validity which ensconces in value terms and value judgments. If, as in our view, universal validity finds its seat and explanation in the law-order, this situation with its dilemmas does not arise. One can recognize the indispensable function which the subject has in formulating norms and, at the same time, argue that norms have universal validity in *that* and only *insofar* as they are particularizations and positivations of the structural norm-law. The subject is not sovereign, but his key part in the process of positivation and evaluation cannot be denied or minimized. The attempt on the part of ethicists to fix the origin and seat of normativity in subject or object betrays a confusing of the two sides of reality.

In conclusion, the "objectivists" à la Moore are guilty of absolutizing the norm-laws. They cut them off from the subject, the object and the law-order itself with the consequence that the norm-laws (now called values) are value-less for life on earth. Hovering above reality, loose from the anchor-relation which gives them meaning, values are related in some way to objects. The "subjectivists" absolutize the real subjective freedom which man enjoys in positivizing. However, this element of subjective freedom and responsibility which, as we shall later explain, comes into its own in positivation and evaluation must not be taken from under the law and absolutized. In such instances the subject is elevated to the position of creator, rather than of actualizer or unfolder of meaning. The norm-laws, robbed of their holding power by being transformed into subjective creations of mankind, stand antithetically over against the "facts" (natural, pre-logical reality). Meta-ethical attempts by means of the techniques of formal logic to (dis)solve the problems are, as we have seen, retreats from rather than solutions of the basic difficulties involved.

The concept of "value" in contemporary ethics takes the place of structural norm-laws. Speaking of values (or of value judgments) instead of norms or laws is a modern way of accounting for the inescapable normativity given in reality. By a concept of value meaning-determining law is brought back into the picture. Even if the values are termed "intrinsic" or "objective," they owe their very existence to a subject who "tore" them out of their place in the law-order and "granted" them an apriori objective existence.[18] Any absolutization is a positing (*ponere, positum*) which is in the nature of the case a subjective act. If the subject is not openly considered the law-giver, he is sure to be lurking

[18] As is also evidenced, for example, by the fact that so-called "ranges of values" are seldom in agreement.

in the shadows calmly pulling the strings. A concept of value is the result of a back-door squeeze in which a new (third) element enters in surreptitiously under the guise of being "objective" or "subjective." Thus, although the recognition of the law-order (in contrast to a facts-only approach) which comes to the fore in value philosophies must be applauded, as presently elaborated these theories are unable to justify or explain this recognition.

In outline: A new perspective 7

Contemporary value theory is caught in a veritable thicket of problems. A new "instrument" is required to clear a path through the dense shrubbery. One such philosophical instrument has been forged by the Dutch philosophers Herman Dooyeweerd and D. H. Th. Vollenhoven.[1] In this chapter we propose to test the cutting edge of this new "machete," the Philosophy of the Law-Idea, on the tangled undergrowth. Since a detailed exposition of this expansive as well as elaborate philosophic position is impossible within the confines of this study, we shall only set out to show that the recognition of a structural law-order which *holds for* reality (and thus can never be confused with or identified with empirical reality) provides a perspective for a "way out."

FUNDAMENTALS

The Law-Order

The entire cosmos, including mankind, stands under the structural[2] law-order of creation. This structural law-order is made up of a rich diversity of modal laws which determine, as well as limit the behavior of things, plants, animals and man. One can distinguish various such aspects or modalities of reality; namely, the numerical, spatial, kinematic, energetic, biotic, psychic, logical, historical, lingual, social, economic, aesthetic, juridical, moral and pistical (or the aspect of belief).

---

[1] Only Dooyeweerd has published significantly in English. H. Dooyeweerd, *A New Critique of Theoretical Thought* I-IV (1953-58) (hereafter, *NC*); *Transcendental Problems of Philosophic Thought* (1948); *In the Twilight of Western Thought* (1960). Cf. fn. 2, ch. 3.

[2] Structure in this use has the meaning of structure *for* in distinction from the more usual structure *of*. However, there is an immediate correlation between the two "structures." One only discovers the structure for (law-side) via, through and in the factual structures (subject-side).

182

Each modality expresses itself in all other modalities, and in turn mirrors all the other aspects. This representation takes place according to the fixed irreversible order of the aspects. Each "lower" or "earlier" modality by means of analogies called *anticipations* refers to all the "higher" or "later" modalities, and each "higher" falls back on the lower by means of analogies called *retrocipations*. This "sphere-universality," as it is called, does not in the least abrogate the mutual irreducibility or "sphere-sovereignty" of the aspects. All the analogies retain the *qualification* of the aspect concerned; they only approach or remind one of the *other* modalities.

These modalities do not as such refer to concrete "whats" (things, events, etc.) but to the "how" of these whats, to the diverse *ways* or *modes* in which we can experience them (a thing is experienced as alone/ in pairs/in umpteens, as heavy/light/ big/ small, as fast/slow, as expensive/cheap, as stolen/borrowed/ owned, as lovable /reprehensible, as ugly/beautiful, etc.). Since these aspects, although mutually irreducible, are bound together in an intermodal coherence and thus never appear alone or isolated, they are always experienced as facets or *aspects* of concrete things, events, etc. Thus one can also talk of the various *functions* of a concrete whole. In principle a concrete thing, man, plant or animal functions in every aspect, sometimes as *subject*[3] and sometimes as *object*. Only man, however, has subject-functions in all the aspects. A rose, for example, has a subject-function in the biotic aspect (it lives) but cannot function as a subject ethically (it does not love). Nevertheless, a rose can function as an ethical *object* to the ethical (human) subject ("say it with flowers"). Or again, a physical thing such as a stone is a physical *subject* but at the same time in that it can be seen and distinguished it has a psychical and a logical object-function. If the said stone is a diamond and is part of an engagement ring, its always-present but latent ethical object-function has been actualized. Concrete experience functions by way of this subject-object relation.

Knowledge

The possibility of knowledge and *a fortiori* of theoretical knowledge rests completely in the *given* coherence of the cosmos. Man has no access-to-reality problem because he himself is part of reality. The modal aspects of reality are not alien to him, they are also his. Man is intuitively aware that reality is also *his* reality. This general awareness of reality, including a general conscious-

---

[3] For want of more acceptable terminology the term "subject" has two uses which ought not to be confused. Both *subjects* and objects are *subject to* the law-order. In the first sense subject is employed as a substantive, the second use is adjectival. Thus, Dooyeweerd talks of a subject-side (including both subjects and objects) which is subject to and correlated with the law-side.

ness of norms, comes over man in intuitive self-reflection.[4] Mankind's recognition of justice and morality, for example, is evidence of the everyday, concrete, non-scientific, intuitive grasp of the meaning of the ethical and juridical principles. Since man is taken up in the full reality, he only grasps the modal aspects implicitly within the total structures which he experiences, and does not bring to conscious articulation the explicit character of ethical norms in contrast to logical or social norms etc. In more technical language (attaching to the previous paragraph), mankind is able to distinguish logically and come to knowledge through what is called the logical object-side of reality.[5]

Norm-Laws

For our study it is important to notice that not all the modal laws *obtain* or *hold* in the same way. The "natural" laws (laws for the pre-logical aspects) hold *without* human recognition. That which is subject to these laws (things, plants, animals and man to a certain extent) cannot withdraw from them. But in regard to the laws for the logical and post-logical aspects the matter is different. These laws — we shall call them norm-laws[6] (in contrast to the "natural" laws) — demand human recognition and require concretization (positivation) and formulation. It is precisely because these laws demand human recognition before they can be fulfilled that they are called norm-laws. It is not that norm-laws are any less law because they require recognition. Rather, exactly in *requiring* they reveal their law-character. The requisite human acknowledgment is the law-ordained means by which such laws are subjectively realized and effectuated.

Neither does the possibility of the non-observance or trespassing of norm-laws in the least endanger their holding-force. Much rather, such disobedience can only take place within the cadre and framework of the law and the possibilities it affords. Thus, adultery is an *im*moral (not *a*moral) act. Ethically-good as well as ethically-bad acts are both ethical in character; that is, they both find their meaning in relation to the ethical norm-law.

In other words, recognition of the norm-laws always takes place — be it in

---

[4] Intuition as immediate insight into states of affairs cannot be separated from the analytical function as if it were a mysterious non-logical faculty. Dooyeweerd conceives of intuition as "the bottom layer" of the logical function which "is in continuous temporal contact with all the other modal functions" (Dooyeweerd, *NC* II, 473; cf. 472-85). It is however at least open to question if one, as Dooyeweerd seems to do, can limit intuition to the logical. Is not all conscious human activity, regardless of qualification, through and through intuitive?

[5] Since an act or a state of affairs has *all* the aspects of reality, it always has a logical object-function and is thus logically distinguishable.

[6] It is perhaps necessary to stress that in our view the normative is not equivalent (even roughly) with the ethical or moral.

abeyance. Without such recognition human existence would be impossible. Yet, it belongs to the distinctiveness of these norm-laws that man is free to disobey these laws (within certain limits, namely, the limits marked out by the norm-law). Having recognized the norm-laws, one must positivize and formulate them into positive laws or norms. These positive laws, it is obvious, derive their validity, their compelling character, their binding force, from the firmness and steadfastness of the law-order. Without the anchor-relation to the law-order, positive law is adrift, and sooner or later would dash itself to pieces on the rocks of naturalism, historicism, relativism and subjectivism. In actual fact, this "breaking to pieces" is always hampered, and ultimately defeated by the presence of the anchor. However, in that theoretical accounts seek to do without the "anchor," they are fraught with tensions.

Positivation

By observing certain regularities, certain law-conformities given in experience, one acquires insight into the norm-laws to which they refer. On the basis of such knowledge one is able to concretize (positivize) positive laws. However, since this knowledge of the law is indirect (the norm-laws, as structural laws holding *for*, are never present at hand, but are the very condition of that which is present at hand and which can be grasped), the resultant positive laws are always open to correction and revision. In addition, positive laws must be revised from time to time in accordance with the stage of cultural integration and differentiation.

Positivation or concretization is an inherent element of the post-historical law-spheres. It is the historical retrocipation of these spheres (underlining the point that positivation depends on the stage of cultural development). The historical and logical analogies of the post-historical spheres reveal themselves in the possibility of free human choice and judgment in positivation. Positivation (of whatever kind) is a human act and as such it takes place on the subject-side of the cosmos.[7] However, the intended *results* of human positivizing are taken up in the normativity complex and receive normative status. Although it remains difficult to explain, it can be said that the possibility (as well as the

[7] Although this process of positivation has always been stressed in the *Wijsbegeerte der Wetsidee* (Philosophy of the Law-Idea), there is no clear understanding as to its nature and scope. In positivation, according to Dooyeweerd, "the human formative will is then to be conceived of as a *subjective moment* on the law-side of these law-spheres themselves." In view of his own repeated insistence that the acting subject is always under law, it appears that this definition is open to misunderstanding: can one talk or even conceive of the human formative will acting, albeit only as a subjective moment, on the law side? It would seem, and the context warrants this interpretation, that Dooyeweerd only intends to underline the "appeal" of the historical and post-historical laws to the human formative will. Cf. *NC* II, 239, also 235, 238, 243.

185

fact) that human "positivations" acquire normative status rests as a given in the creation-order. It stands as the corollary of the "built-in" requirement of the norm-laws of creation that they be recognized and concretized *before* they function properly. For their realization the norm-laws[8] demand even as they induce formative activity. This appeal to the subjective formative will is part and parcel of their very nature. On the one hand, it is not that these laws lose their holding power without the cooperation of the subject, much rather that their power cannot rightly come into force. On the other hand, a subject in his law-bound condition cannot resist positivizing. In brief, one *must will* to positivize. Any failure in this respect is not in the first place impotence but wilful disobedience. The glory of man's task as man — as distinct from the rest of the creaturely — in that he is called upon to take a free, responsible, spontaneous role in the opening-up of the meaning of creation comes into unique focus in the process of positivation.

Facts and Values

Turning to the problematics which we have been discussing, the first matter which requires emphasis is the nature of "facts." Facts do not enjoy an objective, self-sufficient, *an sich* existence. There is no such thing as a "brute fact." It is not that facts stand by themselves and as the occasion affords are perceived as such. Facts can only be known in their meaning-character in relation to a law-order, and can only exist as law-conformable. A certain fact is a fact when and because it answers to a certain law-structure (holding for facts of a typical kind). Facts and law-order are in correlation. Without the law-order te define and determine, there could be no facts. Without the facts as those which answer to and subjectively realize the demands of the law, the law-order would be meaningless. Facts only speak when structured. An awareness of law-order is a prerequisite for the acquistion of any knowledge of the facts. Without at least an implicit sense of the diverse law-spheres, one could not assimilate physical, economic, ethical and all the other kinds of facts. Nor could one distinguish one kind of fact from another. Any reference to fact is by definition a reference to *some kind* of fact. This means that there are not only so-called "natural" facts (the rustling of leaves, the flowering of a tree, the purring of a cat) but also facts bearing a normative qualification; economic, ethical, aesthetic, etc. (buying a car, caressing a child, enjoying a concert). Apart from normative structures, there is no way to acknowledge the institutions one confronts in reality, such as state, church and family. The relationship or

---

[8] For the exceptional position of logical norms, cf. *NC* II, 237, 241.

correlation of fact and norm is obvious, for example, when one talks of a *good* family. But it is just as real when one names a certain group of individuals a family. How does one know that this particular group is a family? There is only one answer: it meets the norm for the family.

In view of the historic ballast burdening the term, one is advised to use extreme caution in any mention of the term "value." Values in our view must simply be facts, acts, things, events which in a high degree live up to the relevant norms.[9] These values in no wise exist by themselves. Values are *referential* in character and only in this reference to the law-order do they possess meaning. As such, they are only possible as a result of prior subjective recognition of the structural law-order of creation. In order to guard against the danger of substantialized values, it is the better part of caution to speak of having value: certain subjective conditions answer to the norm. When something is said to have value, there is, as we have seen, no sense in which the thing is intrinsically valuable. On the other hand, it is not valuable simply because of a subjective arbitrary human choice. Certainly, subjective judgment or valuation is involved. But the key element is the *norm* according to which subjective evaluation examines the object and decides its value.

Thus, when someone remarks that this lamp or that plant etc. is valuable, the first question that must be answered is this: in *what* way is this valuable? Is the lamp worth a great deal of money? Or is it valued because it is a gift from a friend? Perhaps it is beautiful? Does it add something to the atmosphere of the room? In the same way one can judge the value of a highway economically (too expensive), aesthetically (beautiful; follows the contours of the landscape), technically (asphalt or concrete), etc. In each case, although a thing or an act can be evaluated according to various criteria, all such evaluations are more or less directly related to and affected by a "primary" valuation as to how well it lives up to its nature as thing or act qualified in a particular way with a typical internal structure. Thus, for example, an evaluation of a lamp (of whatever kind) is bound by the fact that a lamp has a *socially* qualified objective destination.

---

[9] Thus, in denying that values are peculiar "existents" wholly different from facts, current theorists are undoubtedly right. But in that values for the thinkers concerned take the place of the law-order, the rejection of their existence leaves one without any reference point outside the subject which is not factual. In such a situation extreme "subjectivism" or "naturalism" are the only alternatives. The mistake of the "objectivist" was not that he maintained the existence of a law-order (for him values), but that he treated the law-order as if it were just another object or thing, be it of a non-natural kind. Much rather the law *holds for* things, objects etc.

As is obvious, we have done away with any fact-value dualism with its split of the cosmos into a norm-saturated and a norm-free area. In our view facts (of whatever kind) answer to a law-structure, and in the degree that such subjective realities answer to the law-structure, they bear value (again of various kinds). All this implies that description cannot stand over against evaluation as objective over against subjective. Description of facts, just as much as their evaluation, is an act of judging, of valuing. That a rectangular scrap of paper imprinted with colored ink is on occasion rightly *described* as a "ten dollar bill" is only possible because of the existence of the so-called "institution of money." That an exchange of "I do's" is on occasion to be described as the act of marrying is made possible by the existence of the institution of marriage. When the relevant criteria are fulfilled; that is, when the circumstances are to be *described* in a certain way is a matter dependent on human evaluation. Even describing X as rock, sand, rain or wind demands evaluation in reference to a law-structure.

Whether a certain act is to be described as adultery, fornication or married love depends on the existence of the institution of marriage. If one does not accept the institution, the form it has assumed in our society, and the ethical norms involved, it makes no sense to speak of adultery, fornication or married love. However, to limit the description to the physical, biotic and psychical aspects involved is to do injustice to the "facts" of the situation: human intercourse is reduced to animal copulation. Not only is it impermissible to dehumanize a human act, it is actually impossible. Such attempts always, in the first place, presuppose the essential humanness of the act described. This is most obvious perhaps in the manuals for love-making. Animals do not need and have no use for such manuals. Moreover, even when reducing intercourse to copulation, the act is called love-making. But animals do not love. And thirdly, one discovers as a compensating factor, a mystical pean to the praise of romantic love which has no real connection with the description itself. Love and intercourse are of one piece in marriage. If once separated, all attempts to recover the lost-unity are precarious and inadequate.

It is impossible to suppose that facts can be described without evaluation, objectively so to speak, without incorporating any subjective element. The difference between what is customarily termed description and evaluation lies only in the purposes for which, and the criteria by which one judges. In both cases criteria are required. One either seeks to ascertain with the use of the relevant criteria whether X belongs to groups A, B, C or he is out to gauge, again with the proper criteria, how well X lives up to its function or purpose as member of group A, B, or C.

One must judge in the *same* way when he has to decide whether a stout solid club, one end thicker than the other, is to be *described* as a baseball or cricket bat as when he must decide whether a bat is to be evaluated as good, average or poor. But in the former case since bats are always made according to certain specifications (they are all very much alike) one evaluates that X is a baseball bat without explicitly going through the process — with the proviso that once upon a time one was explicitly taught the characteristics of a baseball bat. In the latter case, since one can rate a bat according to various criteria, including suitability for the type of batter, there is bound in general to be much more explicit attention to the moment of valuation involved. This need not, however, be the case. Thus, for example, whereas someone unacquainted with the game of baseball would have difficulty in judging which club to describe as a baseball bat, a professional player would not hesitate a moment before judging which bat he evaluated as good.

At this point it is well to remember that a complexity of enormous proportions arises in the description (as well as evaluation) of facts bearing a normative qualification. Although the "natural laws" do not require human recognition before they function properly, norm-laws do require this human cooperation. Thus, even before economic, aesthetic or ethical facts etc. can be established, the norms in correlation with which these facts can be ascertained must be positivized. And since this positivation depends on human insight which varies from individual to individual, from community to community, and from generation to generation, there is more possibility for disagreement in ascertaining an ethical fact (X is an act of murder) than in ascertaining, for example, a biotic fact (Y is a rose).

Nevertheless, one must not give in to the temptation to maintain that evaluation is only involved in the *former* case and not in the *latter*. As if an act of murder is not just as factual as a rose! Subjective valuation is involved in both instances. Thus, one not only can challenge whether X was murder, he can also challenge whether Y is a rose. Since evaluation is involved in both instances, debate as to the nature of Y is by no means imaginary. The fact that there is relatively more agreement in the latter case does not plead for the reality of a descriptive-evaluative contrast.

Evaluation as Logical Distinguishing

Evaluation is a completely subjective human act in which man enjoys freedom and responsibility under the law-order of creation. It may not be conceived of as an act in which the autonomous subject calls "values" into being, nor may it be deprived, on the other hand, of the real element of freedom involved. Whether one describes or judges, appraises or estimates, evaluation is involved.

The all-important point for our discussion is that evaluation as such never takes place. It always bears a more precise law-oriented qualification; one

189

speaks of ethical evaluation, economic, social, legal evaluation etc. There can be as many qualifications as normative law-spheres. This is not in the least to deny that every act of evaluation, regardless of its qualification, includes the element of logical distinguishing. It necessarily has such a logical basis and is never a-logical. Evaluation is simply impossible without knowledge of norms, and such knowledge, possible because of the intermodal coherence between the analytic aspect and the non-analytic aspects, depends in the first place on logical distinguishing. It is precisely the logical basis which raises the post-logical spheres above the pre-logical spheres and ushers in for the first time, modally speaking, the moment of human freedom and choice.

The heart of the matter is that in both descriptive and evaluative acts of whatever qualification the moment of logical distinguishing plays a crucial foundational or conditioning role. The difference between description and evaluation, between knowing and valuing, has *nothing* to do with the nature of the acts involved. It is not that a so-called descriptive or logically qualified judgment can (in a normal situation) claim universal validity and thus truth in contrast to an evaluative judgment which remains basically irrational, subjective and individual. Every judgment qua judgment has an analytic aspect. There is no contrast possible between acts of (logical) "knowing" and (post-logical) "valuing" in the sense that one is logical and the other a-logical, the one analytically qualified and the other (usually) psychically. Logical truth-judgments are in every sense as subjective as post-logical, e.g. ethical, or economic truth-judgments. Logical evaluation and ethical evaluation differ only in the qualifying aspect of the act. A knowing and valuing contrast is simply an impossible division: the results of theoretical thought as knowledge must always be evaluated in order to be of use, and not only is the scientific inquiry guided and directed by evaluative considerations, it is in itself, as inquiry, an evaluative matter.[10] Ethical (economic, aesthetic, etc.) judgments are not indifferent to the logical norm of contradiction. They cannot (legitimately) be self-contradictory. The difference is that they are not, as theoretical judgments are, logically qualified.

Of course, a judgment which simply expresses the opinion of an individual does not claim universal validity. But when the same individual, no longer asserting that "I at least think that this is beautiful," simply exclaims, "this is beautiful," he is claiming that his judgment holds – at least ought to hold – for every (normal) subject. It claims to be true, and if it is, it has universal validity.

If someone not only rejects our claim that practical, that is, pre-theoretical

---

[10] Thus Stevenson is forced to recognize that no inquiry "can divorce itself from the evaluative considerations that directly concern and guide the process of inquiry itself" (*EL*, 161, 286ff.). Hare too is aware that "almost every word in our language is capable of being used on occasion as a value-word (that is, for commending or its opposite)" (*LM*, 79).

evaluative judgments can have universal validity, but also asserts that there is no universally valid norm for, say, ethical valuation, he is skating on perilously thin ice. For then he must refrain from any kind of ethical evaluation which is to apply to anyone other than himself. If such an individual claims, for example, that adultery in certain instances is moral, he is contradicting himself. It is self-contradictory to deny the existence of universal norms and then to claim that a certain thing is good or bad, true or false, efficient or inefficient, valuable or valueless, etc. If it is accepted that marital fidelity is an ethical good, if it is valued highly, then, to judge that adultery is immoral, or fidelity moral, has *universally valid meaning*. But if such judgment lacks universal meaning, then it makes no sense to consider fidelity a morally good act. It is all or nothing.

Ethical Evaluation

As has been suggested earlier, an act of valuation always bears a more precise qualification. What is now to be said about an act of ethical evaluation applies *mutatis mutandis* to all non-theoretical acts bearing a normative qualification. Ethical evaluation is to be seen as an ethically qualified act in which the (always-present) analytical function comes to the fore in such a manner and with such emphasis that it "determines" or "specifies" the distinctive individuality of the act. This in contrast to other "types" of ethical(ly qualified) acts in which another function "determines" or "specifies" the typical individualness. For example, an act of kissing — although the analytic aspect (along with all the others) continues to play its peculiar role in accordance with its place in the law-order — receives its uniqueness, its particular character from the determining or conditioning role of the psychical function and thus has a typical ethical-psychical structuration. In a similar way an act of evaluation, e.g. when one considers the advisability of kissing someone, or has "second thoughts" as to the wiseness of a past action, receives its "mark of distinction," its "individual face" as an ethical act from its ethical-*analytical* structuration. In the first instance, the analytic aspect plays a rather unobtrusive albeit still important role within the act of kissing. Unobtrusive in that it finds its place between the aspects — the ethical and psychical — which determine the act in its main lines. Important in that it fulfills its own inconvertible role as the foundational or conditioning moment in any human activity. Demonstrations of love are not instinctive or mechanical; they always presuppose logical insight.

During the execution of such ethically qualified acts, one from time to time deliberately and purposively pulls back and judges the propriety of his actions in various respects according to the relevant norms. Then we have instances of evaluation. In such cases the analytic aspect comes to the fore in such a way that the "individual face" of the act changes even though the ethical qualification clearly remains. The same holds true for acts of valuation bearing another

191

qualification: one has to do with aesthetic-analytic, economic-analytic, etc. structurations. In such an act of evaluation, one distinguishes, describes, arranges, combines, eventually judges and decides under the leading of the qualifying function. Although it is the qualifying function which, so to speak, colors the evaluation, it is the logical base moment which fleshes out the color as to tone and hue.

The relation of the ethical and analytical aspects in acts of ethical evaluation, or in general the relation of the qualifying and founding function in evaluative acts, deserves further attention. In tandem these functions determine such acts in their main lines. From the viewpoint of the qualifying function: it leads the unfolding of the foundational function but at the same time it must resort to this function for further delineation of the typical character of the ethical act. When, in Dooyeweerd's technical terminology, the qualifying function lacks an original or nuclear modal type of individuality, one must for a more precise determination of an act fall directly back upon some other original or peculiar modal type of individuality.[11] Returning to our examples: In the case of the ethical(ly qualified) act of kissing, since there is no ethical nuclear type of individuality, one must fall back upon the nuclear individuality type of the psychical. In the case of ethical evaluation, one must have recourse to the nuclear individuality type of the analytic.

From the side of the foundational function: it is opened up by the qualifying function even as its modal individuality provides the typicalness of the act. This opening-up is imperative since a foundational function "cannot be in a closed condition . . . . [but] can only be conceived in an anticipatory coherence with the leading function."[12] For a more precise determination as well as classification of ethically qualified acts, one is referred to a foundational function. Such a function is relatively easy to locate in that it furnishes the "typical individuality" of the act in question.[13] At the same time, the qualifying function opens up the foundational function without, however, thereby disturbing its nuclear type of individuality.[14]

[11] Cf. Dooyeweerd, *NC* II, 424. At this point it is well to remember that the discussion does *not* concern the foundational role which the analytic plays in the modal order in general and thus in every act, but we have to do with variation in the *individuality* of ethically qualified acts.

[12] Dooyeweerd, *NC* III, 91.

[13] The fact that it is the nuclear modal type of individuality of the analytic aspect which gives the "individual face" to acts of evaluation explains why the *similarity* of all evaluative acts urges itself upon us more than the radical modal differences in qualification.

[14] The fact that the foundational function, in our case the logical, must be opened up does not speak against our earlier contention that it was just the nuclear individuality of the logical which gave the individual face to acts of evaluation. To cite Dooyeweerd: the necessity of an opened-up foundational function "does not affect the nuclear character of the type of individuality of the foundational function" (*NC* III, 91).

192

For an explanation of the regularity and frequency with which, relatively speaking, acts of valuing, pondering, reflecting, judging, considering, etc. occur, one need only remember that the analytic plays a *general, foundational* role in the normative spheres. Indeed, just because of this "lower" or "earlier" place in the law-order, the analytic aspect can be unfolded in more ways than the other normative aspects. Or one could put it this way: it is part of the very character of human acts that they contain that which *induces, evokes,* or *elicits* further (or previous) deliberation and evaluation. But such valuation remains within the "cadre" or "framework" of the act which elicited it in the first place. And even though evaluation involves a "falling back" to the analytic as foundational aspect, it must be stressed that this "retreat" takes place with the express purpose of unfolding and deepening the meaning of the original act.

Description and Evaluation: Their Difference

Having thus far maintained that acts of ethical description and ethical evaluation are both to be explained by ethical-analytic structurations, it is clear that there is no sharp contrast between description and evaluation — both involve valuing. However, this is not to say that the terms ought to be employed interchangeably. Although evaluation is involved in observing the existence of a *family* as well as in judging that it is a *good* family, there is a typical difference involved which may not be overlooked. It is this difference which provides the descriptive-evaluative opposition with a semblance of truth.

Certainly, one must distinguish between activities in which one determines whether X belongs in category A, B, and C, and undertakings in which one notes the value of the members of categories A, B, and C respectively. In the former case one examines if X fulfills the criteria, or has the constitutive properties necessary for it to be a member of a certain kingdom, class or group. In the latter case, one examines in how far X fulfills or fails to fulfill the criteria, or has or fails to have the adherent properties necessary for it to be regarded respectively an excellent, very good, good, or average member of the certain kingdom, class or group. In the first case of description the concern is whether or not an "object" answers to the structural norms which must be met if such a "thing" is to exist. Either it has or fails to have the necessary *constitutive* factors. It either conforms, to take an example, with the aesthetic norms for an art object, or it fails to conform; it is either an art object (poem, novel, etc.) or it is not. In the second instance (valuation) the concern is whether the object meets the "additional" norms which are positivized as insight deepens into what it *means* to be an art object. Granted that "it" fulfills the necessary and sufficient requirements valid for a poem, the issue is now whether it meets the "additional" demand or demands, whether it has the "adherent" aesthetical quality or qualities which make it in one or more respects a *great* poem.[15] However, and this is the most important consideration, evaluation is involved in both description and evaluation — only the criteria differ as the purposes vary.[16]

Evaluation and Positivation

It remains to relate our discussion of description and evaluation to the matter of positivation which we briefly mentioned towards the beginning of this chapter. Since positivation as well as description and valuation are subjective acts involving valuing, these activities form one process. Positivation can be seen as the last phase or last step of a series of descriptions and evaluations. That is: on the basis of knowledge gained in valuation-description, one decides to concretize a positive law. There is an on-going, never-ending interaction of valuation-description and positivation. A positive law or norm, as a specification of the structural norm-law, is valid as long as it has (or is thought to have) value in relation to previously positivized norms and in the final analysis to the norm-law itself. A norm has value when it is recognized as valid. When, in the anticipatory direction, it becomes obvious that a certain norm no longer meets the requirements, it has lost its value and a new norm must be positivized which better embodies the norm-law.[17]

Validity and Evaluation

The actualization of norms and the evaluation of states of affairs finds its origin in the person who is the executor of the act. This evaluation and positivation is *unfolding* — not giving — of meaning and occurs as a necessary subjective answer to the law-order which in its revelatory, impinging character demands recognition. Acts are always answers to the Law. Human evaluation takes place in the *givenness* of the cosmic law-order, but it *begins* in (transcendental) self-reflection. This implies that the states of affairs open up, truly of falsely, to the evaluating subject in the anticipatory direction under the leading of the pistical aspect (either in belief or disbelief). For belief, as the terminal function, "is driven on directly by impulses from the religious root of human

[15] For a charting of such "constitutive" and "adherent" factors in regard to art objects, see Calvin Seerveld's *A Christian Critique of Literature*, Christian Perspective Series 1964, especially the chart on page 56.

[16] In more technical terms: When one describes a family, he is dealing with the (primary) retrocipatory, closed, restrictive structure. When he goes on to judge whether the family is good or bad, he is dealing with the anticipatory, opened-up, regulative structure. In both instances evaluation is involved. Cf. Dooyeweerd, *NC* II, 181 ff.

[17] In the act of positivation as the climax of evaluative acts, the formative aspect stands out along with the qualifying function. In this case perhaps one could talk of an ethical (etc.) -formative structuration.

194

existence, either for good or for evil."[18] Evaluation receives its full meaning and unity from the central choice of a man's heart in answer to the Law of Love. This choice of obedience or disobedience gives the *direction* to the evaluation. How one evaluates and positivizes depends in the last analysis on the central direction (Good or Evil)[19] which "lives" in man's heart and which directs man's bodily (functional) life. The *validity* of human evaluation; that is, whether one truly recognizes what has value and what does not, depends on its agreement with the law-order. Complete agreement with the law-order (in principle possible) is only possible when the evaluator stands *right* over against the Law of God and thus is *good* and up-right. Only when rightly directed is one's evaluation in the last instance and in the full sense of the word valid.

Since Evil is parasitic on the Good, there is always and everywhere, regardless of personal status, a fragmented and relative recognition of true states of affairs. However, since it finds or rather attempts to find certainty in cosmic reality, disbelief sooner or later strangles or petrifies the process of valuation and positivation in its dynamic directedness to the Fullness of Meaning in Jesus Christ and through Him to God the Father. This is immediately obvious when it is realized that certainty implies a *resting-place*. If rest is found in some aspect or segment of reality, there is no impetus to further movement. The "complication" which shatters every such effort to find rest within reality is the fact that "nothing" in creation rests in itself, but only finds its meaning — is meaning — in an interwovenness with all of creation in a continuous outward moving and pointing towards the Fullness of Meaning. Rest cannot be found in a rest-less creation.

ETHICS AS A SPECIAL SCIENCE

The Possibility of (Ethical) Theory

The acts of evaluation described in the preceding section are pre-theoretical in character, that is, practical judgments which leave the concreteness and integrality of reality intact. One evaluates under the leading of ethical, economic, or whatever interests, but not theoretic. However, in that the analytic

---

[18] Dooyeweerd, *NC* II, 293.
[19] The good-evil distinction is the "third determination" in addition to the individual and modal distinctions. Cf. Vollenhoven, *Isagoogè* (1967) p. 53ff. and Dooyeweerd, *NC* II, 148. This basic distinction, although certainly related, may not be confused or identified with the concept of value (as does H. G. Stoker in "Die kosmiese dimensie van gebeurtenisse," *Phil. Reformata* XXIX, 1964, p. 30). "Living" in human hearts, "Good" (or "Evil") influences what is chosen to be modally valuable. Without awareness of the religious character of good in its full meaning, one is at a loss when he must interpret modal good-evil distinctions.

plays an out-standing (foundational, *not* qualifying) role in all acts of pre-theoretical evaluation, such acts can easily function as the "corridors," so to speak, by which pre-theoretical activity can pass over into theoretical thought.

Perhaps it is more accurate to say that such evaluative acts, especially in times of increasing cultural integration and differentiation, can serve as the occasions for or the inducements to new acts in themselves analytically qualified. The scientific investigation characteristic of the special sciences of ethics, economics, aesthetics, etc. begins precisely when one puts other interests aside and is in the first place theoretically interested in the matters at hand. Since our chief concern in explaining the make-up of evaluative acts was explanatory, we have been occupied theoretically, sketching in a *theory* of values and valuation.

The possibility of such scientific judgments and of scientific thought as a whole lies as an objective possibility given in creation. That is to say, reality has a logical object-side which can be opened up in scientific thought. In our theorizing about acts of evaluation the logical object-side of such acts is brought into the logical range of vision of the act of thought. In this process of abstraction from the knowable, intent on tracing out the law-structures, one turns away from the particular to the general, from the fullness of reality to a certain aspect of it.

The distinction between pre-theoretical judgments which participate part and parcel in the wholeness of experience and theoretical judgments which are abstractions from this wholeness, both in themselves valuational, is of decisive significance. It is the difference between a father's advice to his son and an ethicist's generalizing reflection on the *ethical aspect* of such fatherly advice; between a woman judging that the coat is a good buy and the economist reflecting on the buying habits of women. Whereas in the former instances one has to do with ethically and economically qualified judgments uttered in respectively ethical and economic situations, in the latter instances one has to do with scientific (analytically qualified) judgments *about* respectively an ethical and economic state of affairs. The failure to recognize the distinction at issue is abetted by the ambiguous use of terminology. The judgments of the father and the ethicist are both customarily considered "ethical judgments." In the same way the judgments of the purchaser and of the economist are misleadingly grouped together as "economic judgments."

Confusion on this matter has misled value theorists repeatedly. Value judgments (of the every-day variety) have been measured by the standards obtaining for theoretical value judgments. Failing to meet these requirements they have been dismissed as unscientific and irrational, or at least, as substandard. Only when one, it is said, speaks scientifically is he speaking truthfully — at least, in the full sense of the word. Value judgments are shunted aside as intellectually disreputable. Reaction challenging this scientism has set in, as we have seen, in the work of Moore, the later Wittgenstein and the school of Ordinary

Language. Non-scientific life and its value judgments have received reprieve. Nevertheless, this laudatory appreciation of ordinary life and the respectability accorded its value judgments has not resulted in a proper understanding of the theoretic/non-theoretic relationship. Indeed, the danger is not unreal that the pendulum will swing to the opposite pole in which everyday judgments expressed in ordinary language are assigned normative status in scientific investigation. Here again the typical differences between non-theoretical and theoretical judgments are ignored.

The Science of Ethics

According to the theory of law-spheres which we have previously explained in outline, ethics must be seen as a *special* (modal) science. No longer does it have as its field of investigation the whole range of human conduct, no longer does it have a monopoly on matters of goodness and on normativity in general; it is restricted to the *irreducible* aspect of experience called the ethical. Ethics as a science must investigate 1) the ethical norm-law, 2) that which is subject to the law, and 3) the correlation between the law-side and the subject-side. The ethical law holds for, it is universally valid for, all that is ethical, but *only* for that which is ethical. Neglect of the *modal* limitation of the ethical law results in the hegemony of the ethical over other modal areas or in the (mis)application of other modal laws in the ethical area. In the one case we have a moralism, in the other a psychologism, logicism, etc. Later we shall have opportunity to expand on these matters.

It is the aspectual character of the ethical which guarantees the possibility of ethical science. Since ethics is one of the sciences dealing with territories subject to norm-laws, in this case the ethical, the question as to whether ethics is descriptive, normative or meta- is altogether irrelevant. In all her activities, in description and in evaluation, ethics must take account of the norm-law. Even ascertaining ethical facts, as we have seen, involves evaluation in relation to norms. This concern for the norm-law does not mean leaving reality (metaphysically) for the regions beyond. Rather it demands that one go to work empirically (not empiri*cist*ically), for it is only through contact with the regularities in experience that we gain knowledge of these norm-laws. The conformities point to the laws themselves which are the very conditioning factors necessary for the occurrence of such regularities.

It is also this law-aspect which enables ethics to speak in universally valid terms. For only in relation to a norm is it possible to speak of universal validity. In the proportion that an ethics refuses to speak of norms, in that degree there always remains an unbridgeable chasm between the individuality of ethical phenomena and the scientific desire to trace out the universally valid laws involved. At this point stress must again be laid on the fact that the ethical aspect is only *one aspect* of reality. This implies, on the one hand, that ethics studies the ethical aspect of *concrete realities* which in principle can also function in all other *aspects* of reality. Thus ethical science cannot ignore the other aspects (and the respective sciences involved) which also co-determine the meaning of the act, event, fact, etc. On the other hand, this also makes clear that, although ethics is an aspectual science, nothing in reality is in principle off-limits for her. Every human activity functions in all the law-spheres, and every thing, plant or animal has a potential object-function in the ethical. However, as a science ethics has a first and particular responsibility to investigate the states of affairs in which the ethical aspect plays a *leading or qualifying* role, as for example in certain communal relations (marriage and the family), certain inter-communal relations (friendship) and in certain subject-object relations (love of country, love of animals, etc.).[20]

Although it is incontrovertible that reality has an ethical aspect, it is difficult to describe and in the last analysis impossible to define its kernel moment (that point of commonness and cohesion in all that one qualifies as ethical). This is due to the very a-logical, irreducible nature of kernel moments. Indeed, if such moments could finally be defined logically, there would be *nothing* to analyze. This would mean at the same time the absolutization and abolition of the logical. Although science must recognize its impotence to grasp the kernel-moment, it is just the existence of such non-logical moments which makes science possible.

In spite of the impossibility to capture logically the kernel moment, it is known, experienced and sensed *intuitively* by everyone. Notwithstanding the irreducibility of the aspects, there is an indissoluble coherence among them which comes to expression in their analogical moments. And since the ethical (as all aspects) has, among others, a logical analogy, it can be logically distinguished. Whether one should further choose to describe the kernel as "love"[21] or "troth" is a difficult question. While Dooyeweerd, Mekkes, Van Riessen and Troost choose for love in temporal relations,[22] Vollenhoven, Popma and

[20] Cf. Dooyeweerd *NC* II, 140-62 for a discussion of the modal aspect of love; III, 304-42 in regard to marriage and III, 266-304 in regard to the family.
[21] Love in this sense is not to be reduced to a feeling or an emotion. The "love-feeling," as a psychical retrocipation of the ethical, has a *normed* character not shared by psychic feeling in its original or initial occurrence.
[22] Cf. Dooyeweerd, *NC* I, 48; II, 152 ff., 158 ff. and Van Riessen, *Op Wijsgerige Wegen* (1963²), p. 82; and Mekkes in *Philosophia Reformata* XXIII (1958), p. 185. Although Troost in general agrees with Dooyeweerd (*Casuïstiek en Situatie-Ethiek*, 1958, pp. 40, 48, 110, 377), he also describes the ethical as neighborly-love ("naastenliefde") (*Ibid.*, pp. 116, 181, 357 and more clearly in *Vermogensaanwasdeling en Sociale Ethiek*, 1964, pp. 18, 33, 39-40). In a later unpublished paper he talks of "specific" and "relative" neighborly-love. In view of the fact that love of neighbor is a Total, Absolute Command (cf. fn. 24), it is at least misleading to speak of neighborly-love as the mark of the relative ethical aspect.

Taljaard prefer to speak of fidelity or troth, in marriage and friendship.[23] Provisionally, partly because of terminological considerations, partly because love is often reduced to a feeling, and partly because love is generally confined to marriage and the family, it seems to this writer preferable to describe the kernel moment as "troth" (or fidelity).[24]

In Comparison With Traditional Views

In the concluding sections of this study, attention will be called to a number of difficulties in traditional theories of ethics which dissolve when ethics is considered a special science. It is our thesis that perspectives can only be fruitfully opened up if one accepts (pre-theoretically) the *givenness* of a law-order. One advantage of such an acceptance is obvious: scientists are no longer left to mark out arbitrarily and thus artificially the fields of investigation of the various sciences. Without such a law-order there is in principle no barrier preventing the sciences from extending their borders as they see fit. Edel has clearly seen the predicament facing the great majority of contemporary ethicists. "There is a pie to be cut, but there is no injunction about the number and size of the slices." In reference to the *mark* of the ethical, he concludes that there "is no adequate ground for decisive judgment. . . . To waste energy in claims of primacy at this stage . . . is folly."[25]

[23] Vollenhoven, *Isagoogè*, p. 24. Popma, *Inleiding in de Wijsbegeerte* (1956), p. 17; and Taljaard, *Die mens, die liefde en die sedelike* (reprint from *Koers*, June 1956), p. 19. Cf. also Du Plessis *Opskorting van die Etiese*? (1965), pp. 198, 199.

In "solidarity" Von Meyenfeldt seems to have described the kernel in terms of its social or psychical retrocipations (*The Meaning of Ethos*, 1964, p. 38). However, in relating solidarity very intimately with "human relations" and "sense of responsibility," ethos becomes, it seems contrary to his intentions, much more than "one sphere of our existence" (p. 24).

[24] Troth "in marriage and friendship" is too concrete to serve as the designation for the ethical *aspect* of experience (cf. Troost, *Casuïstiek*, pp. 345ff.). An argument against choosing for "love" as the designation is the fact that one must employ the word "love" twice. Love with a capital "L" is used to describe the all-encompassing Total concentrated requirement of the Law in regard to mankind. Love with a small "l", as moral love, must then be seen as only one aspect of this central, radical Law of Love. Cf. Dooyeweerd, *NC* II, 154-61.

[25] Edel, *Method in Theory* (1963), pp. 179-80. He has also tabulated in summary fashion different ways which are employed to describe the specific mark of the ethical (pp. 178-79).

(a) Phenomenal marks of the distinctively moral:
   a directly apprehended quality of requiredness
   the quality of precedence or decisiveness characterizing one rule in comparison with the competing ones
   the characteristic of superiority and legitimacy in a prescription

199

A strong, be it negative, proof for the correctness of our view that ethics is a special, limited science is the inadequacy of the traditional views. If, as has been customary since the time of the Greeks,[26] ethics is taken to have reference to the practical life, with what one ought to do, with that which is good, the science of ethics stands for unsolvable problems. This is not difficult to explain. A man ought to do many things: he ought to love his family, he ought to promote justice, he ought to follow social conventions, and so forth. "Ethical" life in this sense is clearly not uniform or of one kind. There is patently a high degree of diversity. In this situation ethical science must break up into a number of different sciences (in which case they cannot all be called ethics) or ethics must attempt to capture this diversity in terms of one area (but such reduction is impossible as this diversity is the result of a plurality of irreducible norm-laws).

Once the traditional view is adopted, the ethical aspect as such is suspended. It disappears from sight, caught up in a so-called "universal ought." But what is this "universal ought" with which ethics is to deal? Upon investigation, it falls apart into various "oughts." There is the aesthetic "ought," the jural "ought," the economic "ought," the logical "ought," the lingual "ought," etc. as well as the ethical "ought." An "ought" is not as such necessarily ethical, it is not constitutive for the ethical.[27] "Ought" is just as original or non-original in any of the normative aspects. It always bears a more precise

(b) A set of distinctively ethical terms:
   in English, clearly, "good," "ought," "duty," etc.

(c) A set of distinctively ethical uses for ethical terms:
   to express certain emotions
   to command
   to decide or subscribe to courses of action and principles
   to persuade

(d) A set of behaviorally and phenomenally described activities or functions:
   valuing (whether being pleased by or having interest in etc.)
   reflective concern with whole of life
   appraising
   evaluating and ascribing obligations

[26] According to Sextus Empiricus (*Adv. Math.* VII, 16), it was a pupil of Plato, Xenokrates, who first explicitly divided philosophy into Physica, Logica and Ethica.
[27] The state of affairs has not left contemporary thinkers untouched. There is a general recognition that value judgments are not the exclusive property of ethics. But, the distinction is usually made in passing, and thereafter ignored or regarded as unimportant. Cf. Stevenson *FV*, 58-60 and Hare *LM*, 172; *FR*, 26-27, 172. Thus, for example, although he points out that the idea of good is not a "moral idea," Moore considers it "certainly an idea which it is the business of Moral Philosophy to discuss" (*PS*, 326).

qualification. It is the specific sense of the ethical which, in qualifying the ought, gives rise to the "ethical ought."[28]

If nevertheless "ought" is still considered the field of investigation for ethics, a confused situation develops. On the one hand this means that the structural boundaries between the ethical and the juridic, between the ethical and the logical, between the ethical and all of the other normative aspects are shifted — with all the consequences that such violations entail, not only for ethics, but for the other sciences concerned. On the other hand, since an ought only appears with a more specific qualification, in order to develop a tenable ethical theory one is forced to introduce a supplementary criterion[29] and thus deal with more than an "ought." And since there are no restrictions as to which particular ought one is to choose, it is possible that any of the "oughts" be auctioned off as "ethical." The ethical ought itself is lost, or is at least suspended in the confusion.[30] The ethical evaporates as it were in thin air and a thinly disguised logicism, historicism, psychologism or some other "ism" remains. Lacking any structural restrictions, the ethical "box" is given any shape, size or content: anthropology (Binswanger), cultural philosophy (Scheler), dogmatics (Barth), logic-linguistics (Hare), pedagogy (Bollnow), psychology (Schlick), politics (Brunner), sociology (Neurath), etc.

The outcome is the same when one prefers "goodness" as the mark of the ethical. Just as one discovers various "oughts," one discovers that good and evil bear different meanings dependent on the area of concern. Besides being considered morally good or bad, an act can be economically good or bad, socially good or bad, technically good or bad, etc. To compose a bad (grammatically incorrect) sentence is not to be guilty of an immoral act. This obviously means that the general good-evil distinction cannot serve as the criterion for moral good and evil.[31]

---

[28] This is not to deny the universal coherence of "oughts." The point is that an "ought" always reveals itself in a *typical* way. That an ought always requires a more precise "material" qualification speaks volumes against a purely formal theory of ethics.

[29] Hare, for example, considers that moral judgments in the final analysis are "overriding" judgments (*FR*, 169). But, as Warnock responds, it certainly seems possible that non-moral considerations are often overriding. Cf. Warnock, *Contemporary Moral Philosophy*, p. 49. Demonstrating that "use" is by itself an insufficient criteria, Toulmin calls a judgment ethical when "it is used to harmonise people's action" (*The Place of Reason in Ethics*, p. 145). At the same time it is clear that a meta-criterion is required in order to determine when harmonization takes place.

[30] The suspension of the ethical in relation to the existentialistic philosophies of Heidegger, Jaspers, Sartre and De Beauvoir is clearly shown by P. Du Plessis in his *Opskorting van die Etiese?*

[31] Cf. Troost, *op. cit.*, p. 342. It is interesting to note that already Aristotle had employed this argument, i.e. the multi-functionality of the word "good," in refuting Plato's notion of a Universal Good (Cf. *Nicomachean Ethics*, 1095 a 25f.).

If one begins, as we argue he ought, from the givenness of an ethical aspect in reality, the perplexing problem of how to move from the factual to the evaluational (logically or otherwise) becomes a pseudo-issue. An act is by its very nature ethically qualified or it is not. The same can be said for acts bearing other qualifications. To ascertain what is ethical in nature in contrast to what is a-ethical one has recourse to a general modal law which determines and obtains for such activities ethically. Because man by his very nature has this ethical aspect to his existence, whether he performs ethically-commendable or ethically-disgusting acts does not in the least affect their ethical status. The *subsequent* question is whether the act is moral in the sense of answering to the norm or anti-normative and thus immoral. The norms by which this is determined presuppose the norm-law. There is thus a primary (call it "structural") question: Is X to be qualified as an ethical or non-ethical act? The secondary (call it the "directional") question follows: Is the ethical act moral (in accord with the norms) or immoral (not in tune with the norm)?

Failure to distinguish these questions, as is the case with traditional theories, makes it impossible to draw a clear distinction between that which is *im-moral* (ethically-bad) and that which is *a-moral* (non-ethical). That which lives up to the "ought" is, as we have seen, said to be moral. But what if the ought is non-ethical? Is it still moral? And what if X does not live up to the ought? It is reportedly immoral. But perhaps X was a violation of the economic norm. Further, if to be moral is per se to be good, to be non-moral is tantamount to being immoral or bad. But this is obviously not so: how can an economic activity such as buying and selling automatically be branded as *im*moral (bad) simply because it is not morally qualified?

The confusions involved take on two main forms. One either (for example, in the trend of the existentialist) gives the *a*moral the connotation of the *im*moral or inauthentic, or (for example, in the trend of the neo-positivist) one gives the *im*moral the connotation of the *a*moral. Whereas in the first situation "ordinary" everyday activities become suspect and are more or less disqualified as unworthy of man, in the second situation anti-normative behavior loses much of its stigma by being considered not so much wrong as underdeveloped, or on a different, even lower (but in itself legitimate) level. In the former complex living ethically is authentic existence, anything less has the taint of the inferior or inauthentic. In the latter complex living ethically has the quality of the sublime, of an exalted condition. Here there is no suggestion that the natural is inferior, only that the non-natural is an "extra" dimension. In the first instance the amoral, standing in the penumbra of the immoral, shares in the disapprobation accorded the immoral; in the second instance the immoral, standing under the panoply of the amoral, has lost much of its odium.

In the former case — to express it in fact-value terms — only values are given their due, facts must bear the stigma of being grouped together with disvalues. In the latter case, disvalues are treated more as facts than as embodiments of the immoral. In both cases the real and important distinction between the immoral (morally-bad) and the amoral (non-moral) is elastic, hazy and fluid. In both cases, this identification or confusion is an evasion of the problem of evil on the *ethical* niveau. To be moral is to be good.[32] In the one case, it leads to the disqualification of the natural life (that is where "evil" resides); in the other it leads to a playing down of the seriousness of anti-normative behavior (after all, the natural has its own legitimacy).

To illustrate the dire results of a failure to distinguish clearly amoral ("structure") from immoral ("direction"), we shall examine Hare's famous "sincerity" problem. The criterion for employing prescriptive language, we remember, is sincere assent to an imperative entailed by the supposed proposition, and the criterion for assent to an imperative is to act on it. If one accepts a moral judgment that he ought to do X, he is logically committed to doing X (*LM*, 168-69). Failure to do X entails, conversely, that one did not truly assent to the moral judgment in the first place. It is thus logically impossible for Hare that someone can *freely* and *deliberately* perform an act which he knows or thinks is wrong. But such cases appear to be by no means exceptional. In reply Hare argues that backsliding or the failure to act on judgments to which one has sincerely assented is caused by physical or psychological weakness (*LM*, 20; cf. *FR*, 80ff.) rather than by wilful disobedience or ingrained perversity.

In so doing, whether or not he fully realizes the far-reaching implications at stake, Hare has virtually banished the possibility of anti-normative, that is for him, of morally wrong behavior. When one assents and lives up to the assent, he is acting morally and morally *good*. When one assents but fails to live up to the commitment, his actions cannot bear the qualification moral. Either he did not sincerely assent (and thus did not enter the moral arena) or he was physically or psychically impotent (in which case he is free from any kind of *moral* blame). Thus, for example, one is engaged in moral activity and by the same token morally good activity if he sincerely assents to the judgment "love your wife" and also indeed loves her. However, if he hates rather than loves his wife, either he did not sincerely assent to the judgment "love your wife" or some physical disorder or psychic aberration made this impossible. In neither case can one within Hare's view talk of *morally* wrong

---

[32] For Baier the moral point of view is "independent, unbiased, impartial, objective, dispassionate, disinterested observer . . . a God's eye-point of view" (*The Moral Point of View*, p. 201). Likewise Warnock asks: "Does not the 'moral point of view' involve precisely the abandonment of such egoism?" (*op. cit.*, p. 49). Cf. also Taylor, *Normative Discourse*, p. 145 ff.

behavior. Yet certainly hating as well as loving one's wife is a morally qualified affair, and just as loving one's wife is *morally right*, hating her is *morally wrong*.

By the same token, lacking the distinction, Hare is unable — contrary to his deepest intentions — to condemn fanatical views as immoral. If the fanatics are consistent, their views are moral and beyond reproof, they are morally *good*. Hare knows this is absurd, but his method allows him no way out. He attempts to side-step the issue by stressing the paucity of such fanatics.

In conclusion: Since the ethical is not co-extensive with the normative, in order to be scientific ethics must take as its field of investigation only one of the normed-areas of reality. "Goodness" or "oughtness" are not such clearly marked-out fields. The teacher, the artist, the jurist, the linguist, etc. all ask what they ought to do *as* teacher, artist, jurist, linguist. In none of these cases is the query specifically ethical (although it does have such an aspect). In fact it never is exclusively ethical. In the last analysis the what-ought-I-to-do question is a *total* question having various aspects, among them an ethical. It is only the ethical aspect, albeit in its indissoluble coherence with all the other aspects as they together express themselves in the totality of an act, which is the concern of the ethicist.

Bibliography

PRIMARY SOURCES

A. *George Edward Moore*

This bibliography contains, as far as I know, all Moore's published books and articles in chronological order. For a list of his reviews one should consult *The Philosophy of G. E. Moore* (ed. P. A. Schilpp), pp. 680-89.

MOORE, GEORGE EDWARD. "In What Sense, if any, do Past and Future Time Exist?" (Symposium), *Mind* VI (1897), pp. 235-40.
— "Freedom," *Mind* VII (1898), pp. 179-204.
— "The Nature of Judgment," *Mind* VIII (1899), pp. 176-93.
— "Necessity," *Mind* IX (1900), pp. 289-304.
— "Identity," *PAS* I (1901), pp. 103-27.
— "The Value of Religion," *International Journal of Ethics* XII (1901), pp. 81-98.
— "Mr. McTaggart's 'Studies in Hegelian Cosmology'," *PAS* II (1902), pp. 177-214.
— Articles in Baldwin's *Dictionary of Philosophy* I s.v. "Cause and Effect," "Change"; II "Nativism," "Quality," "Real," "Reason," "Relative," "Relativity of Knowledge," "Spirit," "Substance," "Teleology," "Truth" (1902).
— *Principia Ethica*. Cambridge: Cambridge University Press, 1903.
— Review of F. Brentano, "The Origin of Knowledge of Right and Wrong," *Int. Journ. of Ethics* XIV (1903), pp. 115-23.
— "Experience and Empiricism," *PAS* III (1903), pp. 80-95.
— "Mr. McTaggart's Ethics," *Int. Journ. of Ethics* XIII (1903), pp. 341-70.
— "Kant's Idealism," *PAS* IV (1904), pp. 127-40.
— "Jahresbericht über 'Philosophy in the United Kingdom 1902'," *Archiv für Systematische Philosophie* X (1904), pp. 242-64.
— "Mr. Joachim's 'Nature of Truth'," *Mind* XVI (1907), pp. 229-35.
— "The Subject Matter of Psychology," *PAS* X (1909), pp. 36-62.
— *Some Main Problems of Philosophy* (written in 1910-11). London: George Allen & Unwin Ltd., 1953.
— *Ethics*. London: Oxford University Press, 1912 (reset 1947).
— "The Implications of Recognition," (Symposium) *PAS* XVI (1916), pp. 201-23.
— "Are the Materials of Sense Affections of the Mind?" (Symposium) *PAS* XVII (1917), pp. 418-29.
— "Is there 'Knowledge by Acquaintance'?" (Symposium) *PASS* II (1919), pp. 179-93.

- "Is the 'Concrete Universal' the True Type of Universality?" (Symposium) *PAS* XX (1920), pp. 132-40.
- "The Character of Cognitive Acts" (Symposium) *PAS* XXI (1921), pp. 132-40.
- *Philosophical Studies*. London: Kegan Paul, Trench, Trubner & Co. Ltd., 1922. (This reprints the following earlier published papers: "The Refutation of Idealism" (1903), "The Nature and Reality of Objects of Perception" (1905), "William James' 'Pragmatism'" (1908), "Hume's Philosophy" (1909), "The Status of Sense-Data" (1914), "The Conception of Reality" (1917), "Some Judgments of Perception" (1918), "External and Internal Relations" (1919). It adds "The Conception of Intrinsic Value," and "The Nature of Moral Philosophy.")
- "The Nature of Sensible Appearances" (Symposium) *PASS* VI (1926), pp. 179-89.
- "Indirect Knowledge" (Symposium) *PASS* IX (1929), pp. 175-88.
- "The Justification of Analysis" (a lecture note) *Analysis* I (1933), pp. 28-30.
- "Autobiography," *The Philosophy of G. E. Moore* (ed. P. A. Schilpp). Evanston: Northwestern University Press, 1942.
- "A Reply to my Critics," *The Philosophy of G. E. Moore* (ed. P. A. Schilpp). Evanston: Northwestern University Press, 1942.
- "Addendum to Reply to my Critics of 1942," *The Philosophy of G. E. Moore*. 2nd. ed., 1952.
- "Visual Sense-Data," *British Philosophy in Mid-Century* (ed. Mace). London: George Allen & Unwin, 1957.
- *Philosophical Papers*. London: George Allen & Unwin, 1959. (This reprints the following earlier published papers: "Are the Characteristics of Particular Things Universal or Particular?" (1923), "A Defense of Common Sense" (1925), "Facts and Propositions" (1927), "Is Goodness a Quality?" (1932), "Imaginary Objects" (1933), "Is Existence a Predicate?" (1936), "Proof of an External World" (1939), "Russell's Theory of Descriptions'" (1944), "Wittgenstein's Lectures in 1930-33" (1954-5). It adds "Certainty" and "Four Forms of Scepticism.")
- *Commonplace Book* 1919-1953 (ed. C. Lewy). London: George Allen & Unwin, 1962.
- *Lectures on Philosophy* (ed. C. Lewy). London: George Allen & Unwin, 1966. (This contains selections from three courses of academic lectures: 1925-26, 1928-29 and 1933-34.)

B. *Post-Moorean Developments*

AYER, A. J. *Language, Truth and Logic*. London: Victor Gollancz, 1936; 2nd. ed., 1946.
EWING, A. C. *Second Thoughts in Moral Philosophy*. London: Routledge and Kegan Paul, 1959.
FOOT, PHILIPPA. "Moral Arguments," *Mind* LXVII (1958), pp. 502-13.
HAMPSHIRE, S. "Fallacies in Moral Philosophy," *Mind* LVIII (1949), pp. 466-82.
HARE, R. M. *The Language of Morals*. Oxford: Clarendon Press, 1952.
— *Freedom and Reason*. Oxford: Clarendon Press, 1963.
NOWELL-SMITH, P. H. *Ethics*. London: Pelican Books, 1954.
ROSS, W. D. *The Right and the Good*. Oxford: Clarendon Press, 1930.
STEVENSON, C. L. *Ethics and Language*. New Haven: Yale University Press, 1944.
— *Facts and Values*. New Haven: Yale University Press, 1963.
TOULMIN, S. E. *The Place of Reason in Ethics*. Cambridge: Cambridge University Press, 1950.
URMSON, J. O. "On Grading," *Mind* LIX (1950), pp. 145-69.

VON WRIGHT, G. H. *The Varieties of Goodness*. London: Routledge and Kegan Paul, 1963.
WARNOCK, G. J. *Contemporary Moral Philosophy*. London: Macmillan, 1967.

FURTHER SELECTED BIBLIOGRAPHY

ABELSON, R. (ed.) *Ethics and Meta-Ethics*. New York: St. Martin's Press, 1963.
ADDIS, L. and LEWIS, D. *Moore and Ryle: Two Ontologists*. The Hague: Martinus Nijhoff, 1965.
AIKEN, H. D. *Reason and Conduct*. New York: Alfred A. Knopf, 1962.
ALBERT, HANS. "Ethik und Meta-ethik. Das Dilemma der analystischen Moralphilosophie," *Archiv für Philosophie* XI (1961), pp. 28-63.
AMBROSE, A. *Essays in Analysis*. London: George Allen & Unwin, 1966.
ANSCOMBE, G. E. M. *Intention*. Oxford: Blackwell, 1957.
— "Modern Moral Philosophy," *P* XXXIII (1958), pp. 1-19.
AUSTIN, J. L. *How to Do Things With Words*. Ed. J. O. Urmson. Oxford: Clarendon Press, 1962.
AYER, A. J. *Philosophical Essays*. London: Macmillan, 1954.
— (ed.) *The Revolution in Philosophy*. London: Macmillan, 1956.
— (ed.) *Logical Positivism*. Glencoe Ill.: The Free Press, 1959.
BAIER, K. *The Moral Point of View*. Ithaca: Cornell University Press, 1958.
BAYLIS, C. A. "Intrinsic Goodness," *Philosophy and Phenomenological Research* XIII (1952), pp. 15-27.
BERGMANN, G. "Inclusion, Exemplification, and Inherence in G. E. Moore," *Logic and Reality*. Madison: University of Wisconsin Press, 1964.
BINKLEY, L. J. *Contemporary Ethical Theories*. New York: Citadel Press, 1961.
BLACK, MAX. (ed.) *Philosophical Analysis*. Ithaca: Cornell University Press, 1950.
BLANSHARD, B. *The Impasse in Ethics and a Way Out*. Berkeley: University of California Press, 1955.
— *Reason and Goodness*. London: George Allen & Unwin, 1962.
BRAITHWAITE, R. B. *Theory of Games As a Tool for Moral Philosophy*. Cambridge University Press, 1955.
— "George Edward Moore," *Proceedings of the British Academy* XLVII (1961), pp. 293-309.
BRANDT, R. B. *Ethical Theory*. Englewood Cliffs: Prentice Hall, 1959.
BRENTANO, F. *Vom Ursprung Sittlicher Erkenntnis*. Leipzig, 1889. (Eng. trans. *The Origin of the Knowledge of Right and Wrong*. Constable, 1902).
BROAD, C. D. *Five Types of Ethical Theory*. London: Kegan Paul, 1930.
— "G. E. Moore's Latest Published Views on Ethics," *Mind* LXX (1961), pp. 435-57.
CARNAP, R. *Philosophy and Logical Syntax*. London: Kegan Paul, 1935.
CARRITT, E. F. *Theory of Morals*. London: Clarendon Press, 1928.
— *Ethical and Political Thinking*. Oxford: Clarendon Press, 1947.
CHARLESWORTH, M. *Philosophy and Linguistic Analysis*. Pittsburgh: Dusquesne University, 1959.
D'ARCY, E. *Moral Acts*. Oxford: Clarendon Press, 1963.
DEWEY, J. *Theory of Valuation*. Chicago: University of Chicago Press, 1939.
DOOYEWEERD, H. *A New Critique of Theoretical Thought*. 4 Vols. Amsterdam: H. J. Paris; Philadelphia: The Presbyterian and Reformed Publishing Company, 1953-1958.

— *In the Twilight of Western Thought.* Philadelphia: The Presbyterian and Reformed Publishing Company, 1960.

DUNCAN-JONES, A. "Intrinsic Value: Some Comments on the Work of G. E. Moore," *P* XXXIII (1958), pp. 240-73.

DU PLESSIS, P. G. W. *Opskorting Van Die Etiese?* Potchefstroom: Pro Rege-Pers Beperk, 1965.

EDEL, A. *Method in Ethical Theory*, London: Routledge & Kegan Paul, 1963.

EDWARDS, P. *The Logic of Moral Discourse.* Glencoe Ill., The Free Press, 1955.

EMMET, D. *Facts and Obligations.* London: Dr. William's Trust, 1958.

EWING, A. C. *The Definition of Good.* New York: Macmillan, 1947.

FEIGL H. and SELLARS W. (eds.) *Readings in Philosophical Analysis.* New York: Appelton-Century Inc., 1949.

FIELD, G. C. *Moral Theory.* London: Methuen, 1932².

FINDLAY, J. N. *Values and Intentions.* London: George Allen & Unwin, 1961².

— *Meinong's Theory of Objects and Values.* Oxford: Clarendon Press, 1963².

FLEW, A. G. N. (ed.) *Logic and Language*, First Series. Oxford: Blackwell, 1951.

— (ed.) *Logic and Language*, Second Series. Oxford: Blackwell, 1955.

— (ed.) *Essays in Conceptual Analysis.* London: Macmillan, 1956.

FLEW, A. G. N. and MAC INTYRE, A. (eds.) *New Essays in Philosophy and Theology.* London: SCM Press, 1955.

FOGELIN, R. S. *Evidence and Meaning.* London: Routledge and Kegan Paul, 1967.

FOOT, P. "When is a Principle a Moral Principle?" *PASS* XXVIII (1954), pp. 95-110.

— "Moral Beliefs," *PAS* LIX (1959), pp. 83-104.

— "Goodness and Choice," *PASS* XXV (1961), pp. 45-61.

FRANKENA, W. K. "The Naturalistic Fallacy", *Mind* XLVIII (1939), pp. 464-77.

— "Obligation and Motivation in Recent Moral Philosophy," In *Essays in Moral Philosophy*, ed. A. I. Melden. Seattle: University of Washington Press, 1958.

— *Ethics.* Englewood Cliffs: Prentice Hall, 1963.

GARVIN, L. *A Modern Introduction to Ethics.* Boston: Houghton Mifflin Co., 1953.

GAUTHIER, D. *Practical Reason.* Oxford: Clarendon Press, 1967.

GELLNER, E. *Words and Things.* London: Victor Gollancz Ltd., 1963.

GEWIRTH, A. "Meta-ethics and Normatives Ethics", *Mind* LXIX (1960), pp. 187-205.

GINSBERG, M. *Reason and Experience in Ethics.* London: Oxford University Press, 1956.

HALL, E. W. *What is Value?* London: Routledge & Kegan Paul, 1932.

HAMPSHIRE, S. *Thought and Action.* London: Chatto and Windus, 1959.

— *Freedom of the Individual.* London: Chatto and Windus, 1965.

HANCOCK, R. "The Refutation of Naturalism in Moore and Hare," *JP* LVII (1960), pp. 326-34.

HARE, R. M. "Imperative Sentences," *Mind* LVIII (1949), pp. 21-39.

— "Universalizability," *PAS* LV (1954), pp. 295-312.

— "Geach on Good and Evil," *Analysis* XVII (1957), pp. 103-11.

— "Descriptivism," *Proceedings of the British Academy* XLIX (1963), pp. 115-34.

HART, H. *Communal Certainty and Authorized Truth.* Amsterdam: Swets & Zeitlinger, 1966.

HARTMAN, R. S. "The Analytic, Synthetic and the Good: Kant and the Paradoxes of G. E. Moore," *Kant Studien* XLV (1953-54), pp. 67-82 and XLVI (1954-55), pp. 3-18.

— "Definition of Good: Moore's Axiomatic of the Science of Ethics," *PAS* LXV (1964-65), pp. 235-57.

— *The Structure of Value.* Carbondale, Ill.: Southern Ill. University Press, 1965.

208

HILLIARD, P. *The Forms of Value*. New York: Columbia University Press, 1950.

HOCHBERG, H. "Moore's Ontology and Non-Natural Properties," *Review of Metaphysics* XV (1962). (Reprinted in *Essays in Ontology*. Hague: Martinus Nijhoff, 1963).

HUBBELING, H. G. "De betekenis van de analytische filosofie voor de wijsgerige theologie." *Tijdschrift voor Filosofie* XXIX (1967), pp. 734-71.

HUDSON, W. *Ethical Intuitionism*. London: Macmillan, 1967.

JOACHIM, H. H. *The Nature of Truth*. Oxford: Clarendon Press, 1906.

JOHNSON, O. A. *Rightness and Goodness*. Hague: Martinus Nijhoff, 1959.

JOSEPH, H. W. B. *Some Main Problems in Ethics*. Oxford: Clarendon Press, 1931.

JURY, G. S. *Value and Ethical Objectivity*. London: George Allen & Unwin, 1937.

KERNER, G. *The Revolution in Ethical Theory*. Oxford: Clarendon Press, 1966.

KNEALE, W. "Objectivity and Morals," *P* XXV (1950), pp. 49-66.

— W. & N. *The Development of Logic*. Oxford: Clarendon Press, 1962.

KÖHLER, W. *The Place of Value in a World of Facts*. London: Kegan Paul, 1938.

KOOISTRA, R. *Facts and Values*. CPS, 1963. Hamilton: Guardian Publishing Co., 1963.

LAIRD, J. *A Study in Moral Theory*. London: Allen & Unwin, 1926.

LAZEROWITZ, M. "Strong and Weak Verification" I and II, *Mind* XLVIII (1939), pp. 202-13, LIX (1950), pp. 345-57.

— "Moore and Philosophical Analysis," *P* XXXIII (1958), pp. 193-220.

LEHMANN, P. *Ethics in a Christian Context*. London: SCM Press, 1963.

LENK, H. "Kann die sprachanalytische Moralphilosophie neutral sein?" *Archiv für Rechts- und Sozialphilosophie* LIII (1967) pp. 367-86.

LEPLEY, R. (ed.) *Value: A Cooperative Inquiry*. New York: Columbia University Press, 1949.

LEVI, A. W. "The Trouble With Ethics," *Mind* LXX (1961), pp. 201-15.

LEWIS, C. I. *An Analysis of Knowledge and Valuation*. La Salle: Open Court Publishing Co., 1946.

LEWIS, H. E. (ed.) *Contemporary British Philosophy* Third Series. London: George Allen & Unwin, 1956.

— (ed.) *Clarity Is Not Enough*. London: George Allen & Unwin, 1967.

LEWY, C. "G. E. Moore on The Naturalistic Fallacy," *Proceedings of the British Academy* L (1964), pp. 251-62.

LILLIE, W. *An Introduction to Ethics*. London: Methuen, 1948.

LINSKY, L. (ed.) *Semantics and Philosophy of Language*. Urbana: University of Illinois Press, 1952.

MABBOT, J. D. *An Introduction to Ethics*. London: Hutchinson, 1966.

MAC DONALD, M. "Ethics and Ceremonial Use of Language" in *Philosophical Analysis*, ed. M. Black. Ithaca: Cornell University Press, 1950.

— (ed.) *Philosophy and Analysis*. Oxford: Blackwell, 1954.

MACE, C. A. (ed.) *British Philosophy in Mid-Century*. London: George Allen & Unwin, 1957.

MACKINNON, D. M. *A Study in Ethical Theory*. London: Adam & Chutes Black, 1957.

MALCOLM, N. *Knowledge and Certainty*. Englewoods Cliff: Prentice-Hall, 1963.

MAYO, B. *Ethics and the Moral life*. London: Macmillan, 1958.

MEKKES, J. P. A. *De Beteekenis van het Subject in de Moderne Waarde Philosophie Onder het Licht der Wetsidee*. Leiden: Universitaire Pers, 1949.

MELDEN, A. (ed.) *Essays in moral Philosophy*. Seattle: University of Washington Press, 1958.

— *Rights and Right Conduct*. London: Routledge, 1959.

— *Free Action*. London: Routledge, 1961.

209

METZ, R. *A Hundred Years of British Philosophy* 1935 (Eng. trans. J. H. Muirhead, London, 1938).

MITCHELL, B. (ed.) *Faith and Logic*. London: George Allen & Unwin, 1957.

MONTEFIORE, A. C. *A Modern Introduction to Moral Philosophy*. London: Routledge, 1958.

MURE, G. R. *Retreat from Truth*. Oxford: Blackwell, 1958.

MURPHY, A. E. *Reason and the Common Good*. Englewood Cliffs: Prentice Hall, 1963.

NELSON, J. O. "Mr. Hochberg on Moore: Some Corrections," *The Review of Metaphysics* XVI (1962), pp. 119-132.

— "G. E. Moore," *The Encyclopedia of Philosophy* V (ed. P. Edwards) New York: Cromwell Collier and Macmillan, 1967.

NOWELL-SMITH, P. H. and LEMMON, E. J. "Escapism, the Logical Base of Ethics," *Mind* LXIX (1960), pp. 289-300.

NUCHELMANS, G. "Metafysica en ethiek in de Analytische Wijsbegeerte," *Tijdschrift voor Filosofie* XXVIII (1966), pp. 399-417.

OGDEN, C. K. and RICHARDS, I. A. *The Meaning of Meaning*. London: Kegan Paul, 1923².

OSBORNE, H. *Foundations of the Philosophy of Value*. Cambridge: University Press, 1933.

PARKER, D. H. *Philosophy of Value*. Ann Arbor: University of Michigan Press, 1957.

PASSMORE, J. A. *A Hundred Years of Philosophy*. London: Duckworth, 1957.

PEARS, P. F. (ed.) *The Nature of Metaphysics*. London: Macmillan, 1957.

PEPPER, S. C. *Sources of Value*. Berkeley: University of California Press, 1958.

PERRY, R. B. *General Theory of Value*. New York: Longmans, Green, 1926.

PITCHER, G. (ed.) *Truth*. Englewood Cliffs: Prentice Hall, 1964.

POPPER, K. R. *Logik der Forschung*. Vienna: Springer, 1935. (Eng. trans. *The Logic of Scientific Discovery*. London: Hutchinson, 1959).

— "What Can Logic Do for Philosophy?" *PASS* XXII (1948), pp. 141-54.

PRICHARD, H. A. *Moral Obligation*. Oxford: Clarendon Press, 1949.

PRIOR, A. N. *Logic and the Basis of Ethics*. Oxford: Clarendon Press, 1949.

QUINE, W. V. *From a Logical Point of View*. Cambridge, Mass.: Harvard University Press, 1955.

RAMSEY, I. (ed.) *Christian Ethics and Contemporary Philosophy*. London: SCM Press, 1966.

RAPHAEL, D. D. *The Moral Sense*. London: George Allen & Unwin, 1947.

— *Moral Judgment*. London: George Allen & Unwin, 1955.

RASHDALL, H. *The Theory of Good and Evil* I and II. Oxford: Clarendon Press, 1907.

REICHENBACH, H. *The Rise of Scientific Philosophy*. Berkeley and Los Angeles: University of California Press, 1954.

RICE, P. B. *On the Knowledge of Good and Evil*. New York: Randon House, 1955.

ROSS, W. D. *Foundations of Ethics*. Oxford: Clarendon Press, 1930.

RUNNER, H. E. *The Development of Aristotle Illustrated from the Earliest Books of the Physics*. Kampen: J. H. Kok, N.V., 1951.

RUSSELL, BERTRAND. "Meinong's Theory of Complexes and Assumptions," *Mind* XIII (1904), pp. 204-19, 336-54, 509-24.

— "The Elements of Ethics," *Philosophical Essays*. London: Longmans, Green & Co., 1910.

RYLE, G. *The Concept of Mind*. London: Hutchinson, 1949.

SCHILPP, P. A. (ed.) *The Philosophy of G. E. Moore*. Evanston: Northwestern University Press, 1942.

SCHLICK, M. *Fragen der Ethik*. Vienna: Springer, 1930. (Eng. trans. *Problems of Ethics*. New York: Prentice-Hall, 1939).

SESONSKE, A. *Value and Obligation* Berkeley: University of California Press, 1951.

SEERVELD, C. *A Christian Critique of Literature.* Hamilton: The Association for Reformed Scientific Studies, 1964.

SELLARS, W. S. & HOSPERS, J. (eds.) *Readings in Ethical Theory.* New York: Appleton-Century-Crafts, 1952.

SINGER, M. G. *Generalization in Ethics.* London: Eyre & Spottiswoode, 1963.

SPARSHOTT, F. E. *An Enquiry Into Goodness.* Chicago: University of Chicago Press, 1958.

STACE, W. T. *The Concept of Morals.* New York: Macmillan, 1937.

STEBBING, L. S. *A Modern Introduction to Logic.* London: Methuen, 1930.

STRAWSON, P. F. "Ethical Intuitionism," *P* XXIV (1949), pp. 209-24.

— *An Introduction to Logical Theory.* London: Methuen, 1952.

— *Individuals.* London: Methuen, 1959.

— "Social Morality and Individual Ideal," *P* XXXVI (1961), pp. 1-17.

— *The Bounds of Sense.* London: Methuen, 1966.

STROLL, A. *The Emotive Theory of Ethics.* Berkeley: University of California Press, 1954.

TAYLOR, P. W. *Normative Discourse.* Englewood Cliffs: Prentice-Hall, 1961.

— (ed.) *Moral Judgment.* Englewood Cliffs: Prentice-Hall, 1963.

TROOST, A. *Casuïstiek en Situatie-ethiek.* Utrecht: Libertas, 1958.

URBAN, W. M. *Valuation: Its Nature and Laws.* London: Swan Sonnenshein, 1909.

URMSON, J. O. *Philosophical Analysis.* Oxford: Clarendon Press, 1952.

VAN DER HOEVEN, J. "Filosofie op het Spel," *Phil. Ref.* XXX (1965), pp. 137-58.

VAN PEURSEN, C. A. *Feiten, Waarden, Gebeurtenissen.* Amsterdam: J. M. Meulenhoff, 1965.

VAN RIESSEN, H. *Op Wijsgerige Wegen.* Wageningen: N.V. Gebr. Zomer & Keuning, 1963².

VOLLENHOVEN, D. H. TH. *Isagoogè Philosophiae.* Amsterdam: Filosofisch Instituut Vrije Universiteit, 1967².

VON MEYENFELDT, F. H. *The Meaning of Ethos.* Hamilton: The Association for Reformed Scientific Studies, 1964.

VON WRIGHT, H. G. *Norm and Action: A Logical Inquiry.* London: Routledge & Kegan Paul, 1963.

WAISMANN, F. *The Principles of Linguistic Philosophy.* Oxford: Blackwell, 1965.

WARNOCK, G. J. *English Philosophy Since 1900.* London: Oxford University Press, 1958.

WARNOCK, M. *Ethics Since 1900.* London: Oxford University Press, 1960.

WEDER, G. *Unity and Utility.* Lund: CWK Gleerup, 1952.

WHITE, A. *G. E. Moore.* Oxford: Blackwell, 1958.

WHITE, M. *Toward Reunion in Philosophy.* Cambridge: Harvard University Press, 1956.

WISDOM, JOHN. *Philosophy and Psycho-Analysis.* Oxford: Blackwell, 1953.

WILLIAMS, B. and MONTEFIORE, A. (eds.) *British Analytical Philosophy.* London: Routledge & Kegan Paul, 1966.

WITTGENSTEIN, L. *Philosophical Investigations.* trans. G. E. M. Anscombe. New York: Macmillan, 1953.

— *Tractatus Logico–Philosophicus* London: Routledge & Kegan Paul, 1922, 2nd. Eng. trans. Pears, D. F. & Mc Guinnes, B. F., 1961.

— "A Lecture on Ethics," *PR* LXXIV (1965), pp. 3-12.

ZIFF, P. *Semantic Analysis.* Ithaca: Cornell University Press, 1960.

ZINK, S. *The Concepts of Ethics.* New York: St. Martin's Press, 1962.

ZUURDEEG, W. F. *A Research for the Consequences of the Vienna Circle Philosophy for Ethics.* Utrecht: Kemik en Zoon, 1946.

Index of persons

214